D1517973

British TV Streaming Guide

US Edition: Autumn 2020

Your guide to streaming roughly 2000 different British TV shows in the US.

See more of our British TV books & news at:

IHeartBritishTV.com

Shop.IHeartBritain.com

Published by IHeartBritishTV.com

Sacramento, California

ISBN:978-1-7332961-4-4

Welcome - and thank you for buying or borrowing this guide! We're a small business, and we genuinely appreciate your support.

Before we get any further, I just want to offer a few comments to help you get the most out of this guide. We put hundreds of hours into researching, writing, and laying it out, and as far as we know, it's the only one of its kind in the world.

That doesn't mean it's perfect.

We've long resisted the idea of putting out a printed streaming guide, purely because the offerings on streaming services change very rapidly. It's literally impossible to put out a guide that will be 100% accurate by the time it goes through printing and shipping.

Though we've done our best to track down the new and leaving shows, even the streaming services themselves don't always know what's leaving in a month's time - and occasionally, premieres get pushed back.

That said, most services change no more than 3-5% of their offerings in any given month. This guide should still be mostly accurate for months to come.

There are a couple other quirks you should be aware of as you dig in:

- Few services offer a list of all their British programming. That means many of these lists were gathered through sheer force, spending hours upon hours clicking around and digging through thousands of shows and related shows to figure out what's British. It's possible we've missed a few.
- For Acorn TV and BritBox, we listed ALL programming - including movies. On other platforms, we stuck to television.
- Our primary focus was on British programming. We've included a handful of shows from Australia, New Zealand, Canada, and Europe, but those are just happy little extras. This guide is far from comprehensive when it comes to shows from those countries.

This is our first time publishing this particular guide, and we hope you like it. We welcome your feedback at stefanie@iheartbritishtv.com.

We hope we're adding something valuable to the British TV community, and we'll certainly put out future editions if it's well-received (and we'll be forever grateful if you tell your British TV-loving friends about it).

Happy Watching!

Stefanie & David
IHeartBritishTV.com

TABLE OF CONTENTS

ACORN TV

Website: http://acorn.tv

Description: Acorn TV describes itself as "world-class TV from Britain and Beyond". British programming dominates, but they also include shows from Australia, Ireland, Canada, New Zealand, Scandinavia, and mainland Europe.

Available On: Roku, Amazon Fire TV, Apple TV, Apple iPhone & iPad, Android TV, Android phones and tablets, Google Chromecast, computer (via web browser). You can also subscribe via Amazon Prime Video.

Cost: $5.99/month, $59.99/year

Now Streaming
Mysteries & Crime Dramas

Above Suspicion - 2009 to 2012 - DC Anna Travis is a rookie detective determined to prove herself. She finds herself quickly tossed into the deep end, working cases where a prime suspect is wealthy or prominent enough to be considered "above suspicion".

Acceptable Risk - 2017 to present – When Sarah's husband is murdered, she realises how little she knows about his past.

The Agatha Christie Hour - 1982 - This series is a collection of one-hour dramas based on Agatha Christie's short stories. Each of the adaptations feature talented casts with British actors like John Nettles (*Midsomer Murders*), Amanda Redman (*The Good Karma Hospital*), and Stephanie Cole (*Doc Martin*).

Agatha Christie's Marple - 2004 to 2013 - Julia McKenzie stars as the iconic sleuth of St. Mary Mead. At present, Acorn TV offers the three-episode Series 6.

Agatha Christie's Partners in Crime - 2015 - David Walliams (*Little Britain*) and Jessica Raine (*Call the Midwife*) star in this updated adaptation of Agatha Christie's Tommy and Tuppence Beresford stories. Together, they solve mysteries and search for enemy spies in Cold War Britain.

Agatha Christie's Poirot - 1989 to 2020 - David Suchet portrays the eccentric Belgian Detective Poirot in this long-running series of Agatha Christie mysteries. Acorn TV has seasons 7 and 8, while BritBox has all the others.

Agatha Christie's The Witness for the Prosecution - 2016 - In 1920s London, a handsome townhouse is the setting for the brutal murder of Emily French, a glamorous young socialite. Toby Jones (*Detectorists*) and Kim Cattrall (*Sex and the City*) are among the members of this feature film's all-star cast.

Agatha Raisin - 2016 to present - Based on the M.C. Beaton novels, Agatha Raisin leaves her high-flying London PR life for a peaceful existence in The Cotswolds - or so she thinks. Though originally cancelled after Series 1, Acorn TV brought this one back for another two seasons, and a fourth is planned.

Alibi - 2003 - Michael Kitchen (*Foyle's War*), Sophie Okonedo (*Hotel Rwanda*), and Phyllis Logan (*Downton Abbey*) star in this thriller about a man discovered with the dead body of his business partner. When a nearby witness helps him dispose of the body, the situation spirals out of control and she wonders what she's gotten herself into. This series is presented in three episodes.

And Then There Were None - 2015 - Based on the Agatha Christie novel, this miniseries sees 10 strangers invited to an island, only to be killed off one by one.

Balthazar - *France* - 2018 to present - This French crime drama revolves around Raphael Balthazar, a brilliant forensic pathologist who's haunted by the memory of his murdered wife. Highly unconventional in his approach, he frequently helps police commander Hélène Bach solve some of Paris' most baffling murder cases.

The Best of Agatha Christie - This collection of Agatha Christie adaptations includes productions of *And Then There Were None, Five Little Pigs, Death on the Nile, Witness for the Prosecution, Three Act Tragedy,* and *Hallowe'en Party*.

Black Work - 2015 - A widowed policewoman tries to figure out who killed her husband during an undercover operation. Sheridan Smith (*Gavin & Stacey*) stars.

Blood - 2018 to 2020 - *Ireland* - Adrian Dunbar (*Line of Duty*) stars as a respected doctor and new widower in a small Irish town. Though everyone else believes his wife's death was an accident, his daughter has her doubts. Carolina Main (*Unforgotten*) stars alongside Dunbar as his daughter, Cat.

The Brokenwood Mysteries - 2014 to present - DI Mike Shepard arrives in the seemingly peaceful New Zealand town of Brokenwood with a classic car, loads of country music, and a string of ex-wives. There, he quickly finds that all is not as it seems, and both secrets and animosities run deep in the local community. He's assisted in his crime-fighting efforts by the highly capable, by-the-books assistant DC Kristin Sims.

The Broker's Man - 1997 to 1998 - An ex-cop now puts his detective skills to work for insurance companies. Kevin Whately (*Lewis*) stars.

Chasing Shadows - 2014 - A difficult but gifted officer works within a missing persons unit to find cases that may be linked to murder.

Code of a Killer - 2015 - This criminal drama tells the story of the first time DNA fingerprinting was used to help solve a murder case. David Threlfall (*Shameless*) stars as DCS David Baker, who heads up the investigation. John Simm (*Life on Mars*) plays Dr. Alec Jeffreys, the scientist who invents the process for fingerprinting DNA.

The Commander - 2003 to 2008 - Amanda Burton (*Silent Witness*) stars in this thriller about the murder investigations of Commander Clare Blake, highest-ranking female officer at New Scotland Yard. The series was written by *Prime Suspect* creator Lynda La Plante.

Dead Lucky - *Australian* - 2018 – When a dangerous armed robber resurfaces in Sydney, two very different detectives are forced to work together to catch him.

Deadwater Fell - 2019 - David Tennant stars in this dark miniseries about a Scottish family that's murdered one night, tearing apart their otherwise peaceful village and bringing secrets to the surface.

Deep Water - *Australian* - 2016 - Yael Stone (*Orange is the New Black*) and Noah Taylor (*Game of Thrones*) star as detectives investigating the vicious murder of a young man. As their investigation progresses, they discover connections to a string of unsolved cases involving gay men killed in the 80s and 90s.

East West 101 - *Australian* - 2007 to 2011 - *Australia* - Malik and Crowley are a study in opposites as they investigate major crimes.

The Field of Blood - 2011 to 2013 - Set in early 1980s Glasgow, a young woman skillfully solves murders on a police force full of men. Unfortunately, her dedication to the truth also puts her in danger. The series stars BAFTA winner Jayd Johnson (*River City*) as Paddy Meehan, working alongside Peter Capaldi (*Doctor Who*) and David Morrissey (*The Missing*).

Five Days: The Train - 2010 - This series follows five non-consecutive days in a police investigation, and Acorn TV offers only the second season, starring Suranne Jones (*Gentleman Jack*) and Anne Reid (*Last Tango in Halifax*). Each series is a standalone story, so there's no need to see the first to enjoy the second.

Foyle's War - 2002 to 2015 - DCS Foyle fights a war against crime in southern England as WWII goes on around him. Michael Kitchen (*The Life of Rock with Brian*

Pern) and Honeysuckle Weeks (*The Five*) star.

Hamish Macbeth - 1995 to 1997 - Hamish Macbeth (Robert Carlyle, *The Full Monty*) is a talented but unambitious Highlands constable who doesn't always follow the rules. The series was filmed in the lovely Highland village of Plockton on the shores of Loch Carron, and it's a great watch for those who enjoy good scenery.

Harry - *New Zealand* - 2013 - Detective Harry Anglesea returns to work just four weeks after his wife's suicide, and it may be too soon.

Hidden - 2011 - This four-part BBC conspiracy thriller stars Philip Glenister (*Life on Mars*) as Harry Venn, a high street solicitor who's unwittingly drawn into the investigation of his brothers murder 20 years prior. Thekla Reuten (*The American*) and David Suchet (*Poirot*) also appear.

Hidden - 2018 - When a young woman's body turns up with evidence that she was held prisoner prior to her death, the investigation leads DI Cadi John (Sian Reese-Williams, *Requiem*) to a string of disappearances in a beautiful but remote part of Wales. Only the first season is currently available on Acorn at time of print.

Injustice - 2011 - A defense barrister has to deal with the consequences of defending an indefensible crime. *Foyle's War* and *Midsomer Murders* screenwriter Anthony Horowitz created the series, and it features an all-star cast with actors like James Purefoy (*Rome*), Dervla Kirwan (*Ballykissangel*), Charlie Creed-Miles (*The Fifth Element*), and Nathaniel Parker (*The Inspector Lynley Mysteries*).

Jack Taylor - *Ireland* - 2010 to 2016 - Resistant to rules, ex-cop Jack Taylor becomes a private investigator after losing his job with the Guard. Iain Glen (*Game of Thrones*) stars in this series set against the city of Galway. It's based on a series of novels written by Ken Bruen.

Jericho of Scotland Yard - 2005 - This period mystery gives us DI Michael Jericho, a WWII veteran who investigates murders while also seeking to figure out the circumstances surrounding his father's death.

Keeping Faith - 2017 to present - A Welsh lawyer cuts her maternity leave short when her husband goes missing. As she tries to solve the crime before she's arrested for it, she finds herself knee-deep in the criminal underworld of her small town. Eve Myles (*Torchwood*) stars, though some might argue her yellow anorak deserves a mention, too.

Killer Net - 1998 - A psychology student becomes obsessed with a computer game about murder, but it gets scary when it suddenly seems to be connected to real murders. Tam Williams (*Spectre*) and Paul Bettany (*The Avengers* films) star in this dark miniseries.

L'Accident - *France* - 2016 to 2017 - When police accuse his wife of drunk driving in the crash that killed her, Gabriel Cauvy (Bruno Solo, *Blood on the Docks*) sets out to clear her name. Unfortunately, the search proves more dangerous than he might have guessed.

Les Petits Meurtres D'Agatha Christie - *France* - 2009 to present - In English, it's "The Little Murders of Agatha Christie", and this one offers a number of single episode Agatha Christie adaptations in French with English subtitles.

The Level - 2016 to 2017 - A detective is the missing witness in the murder of a drug trafficker. The police want her, and the killer wants her dead.

Like Father Like Son - 2005 - Things seem to be looking up for one single mother with a dark past, but then her son learns the truth about his father. Tara Fitzgerald (*Game of Thrones*), Jemma Redgrave (*Holby City*), and Robson Green (*Grantchester*) star in this psychological thriller miniseries.

Line of Duty – 2012 to present - This suspenseful British police series is set in the fictional "anti-corruption unit" AC-12, where the police police the police. Yes, we know that sounds a bit odd. Lennie James, Vicky McClure, Martin Compston, and Adrian Dunbar all feature.

Loch Ness - 2017 to present - Highlands Detective Annie Redford faces her first murder case when a human heart is found.

London Kills - 2019 - This Acorn TV Original follows a team of London's top detectives as they investigate homicides. Hugo Speer (*The Full Monty*) stars as DI David Bradford, the lead investigator whose talents seem to solve every case but the disappearance of his wife. Sharon Small (*The Inspector Lynley Mysteries*) and Bailey Patrick (*Bodyguard*) also star.

We had the opportunity to interview two of the stars from London Kills: Hugo Speer and Bailey Patrick. You can view their interviews at IHeartBritishTV.com/hugo and IHeartBritishTV.com/bailey

Lovejoy - 1986 to 1994 - Ian McShane (*Deadwood*) stars as Lovejoy, the slightly shady antiques dealer and part-time detective. *Downton Abbey* fans will be delighted to see a young Phyllis Logan (aka Mrs. Hughes) in this early role.

Manhunt - 2018 to present - Martin Clunes (*Doc Martin*) stars in this series based on the real investigation into the death of French student Amélie Delagrange. Clunes plays DCI Colin Sutton, the man who led the task force that ultimately brought her killer to justice. Though it feels very much like a miniseries, it's been confirmed that another series will be produced at some point in the future.

>><< We had the opportunity to interview Mr. Clunes prior to the Series 1 premiere, and you can read the full interview at IHeartBritishTV.com/martin1

Mayday - 2013 - When the May Queen disappears just before May Day celebrations, a small town is thrown into chaos.

McCallum - 1995 to 1998 - Pathologist McCallum and his team help the dead tell their stories.

Midsomer Murders - 1998 to present - In Midsomer County, the landscapes are beautiful, the villagers all have secrets, and murder is rampant. This British mystery classic features John Nettles as DCI Tom Barnaby through the first 13 seasons, with Neil Dudgeon as DCI John Barnaby for the later seasons.

Midsomer Murders: 20th Anniversary Special - 2019 - John Nettles presents this look back at Midsomer Murders on its 20th anniversary. The hour-long special features appearances by Neil Dudgeon, Nick Hendrix, Daniel Casey, Jason Hughes, Jane Wymark, and more.

Midsomer Murders: Neil Dudgeon's Top 10 - This special collection doesn't include any new episodes of Midsomer Murders, but it does feature commentary and behind-the-scenes stories from Neil Dudgeon.

Mind Games - 2001 - Fiona Shaw (*Killing Eve*) stars in this television movie about a nun turned criminal profiler who's called in to investigate the deaths of two middle-aged women. She quickly realises that these aren't just home robberies gone wrong - they're the work of a serial killer.

Miss Fisher's Murder Mysteries - *Australian* -2012 to 2015 - In 1920s Melbourne, Miss Phryne Fisher works as a skilled private detective. Essie Davis and Nathan Page star.

Miss Fisher & The Crypt of Tears - *Australian* - 2020 - This movie is a continuation of the original Miss Fisher's Murder Mysteries stories, and it premiered in early 2020. In this one, Essie Davis returns to the role of Phyrne in 1929 Jerusalem. There, she rescues a young Bedouin girl and finds herself on a globe-trotting adventure with her favourite handsome detective, Jack Robinson (Nathan Page).

Mr. and Mrs. Murder - *Australian* - 2013 - A married couple runs a crime scene cleaning business while also helping to solve the murders they clean up.

Ms. Fisher's Modern Murder Mysteries - *Australian* - In this spin-off to the original *Miss Fisher's Murder Mysteries* series, Phryne Fisher's long-lost niece follows in her aunt's footsteps as a 1960s lady detective with her own handsome officer. Geraldine Hakewill stars as Peregrine Fisher, and Joel Jackson plays Detective James Steed.

Murder Investigation Team - 2003 to 2005 - A London-based team of elite investigators handles exceptionally challenging murders.

Murderland - 2009 - This miniseries looks at a murder from the perspectives of the daughter, the detective, and the murder victim.

Murdoch Mysteries - *Canada* - 2008 to present - Set in the 1890s, Murdoch uses early forensics to solve murders. Yannick Bisson stars as Detective William Murdoch, Helene Joy plays Dr. Julia Ogden, and Thomas Craig and Jonny Harris fill the roles of Inspector Thomas Brackenreid and Constable George Crabtree, respectively.

Murdoch Mysteries: The Movies - *Canada* - 2004 to 2005 - Before it was a hit television series, there were three Murdoch Mysteries movies. Also set in 1890s Canada, the movies feature Peter Outerbridge as Detective William Murdoch (as opposed to Yannick Bisson) and Keeley

Hawes (*The Durrells, Bodyguard*) as Dr. Julia Ogden.

Murphy's Law - 2001 to 2007 - James Nesbitt (*Cold Feet*) stars as Tommy Murphy, a charming but tough Northern Irish cop with a tragic past.

My Life is Murder - *Australia* - 2019 - Lucy Lawless (*Xena: Warrior Princess*) stars as retired Melbourne cop Alexa Crowe. Alexa is a mystery, but we know she's tough, smart, hurting from a past trauma, and great at baking bread. She's also slowly warming up to the cat who's invited itself to live with her. In each episode, her old boss (played by Bernard Curry) requests her assistance on a tough case - and on each case, she seeks a bit of extra help from her protégé Madison (Ebony Vagulans).

Mystery Road - *Australia* - 2018 to present - Detective Jay Swan investigates crimes in the Australian Outback.

No Offence - 2015 to 2018 - This gritty Manchester-based police drama showcases the work of some talented serious crimes investigators under the straight-talking DI Viv Deering. Sadly, one of the actors, Will Mellor, made an Instagram post letting people know that a fourth season won't be happening due to changes at the network (Channel 4). The writer, Paul Abbott (*Shameless*), had already been working on ideas for a new season, but unless the show is somehow saved, it looks like we may never see them brought to life.

The Oldenheim 12 - *The Netherlands* - 2017 - A traditional Dutch village is shaken to its core when multiple residents suddenly go missing without a trace.

Pie in the Sky - 1994 to 1997 - When DI Crabbe leaves the police force to open a restaurant, they continue to pull him back in for part-time crime-solving. Richard Griffiths (Vernon Dursley in *Harry Potter*) stars, but you'll also spot guest appearances from actors like Phyllis Logan (*Downton Abbey*), Jim Carter (*Downton Abbey*), Jane Wymark (*Midsomer Murders*), Keeley Hawes (*Bodyguard*), Ian McNeice (*Doc Martin*), Michael Kitchen (*Foyle's War*), Derren Litten (*Benidorm*), Abigail Thaw (*Endeavour*), Nicola Walker (*Unforgotten*), and Joan Sims (*As Time Goes By*).

The Poison Tree - 2012 - Matthew Goode (*A Discovery of Witches*) stars in this psychological thriller about a man who returns home after being released from prison. Though his devoted wife (MyAnna Buring, *Ripper Street*) has always maintained his innocence, he comes to realise she may be hiding more than her fair share of dark secrets.

Prisoners' Wives - 2012 - Gemma thinks she has a perfect life until her husband is arrested for murder.

Queens of Mystery - 2019 - Young Matilda Stone is just beginning her career in law enforcement and she has not one, not two, but three crime-writing aunts. Her quirky aunts raised her after the disappearance of her mother, and they always manage to worm their way into her cases. This series was created by *Doc Martin* writer Julian Unthank, and features appearances by Olivia Vinall (*The Woman in White*), Julia Graham (*Bletchley Circle*), Siobhan Redmond (*Taggart*), and Sarah Woodward (*Gems*).

>><< When Queens of Mystery premiered, we had the opportunity to interview Julie Graham about her role in the new series. You can read it at IHeartBritishTV.com/juliegraham

Rebecka Martinsson - 2017 to present - *Sweden* - This Swedish crime drama follows a young Stockholm lawyer as her life is turned upside down by the violent murder of a childhood friend. She quits her job and returns to her hometown to investigate a world that's not what it seems.

Rebus - 2000 to 2004 - Based on the novels of Scottish author Ian Rankin, Inspector Rebus is an old-fashioned detective in every sense of the word. He smokes, drinks, and doesn't have a lot of luck with his personal life. Set in Edinburgh, the series features John Hannah as DI John Rebus in early episodes, followed by Ken Stott in later episodes.

Reilly: Ace of Spies - 1983 - Sam Neill plays Sidney Reilly, the legendary British spy who inspired James Bond.

Rumpole of the Bailey - 1978 to 1992 - No British TV education is complete without watching this series about the cigar-puffing, cheap wine-drinking, incredibly eccentric defense barrister Horace Rumpole (played by Australian Leo McKern). This classic comedy features relatively early performances from Patricia Hodge (*Miranda*), Camilla Coduri (*Doctor Who*), and Brenda Blethyn (*Vera*).

The Schouwendam 12 - *Netherlands* - 2019

- Decades ago, teenagers Alice and Olaf disappeared from their Dutch village of Schouwendam without an indication of what might have happened. Now, an unknown man has arrived, strongly resembling Olaf but with no memories of his past. It's not long before more deaths start to occur, and the village is forced to confront not just the past, but the possibility there might be a killer in their midst.

The Silence – 2010 - While struggling to integrate into the hearing world, a young girl with a new cochlear implant witnesses the murder of a police officer. Douglas Henshall (*Shetland*) is among the stars of this miniseries.

Single-Handed - 2007 to 2010 - *Ireland* - Jack Driscoll is transferred back to his hometown to take over the Garda Sergeant role his father left.

Sisters, aka Sorelle - 2017 - *Italy* - In this Italian-language mystery, a young lawyer returns to her Italian hometown to investigate the disappearance of her younger sister. As she's drawn further into the case, she realises the main suspect may be closer than she thinks.

The Sommerdahl Murders - *Denmark* - 2020 - In the beautiful Danish coastal town of Helsingør, Detective Chief Inspector Dan Sommerdahl (Peter Mygind, *Flame and Citron*) is the undisputed hero at North Sjælland Police. When the body of a young woman washes up on a beach, Dan and his best friend and colleague, Detective Flemming Torp (André Babikian, *The Protectors*), quickly determine this wasn't an accident, and they are in hot pursuit to find the murderer and the baby the female victim had just given birth to.

Still Life: A Three Pines Mystery - *Canada* - 2013 - In this television movie, Chief Inspector Armand Gamache (Nathaniel Parker) arrives in Three Pines to investigate a strange death in the sleepy village of Three Pines.

Supply and Demand - 1997 to 1998 - This crime drama features an elite team of detectives charged with investigating large-scale smugglers and importers.

Suspects - 2014 to 2016 - Three Greater London detectives investigate serious crimes in this heavily improvised series.

The Poirot Collection - This collections offers Series 7 and 8 of David Suchet's portrayal of the Agatha Christie sleuth.

The Rivals of Sherlock Holmes - 1971 to 1973 - This vintage British mystery series offers up a variety of detective story adaptations from Sir Arthur Conan Doyle's contemporaries.

Thorne - 2010 - This collection of two Thorne movies includes *Scaredy Cat* and *Sleepyhead*. In *Sleepyhead*, DI Thorne (David Morrissey, *Men Behaving Badly*) is in a race against time to find a serial killer who enjoys making unusual attacks on young women. *Scaredy Cat* sees Thorne is working with a new team to tackle a tough double murder case, but it's not long before he's hunting down two different serial killers.

Traffik - 1989 - This drama tells a story about the international drug trade through the lens of three different characters: Jack, the British government minister who sees heroin hurting his constituents; Helen, a woman whose husband has been arrested; and Fazal, a Pakistani man who works for a drug lord. The series was filmed on location in London, Hamburg, and Pakistan.

Trial & Retribution - 1997 to 2009 - DS Walker and his team follow criminals from their crime to the courts.

The Truth Will Out - 2018 to present - Detective Peter Wendel sets out to create an elite task force to help solve cold cases, but when he finally gets his chance, the only available officers seem to be some of Sweden's worst. Meanwhile, he's dealing with the possibility that a noted serial killer may not have killed all his victims - leaving another murderer, or even many murderers, running free.

Vera - 2011 to present - DCI Vera Stanhope investigates murders in the Northumberland countryside. Brenda Blethyn (*Chance in a Million*) stars in this long-running crime drama based on Ann Cleeves' *Vera* novels. This series is split between Acorn TV and BritBox, with Acorn having seasons 1, 2, 6, and 7.

Vexed – 2010 to 2012 - A young male and female detective team frustrate each other with their different attitudes and complicated personal lives.

Winter - 2015 - *Australia* - Eve Winter, a Sydney homicide detective, solves some of the most difficult cases while dealing with bureaucracy and the challenges of being a woman in her field. Rebecca Gibney

(*Packed to the Rafters*) stars.

Wire in the Blood - 2002 to 2009 - An eccentric psychologist helps the police solve murders by getting inside the minds of the killers. Robson Green (*Grantchester*) stars.

Dramas

800 Words - *New Zealand* - 2015 to 2018 - After the death of his wife, a man relocates his family from Sydney to a small coastal community in New Zealand.

A Dance to the Music of Time - 1997 - This miniseries adaptation of Anthony Powell's novel of the same name charts the lives of characters from the 1920s thru the 1960s.

A Place to Call Home - *Australia* - 2013 to 2018 - A mysterious woman begins a new life in Australia after World War II.

A Voyage Round My Father - 1984 - Sir Laurence Olivier stars in this family drama based on the life of John Mortimer, creator of Rumpole of the Bailey.

Accused - 2010 to 2012 - This series consists of self-contained episodes that look at how different people ended up in court. Episodes include performances by Sean Bean (*Lord of the Rings*), Christopher Eccleston (*The Leftovers*), Mackenzie Crook (*Detectorists*), and Peter Capaldi (*Doctor Who*), among others.

Ackley Bridge - 2017 to present - Two struggling schools merge to form one, and it creates big problems for the headmistress.

Alibi - 2003 - Michael Kitchen (*Foyle's War*), Phyllis Logan (*Lovejoy*), and Sophie Okonedo (*Mayday*) star in this series about a woman who helps a man dispose of a corpse, only to find she's gotten herself into something messy.

Amnesia - 2004 - This miniseries tells the story of DS MacKenzie Stone, his tireless search for his wife who disappeared 5 years prior, and an amnesiac who factors into the case.

An Accidental Soldier - 2013 - In this acclaimed WW1 drama, a 35-year-old Australian soldier flees the Western Front and finds love and refuge with a French woman in a remote farmhouse. The film is based on the novel *Silent Parts* by John Charalambous, and it tells the story of two

people who find passion at an age when they thought love had passed them by. *Editor's Note: Is anyone else laughing a bit at the thought of 35 being too old to find love?*

Anglo-Saxon Attitudes - 1992 - This dramatic satire sees an aging historian come to terms with the events of his life.

Anna Karenina - 2000 to 2001 - Helen McCrory plays the title role in this adaptation of Tolstoy's classic novel.

Anner House - 2007 - Based on one of Maeve Binchy's short stories, this film is a romantic drama about two Irish emigrants who begin new lives in Cape Town while struggling to deal with their pasts.

Anzac Girls - *Australia* - 2014 - Heroic women rise to the occasion during the war.

Back Home - *Italy* - 2017 - After spending five years in a coma, an Italian man awakens to find that his wife is now with his best friend, his kids are grown up, and his business is all but ruined.

Bang - 2017 to present - In this bilingual Welsh crime drama, a man comes into possession of a gun and his life is forever changed.

Bed of Roses - *Australia* - 2008 to 2011 - A mother and daughter struggle after the death of their husband and father.

Behaving Badly - 1989 - Dame Judi Dench stars in this funny drama about a woman who decides not to take things lying down after her husband leaves her for a much younger woman.

Black Widows - *Finland* - 2016 to 2017 - Three best friends are going through a mid-life crisis and think that life will be better if their husbands are dead. Unfortunately for them, it's not quite as simple as they had imagined.

The Blue Rose - New Zealand - 2013 - This investigative drama sees a group of law firm employees joining together to figure out what happened in the mysterious death of a co-worker.

11

Bodily Harm - 2002 - Timothy Spall (*Blandings*) stars as a suburban man whose life is changed forever after he loses his job, finds out his father is dying, and catches his wife cheating.

Bomb Girls - 2012 to 2013 - Set during World War II, BOMB GIRLS tells the remarkable stories of women who risked their lives in a munitions factory as they build bombs for the Allied Forces. The series stars Meg Tilly (*The Big Chill*), Jodi Balfour (*Quarry*), Charlotte Hegele (*When Calls The Heart*) and Ali Liebert (*Ten Days in the Valley*).

The Boy with the Topknot - 2017 - This film tells the story of Sathnam, young Indian raised in Britain, as he tries to adjust to his multicultural life.

Brief Encounters - 2016 - When a group of women start selling lingerie and other marital aids through at-home parties in the early 1980s, their lives are transformed.

The Camomile Lawn - 1992 - In August 1939, a family comes together for one last wonderful summer before WWII. Felicity Kendal and Paul Eddington (both of *The Good Life*) appear in this lovely British drama.

Capital - 2015 - When property values soar on a once middle-class London street, residents receive mysterious postcards saying, "We want what you have."

Care - 2018 - Sheridan Smith (*Gavin & Stacey*) stars as a single mother struggling to raise her two children after a family tragedy. After her husband's departure, she's fully reliant on the childcare her mother Mary (Alison Steadman, also from *Gavin & Stacey*) provides. That all changes when Mary suffers a devastating stroke and develops dementia.

The Case - 2011 - This legal drama tells the story of a man put on trial for the murder of his terminally ill partner after he helped her commit suicide.

Cider with Rosie - 2015 - This feature-length drama tells a coming of age story set in rural, post-WWI England.

Cilla - 2014 - Cilla tells the story of British entertainer Cilla Black and her rise to fame in 1960s Liverpool.

Clean Break - 2015 - When a car dealer realises he's in trouble and about to lose everything, he sets out to fix his problems while also exacting revenge on those who have hurt him.

Close to the Enemy - 2016 - After WW2, a German engineer is taken to Britain in hopes of gaining his cooperation. Jim Sturgess (*Across the Universe*) and Charlotte Riley (*Press*) star.

Cloudstreet - *Australia* - 2011 - This period drama is set around Perth, Australia between 1943 and 1963, and it tells the story of two families thrown together in a large house after a series of catastrophes.

The Code - *Australia* - 2014 to 2016 - When two brothers, a hacker and a journalist, are facing the possibility of extradition to the US, the Australian National Security offers them a way out. They're taken to a government facility and told that if they help out out with their efforts, the slate will be wiped clean.

Dear Murderer - *New Zealand* - 2017 to present - This series tells the true story of Mike Bungay, one of New Zealand's most successful and controversial defense lawyers.

Delicious - 2016 to present - Two women in Cornwall try to get on somewhat peacefully after circumstances in their lives change dramatically.

Doctor Finlay - 1993 to 1996 - After WW2 and before the NHS is created, a doctor returns to his Scottish hometown.

Dominion Creek - *Ireland* - 2015 to present - Three Irish brothers dream of striking it rich in the Klondike Gold Rush.

East of Everything - *Australia* - 2008 to 2009 - When an Australian woman dies, she dictates in her will that her two estranged sons must reopen the family hostel in Broken Bay.

Maeve Binchy Echoes - *Ireland* - 1988 - In 1950s Ireland, a young woman longs to escape her tiny village, but local suitors may hamper her efforts.

Elizabeth I & Her Enemies - 2017 - Presenters Dan Jones (*Britain's Bloody Crown*) and Suzannah Lipscomb (Hidden Killers) take a look at those who wanted to bring down the much-respected Queen Elizabeth I.

Family Business - *France* - 2017 - A mother-daughter lawyer pair juggle the ins and outs of running a family law practice, all while balancing and navigating their own issues away from the office.

Fanny Hill - 2007 - Based on the scandalous classic novel, orphaned Fanny Hill is a prostitute who falls in love with a handsome merchant's son who also happens to be her first customer.

The Fragile Heart - 1996 - Nigel Hawthorne (*The Madness of King George*) stars as a successful cardiac surgeon in the midst of a professional and personal crisis. He plays Edgar Pascoe, a man whose world begins to cataclysmically crumble during a visit to China. Confronted by an ethical dilemma over human rights abuses, he's forced into a painful moral awakening which seeps into every area of his life.

From Father to Daughter - *Italy* - 2017 - This Italian saga begins in 1958 and covers nearly 30 years in the lives of the Franza sisters. The three work hard to impress their father, take on the family distillery business, and find love.

Girlfriends - 2018 - A group of middle-aged women experience some strange and dramatic situations, but get through it together. Miranda Richardson (*Good Omens*) stars alongside Zoë Wanamaker (*Love Hurts*) and Phyllis Logan (*Lovejoy*).

Gold Digger - 2019 - Julia Ormond (*Sabrina*) stars as Julia Day, a wealthy 60-year-old woman who falls in love with a handsome man 26 years her junior. As secrets come to light, no one can be sure what's real and what's merely convenient.

The Good Karma Hospital - 2017 to present - After a relationship sours, a young British-Indian woman decides to move to India to work in an impoverished hospital. Little does she know, she's got a lot to learn. Amanda Redman stars alongside Amrita Acharia.

The Great Train Robbery - 2013 - This two-part series tells the story of 1963's Great Train Robbery from two perspectives - the side of the robbers, and the side of the cops. Martin Compston (*Line of Duty*), Luke Evans (*The Girl on the Train*), and Jim Broadbent (*Iris*) star.

The Heart Guy (aka Doctor Doctor) - *Australia* - 2016 to present - When a prominent heart surgeon falls from grace, he's forced to go work as a country GP in his former hometown. At his lowest moment, he'll have to face the things he's spent his life trying to get away from.

The Helen West Casebook - 2002 - Amanda Burton (Silent Witness) stars as crown prosecutor Helen West, a justice-driven woman who pursues tough cases even as her boss recommends dropping them.

The Hour - 2011 - This period drama takes us behind the scenes during the launch of a new London news programme during the mid 1950s. Ben Whishaw (*Spectre*), Romola Garai (*Emma*), Dominic West (*The Affair*), and Peter Capaldi (*Doctor Who*) are among the cast members.

I, Claudius - Sir Derek Jacobi (*Last Tango in Halifax*) and Sir Patrick Stewart (*Star Trek*) star in this BBC television adaptation of Robert Graves' 1934 novel of the same name (along with its sequel, *Claudius the God*). The series covers the early history of the Roman Empire, with an elderly Emperor Claudius narrating.

The Indian Doctor - 2010 to 2013 - An Indian doctor and his wife move to a small Welsh mining village during the 1960s. They have to adjust to culture shock, and Dr. Sharma must win the trust of the locals as their GP.

The Irish R.M. - *Ireland* - 1983 to 1985 - When an Englishman leaves home to become an Irish Resident Magistrate, he quickly learns the normal rules don't apply with his eccentric new neighbours.

The Invisibles - 2008 - A couple of retired master burglars tried living in Spain, but after a bout of homesickness, they returned to England with their wives to live in a Devon fishing village. It's not long before a return to familiar shores sees them taking up the same old bad habits.

Jack Irish - *Australia* - 2012 to 2018 - Guy Pearce (*Memento*) stars as Jack Irish, a talented PI and ex-lawyer with a checkered past. Marta Dusseldorp (*A Place to Call Home*) also appears as his occasional girlfriend and talented journalist helper.

Janet King - Australia - 2014 to 2017 - This spinoff from the legal drama *Crownies* follows Senior Crown Prosecutor Janet King as she returns from maternity leave and progresses through her career. Marta Dusseldorp (*A Place to Call Home*) stars.

Jennie: Lady Randolph Churchill - 1974 – This miniseries tells the story of American-born socialite and mother to Winston Churchill, Lady Randolph Churchill.

Jericho - 2016 - This Yorkshire-based 1870s period drama tells the story of a community dominated by the construction of a new viaduct. Jessica Raine (*Call the Midwife*) stars.

Lady Chatterley - 1993 - Sean Bean and Judy Richardson star in this adaptation of the scandalous DH Lawrence novel.

Land Girls - 2009 to 2011 - Land Girls follows four women in the Women's Land Army during WW2.

The Life of Verdi - 1982 - This biographical miniseries tells the story of Giuseppe Verdi, composer of operas like Aida, Rigoletto, and La Traviata.

The Lilac Bus - *Ireland* - 1990 - This drama tells the story of seven people who share a bus from Rathdoon to Dublin each weekend. It's based on a collection of eight interconnected stories by Maeve Binchy, and the stories explore topics like alcoholism, sexuality, abortion, drug use, and infidelity.

Liverpool 1 - 1998 to 1999 - This gritty, Liverpool-based police drama dives into the city's underworld. We follow the vice squad at Bridewell as they fight drug dealers, paeodophiles, pimps, and porn peddlers in this rough-around-the-edges port city. Samantha Womack stars as DC Isobel de Pauli.

Lorna Doone - 1976 - This miniseries tells the story of star-crossed lovers in 17th century Somerset and Devon.

Love Hurts - 1992 to 1994 - After a messy breakup, an ambitious woman leaves the rat race and finds herself pursued by a wealthy man who seems like trouble.

Love, Lies, & Records - 2017 - Ashley Jensen (*Agatha Raisin*) stars as Kate Dickinson, a woman constantly challenged in her efforts to balance a personal life with the stress of the records she oversees.

Marvellous - 2014 - Toby Jones (*Detectorists*) stars in this drama about a man with learning disabilities who did better than anyone expected.

The Mayor of Casterbridge - 2003 - Ciarán Hinds (*Above Suspicion*) and James Purefoy (*Rome*) star in this adaptation of Thomas Hardy's novel of the same name. It tells the story of a drunken farmer who auctions off his family, only to realise the horror of what he's done and change his life.

McLeod's Daughters - 2002 to 2009 - Two sisters separated as children are reunited when they jointly inherit a ranch in the Australian bush: the independent Claire McLeod (Lisa Chappell, *Gloss*) and her estranged half-sister, Tess (Bridie Carter, *800 Words*), a stubborn city girl with a drive to change the world. Together, they build an all-female workforce and commit to life at Drovers Run. Nearby, the men of the Ryan family help keep things interesting.

Midwinter of the Spirit – 2015 – This creepy drama follows a country vicar as she trains to be an exorcist for the Church of England. Before she's able to get much experience, she finds herself faced with powerful supernatural threats.

Missing - 2006 - Joanne Froggatt (*Downton Abbey*) stars as a young runaway who scams men to survive. When one of them turns up dead, she becomes the main suspect in a string of murders.

Mr. Palfrey of Westminster - 1984 to 1985 - The mild-mannered Mr. Palfrey may seem like "just a civil servant", but he's actually a major player in the world of espionage.

Mrs. Biggs - 2012 - Sheridan Smith (*Gavin & Stacey*) stars as Mrs. Charmian Biggs, the unsuspecting wife of one of Great Britain's most notorious robbers.

The Nest - 2020 - Sophie Rundle (*Bodyguard*) and Martin Compston (*Line of Duty*) star in this Glasgow-based drama about a couple who would do almost anything to have a child. When they meet a troubled young woman, they make her an irresistible offer.

New Worlds - 2014 - Jamie Dornan (*50 Shades of Grey*) stars in this period drama set in the 1680s. The story takes place in both England and the new American colonies, and it focuses on love and conflict in the uncertain time period. It was produced as a follow-up to *The Devil's Whore* (aka *The Devil's Mistress* in North America).

Newton's Law - *Australia* - 2017 - Josephine Newton (Claudia Karvan, *Love My Way*) is a suburban solicitor whose life has hit a few bumps. When an old friend suggests she join Knox Chambers, she decides to take on a new challenge and return to her barrister's robe.

No Tears - 2002 - This Irish legal drama is based on the true story of women who were infected with hepatitis C during childbirth in the 1990s. Brenda Fricker (*My Left Foot*) and Maria Doyle Kennedy (*The*

Tudors) star.

Party Tricks - *Australia* - 2014 - This Australian series follows Kate Ballard (Asher Keddie, *X-Men Origins: Wolverine*), a woman facing her first election for State Premier. Victory seems guaranteed until the opposition brings in a new shock candidate – David McLeod (Rodger Corser, *The Heart Guy*). McLeod is a popular media figure, but more concerning is the fact that she had a secret affair with him years earlier.

Pitching In - 2019 - Larry Lamb and Melanie Walters (both of *Gavin & Stacey*) reunite in this fun family drama about a North Wales holiday camp owner who contemplates selling up after his Welsh wife dies. Though the series has been criticised for inauthentic North Wales accents, it offers a feel-good viewing experience and scenery from a different part of the UK than we typically see in TV and film. Hayley Mills (*Wild at Heart*) also appears as Iona.

Place of Execution - 2008 - Based on the novel by Scottish novelist Val McDermid, this series follows a journalist making a film about the 1963 disappearance of a young schoolgirl.

Poldark - 1975 to 1977 - Based on the Poldark novels by Winston Graham, this series tells the story of a man who went off to fight a war and came back to find everything changed. Robin Ellis stars as Captain Ross Poldark in this older adaptation.

The Promised Life - *Italy* - 2018 - This eight episode series tells the epic tale of a Sicilian family's troubles and their eventual migration from Italy to New York.

Rake - *Australia* - 2011 to 2018 - Defense lawyer Cleaver Greene makes a career out of hopeless cases, perhaps because his own personal life is troubled enough to help him relate.

The Rector's Wife - 1994 - When a stifled vicar's wife tries to assert her independence, she meets resistance from her husband and his parishioners. When she meets a man who understands and supports her, she's easily drawn into an affair. Keep an eye out for performances from Pam Ferris (*Rosemary and Thyme*) and Prunella Scales (*Fawlty Towers*).

Relative Strangers - *Ireland* - 1999 - This drama tells the story of an Irish nurse whose happy life comes to an end when her husband dies and she learns she was living a lie. He was deeply in debt and living a double life in Dublin. After meeting the other family, she learns the other wife's child has leukaemia and needs help from her own children to survive.

Restless – 2012 – This two-part TV movie is based on a bestselling spy novel by William Boyd. It focuses on a young woman who finds out her mother was a spy for British intelligence during WWII, and that she's been on the run ever since.

The Return - 2003 - Julie Walters (*Harry Potter*) stars in this film about a woman released from prison after serving time for killing her husband. Neil Dudgeon (*Midsomer Murders*) also appears.

Run - 2013 - Olivia Colman and Lennie James star in this four-part miniseries about four seemingly unconnected people whose lives intersect after a random act of violence.

The Saint - 1962 to 1969 - Roger Moore stars as Simon Templar, a wealthy adventurer who travels the world solving crimes and engaging in all manner of secret agent hijinks. Though the settings are occasionally exotic, nearly every episode was filmed at a studio in Hertfordshire using "blue-screen" technology. The series was based on the Simon Templar novels by Leslie Charteris.

The Scapegoat - 2012 - Set in 1952, this period drama sees two men with similar faces switching places. The film is based on the novel by Daphne du Maurier, and Matthew Rhys (*The Americans*) stars.

The Scarlet Pimpernel - 1982 - Jane Seymour, Anthony Andrews, and Sir Ian McKellen star in this period drama set during the French Revolution. While many aristocrats are facing the guillotine, quite a few have escaped thanks to the efforts of a young Englishman known as the "Scarlet Pimpernel". The film is based on Baroness Orczy's 1905 novel by the same name.

Seachange - *Australia* - 1998 to 2000 - After her husband is arrested for fraud and has an affair with her sister, Laura Gibson decides to undergo a "seachange" with her children. They move to the coastal village of Pearl Bay and embark on a new kind of life.

Seachange: Paradise Reclaimed - 2019 - This 2019 reboot features original cast members Sigrid Thornton (*The Man from Snowy River*), Kerry Armstrong (*Lantana*) and John Howard (*All Saints*), and takes place 20 years after the final season. After divorce and job loss, Laura Gibson (Thornton) finds herself questioning her place in the world. But when she returns to the beachside paradise of Pearl Bay, she's able to start putting the pieces back together.

The Secret Agent - 2016 - Toby Jones (*Detectorists*) stars in this adaptation of Joseph Conrad's novel of the same name. He stars as Anton Verloc, a Soho shopkeeper who also happens to be a spy for the Russian embassy. Vicky McClure (*Line of Duty*) stars as his unassuming wife Winnie.

Secret Daughter - *Australia* - 2016 to 2017 - When a wealthy man goes out looking for the daughter he never knew, a young singer pretends to be her.

Seesaw - 1998 - David Suchet (*Poirot*) and Geraldine James (*Back to Life*) star in this series about what happens in the aftermath of a kidnapping when ransom has been paid and the loved one is returned home.

Sensitive Skin - 2014 - Kim Cattrall (*Sex and the City*) stars in this dramedy about a mid-life couple who sell their family home and move to an urban condo. Unfortunately, their wish for more excitement brings a little too much of it.

Sisters of War - *Australia* - 2010 - This film follows the lives of two Australian women during WWII - one a nun, the other an army nurse.

The Slap - *Australia* - 2011 - This series explores how one brief event can create waves of repercussions within a group of friends and family. Essie Davis (*Miss Fisher's Murder Mysteries*) and Sophie Okonedo (*Hotel Rwanda*) star in this miniseries based on Christos Tsiolkas' 2008 novel.

Slings & Arrows - *Canada* - 2003 to 2006 - This Canadian dark comedy is set at a fictitious Shakespeare festival in Canada as they embark on a production of Hamlet. Paul Gross (*Due South*) stars as washed-up actor Geoffrey Tennant, along with Rachel McAdams (*Wedding Crashers, The Notebook*), Luke Kirby (*The Marvelous Ms. Maisel*), Stephen Ouimette (*Mentors*), and Mark McKinney (*Kids in the Hall, Superstore*), who is also the co-creator/co-writer.

Straight Forward - *Denmark / New Zealand* - 2019 - After attempting to get revenge for her father's death, a Danish conwoman is forced to flee to New Zealand.

Striking Out - *Ireland* - This Acorn Original stars Amy Huberman (*Finding Joy*) as Tara Rafferty, a successful Dublin lawyer who abandons her safe life after discovering that her fiancé is cheating on her. She cancels the wedding, quits her job, and begins a new and unconventional private practice. Neil Morrissey (*Men Behaving Badly*) and Rory Keenan (*War & Peace*) also star.

Sword of Honour - 2001 - Daniel Craig stars as Guy Crouchman, an Englishman returning home from Italy at the outbreak of WWII. Horrified by Nazis and upset over his divorce, he joins up with the Royal Corps of Halberdiers. The film is based on the *Sword of Honour* novel trilogy by Evelyn Waugh.

The Syndicate: Playing for Keeps - 2013 - Each series of The Syndicate follows a different group of lottery winners as they grapple with personal dramas, newfound wealth, and temptation. Acorn has just one series, but there are two others.

Taken Down - *Ireland* - 2018 - When a Nigerian girl is killed in Dublin, Inspector Jen Rooney is drawn into a refugee community where some may know more than they're letting on.

Tales of the City - 1994 - This British-American miniseries is based on Armistead Maupin's book about colorful people living in San Francisco.

Therese Raquin - 1980 - Based on the novel by Emile Zola, this miniseries tells a tale of passion, obsession, and desperate acts. When first published, the novel was described as "putrid" by the newspaper *Le Figaro*, and it's not recommended for young audiences.

The Time of Our Lives - *Australia* - 2013 to 2014 - This drama follows the lives of an extended family in inner-city Melbourne as they build families, pursue careers, and work on their relationships.

The Trench - 1999 - Daniel Craig stars in this film about young British soldiers stationed on the Western Front during WWI.

Trust - 2000 - Caroline Goodall (*Schindler's List*) stars as Anne, a successful young woman in what seems like a happy marriage. Unfortunately, there's something quite dark on the horizon.

Turning Green - *Ireland* - 2005 - When a teenage boy's mother dies, he's forced to live with his three Irish aunts. He wants nothing more than to return to America, and in pursuit of the funds to do so, he starts a successful business selling illegal magazines.

Under Capricorn - *Australia* - 1983 - When a young Irish immigrant heads to Australia to make his fortune, he soon finds himself mixed up with a wealthy family that's hiding a lot of secrets.

United - 2011 - David Tennant (*Deadwater Fell*) stars in this film based on the true story of Manchester United's 1958 air crash that killed eight of their members.

The Viceroys - *Italy* - 2007 - In 1800s Sicily, the Uzeda family fights to retain control after the unification of Italy.

Vidago Palace - *Portugal* - 2017 - Set in 1936, this Portuguese romance is set at the Vidago Palace hotel where Europe'e elite flee from the Spanish Civil War.

War & Peace - 2007 - Based on the Tolstoy novel, this series follows four aristocratic families during the Napoleonic era. Malcolm McDowell (*A Clockwork Orange*), Brenda Blethyn (*Vera*), Clemence Poesy (*The Tunnel*), and Ken Duken (*Inglourious Basterds*) are among the stars.

The Way Back - 2010 - A group of prisoners escape from a Siberian gulag and trek across four thousand miles to reach freedom in India. Ed Harris, Colin Farrell, and Saoirse Ronan are among the stars.

Wide Sargasso Sea - 2006 - This prequel to Jane Eyre tells the story of the first Mrs. Rochester and how she ended up in the attic at Thornfield Hall. Rebecca Hall (*Parade's End*) and Rafe Spall (*The Big Short*) star.

Wild at Heart - 2006 to 2013 - Stephen Tompkinson (*DCI Banks*, *Ballykissangel*) stars in this series about a British veterinarian who takes his family along to South Africa to release an animal back into the wild. When he sees the area and meets pretty game reserve owner Caroline (Hayley Mills), he ultimately decides to stay.

Wild Decembers - 2009 - Based on Edna O'Brien's novel of the same name, this film tells the story of two young lovers whose relationship is threatened by a centuries-old feud.

What to Do When Someone Dies - 2011 - Anna Friel (*Marcella*) plays schoolteacher Ellie Manning, a woman trying to have a baby with her husband Greg (Marc Warren, *Jonathan Strange & Mr. Norrell*). One night, he doesn't return home from work. Ellie is horrified to learn he has been killed in a terrible car accident, and he wasn't alone – there was a woman in the passenger seat. A tormented Ellie begins to question: who is the mystery woman and was Greg having a secret affair?

Wreckers - 2011 - Benedict Cumberbatch (*Sherlock*), Claire Foy (*The Crown*), and Shaun Evans (*Endeavour*) star in this film about a couple who move to an idyllic town to start a family, only to find new stress on their relationship when husband David's disturbed brother starts sharing old secrets.

Comedies

Ain't Misbehavin' - 1997 - Robson Green (*Grantchester*) and Jerome Flynn star as two bandsmen during 1940s London. Julia Sawalha (*Absolutely Fabulous, Press Gang*) stars as the lovely Dolly Nightingale, Green's character's love interest. *Downton Abbey*'s Jim Carter also appears.

All in Good Faith - 1985 to 1988 - Middle-aged Reverend Philip Lambe decides to relocate from rural Oxfordshire to an urban Midlands parish, inheriting a whole new set of issues. Richard Briers (*The Good Life, Monarch of the Glen*) stars.

Birds of a Feather - 1989 to 1998, 2014 to 2016 - This long-running comedy series follows the lives of two very different sisters left to fend for themselves after their husbands go to prison for armed robbery.

Boomers - 2014 to 2016 - Retired friends make comedy of learning to deal with retirement.

Count Arthur Strong - 2013 to 2017 - A delusional former actor tries to put together his life story with the help of a partner's son.

Cradle to Grave - 2015 - Danny Baker and his friends grow up in 1970s South London.

Decline and Fall - 2017 - After a prank, an Oxford student is wrongly dismissed for indecent exposure, going to work at a sub-par private school in Wales. This series is an adaptation of Evelyn Waugh's novel of the same name.

Detectorists - 2014 to 2017 - Two quirky friends scan the fields of England with metal detectors, hoping for the big find that will finally let them do the gold dance.

The Delivery Man – 2015 - Former police officer Matthew begins work as a midwife. He's the first male midwife to hit the unit, and he hopes his new career will give him more satisfaction than his previous work.

Doc Martin - 2004 to present - Martin Clunes (*Men Behaving Badly*) stars in this comedy about a brilliant but grumpy London surgeon who suddenly develops a fear of blood. He leaves his high-flying career and takes a post in a Cornish fishing village where he spent holidays as a child with his Aunt Joan. His bad attitude and lack of social skills makes it a challenge to adapt to his new life.

Executive Stress - 1986 to 1988 - Penelope Keith (*The Good Life, To the Manor Born*) stars in this sitcom about a couple forced to go undercover to work together, only to have the wife become the husband's boss.

Finding Joy - *Ireland* - 2018 to present - A young Irish woman named Joy struggles in the aftermath of a breakup, but not nearly as much as her dog (who becomes incontinent). At the same time, Joy is promoted to a position that takes her out of her comfort zone.

French Fields - 1989 to 1991 - A British couple moves to France and has difficulties adjusting to French culture. This series is a follow-up to *Fresh Fields*.

Fresh Fields - 1984 to 1986 - A suburban couple must find new hobbies and interests after their children leave the nest.

Golden Years - 2016 - This quirky film sees a couple of pensioners lose their hard-earned retirement funds in a financial crisis, only to turn to robbing banks to replenish the loss.

Henry IX - 2017 to present - King Henry has a mid-life crisis.

Kingdom - 2007 to 2009 - Stephen Fry (*QI*) stars as a country solicitor in the small town of Market Shipborough. Working with his trusty secretary Gloria and reasonably capable assistant Lyle, it should be a peaceful life. The only problem? He has a crazy sister and he recently lost his half-brother in mysterious circumstances. Hermione Norris (*Cold Feet*) and Celia Imrie (*Bergerac*) also star.

Ladies of Letters - 2009 to 2010 - Two widows meet under a table at a wedding, then maintain a friendship via letters.

The Man Who Lost His Head - 2007 - Martin Clunes stars in this film about a curator at the British Museum who gets in over his head while returning an ancient Maori carving to New Zealand.

The Moodys - Australia - 2012 to 2014 - This Australian comedy follows a dysfunctional family over the course of several Christmas holidays. In the second season, it follows the family as they progress through significant events in their year.

Mount Pleasant - 2011 to 2017 - This dramedy dives into the lives of a tight-knit Manchester family, focusing on their everyday struggles and hurdles. The cast includes Pauline Collins (*Upstairs Downstairs*), Sally Lindsay (*Coronation Street, Scott & Bailey*), and Daniel Ryan (*Black Sea*). Robson Green (*Grantchester*) also appears in a handful of episodes.

The Other One - 2017 - After a man drops dead at his birthday party, his family learns he has another, entirely separate family they didn't know about - just 13 miles away. What else can they do but decide to make the best of it?

Over the Rainbow - 1993 - On his wedding day, Neil is arrested for robbery. A year later, he returns to his wife's flat only to learn she's living with his best mate.

Parents - 2012 - A businesswoman finds out her husband has lost their life savings on the day she loses her job, and they have to go live with her parents.

Raised by Wolves - 2013 to 2016 - A single mother raises her large family in a not-so-conventional way.

The Rebel - 2016 to 2017 - A grumpy retired man rebels against everything, leaving his friends and family to clean up whatever messes he makes. Simon Callow stars in this Brighton-based comedy.

Reggie Perrin - 2009 to 2010 - Martin Clunes stars in this remake of the classic Reginald Perrin stories.

Sando - 2018 to present - *Australia* - Sando is the queen of package furniture deals in Australia.

The Simple Heist - *Sweden* - 2017 - When two older women find themselves cash-strapped and overlooked, they decide to turn to crime.

Terry Pratchett's Going Postal - 2010 - This adaptation of Pratchett's novel see con man Moist von Lipwig (Richard Coyl, *Chilling Adventures of Sabrina*) caught by the law and given two choices: suffer a painful death, or take over a derelict post office. Also starring David Suchet (*Poirot*), Charles Dance (*Game of Thrones*), and Claire Foy (*The Crown*).

Together - 2015 - This short-lived sitcom focuses on a young couple in the early stages of their relationship.

Trivia - *Ireland* - 2011 to 2012 - *Ireland* - A highly-dedicated quiz team leader in Ireland knows everything but how to deal with other people.

White Teeth - 2002 - Based on Zadie Smith's popular novel, this series tells the story of three families in Willesden, a neighbourhood in northwest London. The series takes places over three decades in the increasingly diverse modern Britain. Stars include Om Puri (*The Hundred-Foot Journey*), Phil Davis (*Vera Drake*), Naomie Harris (*28 Days Later*) and Archie Panjabi (*The Good Wife*).

Whites - 2010 - Alan Davies (*Jonathan Creek*) stars as a chef in a posh country hotel.

The Worst Week of My Life - 2004 to 2007 - Ben Miller (*Death in Paradise*) stars with Sarah Alexander (*Coupling*) as the world's most disastrously awkward fiancé and husband.

You, Me, & Them - 2013 to 2015 - Anthony Head and Eve Myles star in this sitcom about an age gap romance. Acorn has Series 1, but you can find Series 2 on Amazon's Prime Video.

Documentary & Lifestyle

1900 Island - 2019 - On a deserted island in Wales, four modern families live as people would have lived more than 100 years ago. The series gives us a look at both the hardships and the joys of a simpler kind of life.

A Royal Tour of the 20th Century - 2019 - This docuseries takes a look at the royal tours and state visits of the British royal family over the last century.

A Stitch in Time – 2016 - Amber Butchart takes a look at historical figures through the clothing they wore.

Alexandria: The Greatest City - 2016 - Historian Bettany Hughes explores the once-grand city of Alexandria, founded by Alexander the Great and home to Cleopatra.

Art of the Heist - 2007 - This series takes a look at some of the world's biggest, most audacious acts of art theft.

At Home with the Georgians - 2010 - Over the course of three episodes, prize-winning author Amanda Vickery unlocks the secrets of the Georgian home by investigating the lives of the people who lived in them. The series is based on her highly acclaimed book "Behind Closed Doors – At Home in Georgian England".

The Ballroom Boys - 2016 - This short documentary follows a group of Welsh boys as they prepare for a ballroom dancing competition.

Baroque - 2015 - Noted art critic Waldemar Januszczak traces the history of the Baroque movement from its start as a Vatican-approved religious art style to a bigger global movement.

Barristers - 2014 - This groundbreaking series takes us behind the scenes to see the inner workings of the British courts.

Bollywood: The World's Biggest Film Industry - 2018 - This two-part series examines the world's largest film industry, complete with access to stars and active productions.

The Brilliant Brontë Sisters - 2013 - Sheila Hancock takes us on a journey through Yorkshire, looking at these incredible sisters who changed British literature forever.

Britain's Bloodiest Dynasty - 2014 - Historian Dan Jones tells the story of the Plantagenets, one of Britain's darkest and most brutal dynasties.

Britain's Bloody Crown - 2016 - Dan Jones presents this four-part documentary about the War of the Roses.

Caligula with Mary Beard - 2013 - Cambridge classicist Mary Beard takes a look at the life and times of the scandalous Roman emperor Caligula.

Can a Computer Write a Hit Musical - 2016 - As computers become more and more advanced, they get closer to taking over those creative tasks many of us assumed to be out of their capabilities. In this programme, a team of scientists and musical writers attempt to devise a recipe for a computer-generated musical.

Churchill: Blood Sweat, & Oil Paint - 1970 - Hosted by Andrew Marr, this BBC special tells the fascinating story of Winston Churchill's lifelong love of painting. He meets Churchill's descendants and explores the connections between his private passion for painting and his public career as politician and statesman.

The Churchills - 2012 - David Starkey looks at the links between Winston Churchill and his ancestor John Churchill, a man who dared to go up against Louis XIV of France.

Civil War - 2002 - Dr. Tristram Hunt takes a look at the conflict that briefly toppled the English monarchy back in the 17th century.

Civil War: The Untold Story - 2014 - Elizabeth McGovern (*Downton Abbey*) hosts this documentary about the Civil War and the North/South divide in the United States.

Julia Bradbury's Coast and Country Walks - 2008 - Keen rambler and host Julia Bradbury (*The Magicians, The Greek Islands with Julia Bradbury*) takes viewers on an adventure around historic railway lines in England, Scotland and Wales.

Coastal Railways with Julie Walters - 2017 - Julie Walters travels Britain's most scenic coastal railways, stopping off to visit the people and villages along the way.

David Jason's Secret Service - 2017 - Sir David Jason hosts this fascinating docuseries about Britain's history of espionage.

David Suchet's Being Poirot - 2015 - Generally regarded as the best Poirot of all time, David Suchet held the iconic role for roughly a quarter of a century. In this three-part series, he attempts to share some of his experiences and explain why people have loved Poirot for so long.

The Detectives - 2017 - This docuseries follows specialist units within the Manchester police force as they unravel some of the worst crimes in their area.

Digging for Britain - 2010 to 2016 - Professor Alice Roberts shares her passion for Britain's history as she takes us to a variety of exciting archaeological sites. From Roman burial sites to Viking treasures to history as recent as World War II, there's a bit of everything in this one, along with plenty of expert commentary to help add context.

Discovering Britain - 2018 - In this fun travel series, Maureen Lipman (*Metamorphosis*) and Larry Lamb (*Gavin &*

Stacey) join a number of their fellow British actors as they travel the country exploring its heritage.

Edward & Mary: The Unknown Tudors – 2002 - This two-part special tells the story of King Edward and Queen (Bloody) Mary, eldest daughter of Henry VIII and first English queen since Matilda.

Empire - 2015 - Jeremy Paxman (*The Victorians*) hosts this five-part series about the impact and enduring legacy of the British empire.

The Family Farm - 2018 - BBC presenter Kate Humble visits with three families who leave urban life to live on farms in remote Wales.

The Genius of Roald Dahl - 2012 - Comedian and bestselling author David Walliams delves into Roald Dahl's world, chatting with those who knew him best. He meets Dahl's widow at the family home, and chats with longtime illustrator Quentin Blake as he draws a Dahl villain.

Genius of the Ancient World – 2015 - Historian Bettany Hughes travels the world to study the lives and times of great philosophers like Socrates, Confucius, and Buddha.

Henry IX: Lost King - 2017 - Many have called Henry Frederick, Prince of Wales the best king England never had. Though bright and promising, he died at the age of 18 from typhoid fever. This documentary looks at the achievements in his short life, along with what might of been, had he lived.

Hidden Britain by Drone - 2016 - Tony Robinson (*Time Team*) uses drones to snoop on parts of Britain not normally visible to those of us confined to the ground. The series includes a look at abandoned homes in the Outer Hebrides of Scotland, a WWII shipwreck along the Kent coast, and a peek at an abandoned theme park.

Joseph Campbell: Mythos 1 - 1999 - Watch this series of lectures on the "one great story", filmed shortly before Joseph Campbell's death in 1987.

Keeping the Castle - 2018 - Though it may sound wonderful, managing a stately home can be an enormous financial burden and family obligation. This series takes a look at the challenges of managing these enormous, sometimes crumbling homes in modern times.

King Arthur's Britain - 2015 - Archaeologist Francis Pryor takes a look back to what Great Britain was like during the days of King Arthur.

Living in the Shadow of World War II - 2017 - World War II affected more than just the people on the battlefield. Back home, the war cast a shadow over nearly every aspect of day-to-day life. This series takes a look at the ways the war affected people on the homefront.

Lords and Ladles - 2016 - Three of Ireland's top chefs travel to stately homes and prepare grand dinners as they might have done in centuries past.

Lost Kingdoms of Africa - 2010 - Dr. Gus Casely-Hayford takes us on a journey through the "forgotten" civilisations of Africa.

Magic Numbers: Hannah Fry's Mysterious World of Maths - 2018 - Hannah Fry examines where math came from.

Martin Clunes: Islands of America - 2019 - Martin Clunes travels the islands of the United States, stopping off in Hawaii, Alaska, Washington, California, Louisiana, Puerto Rico, Georgia, North Carolina, Virginia, New York, Massachusetts, and Maine.

Martin Clunes: Islands of Australia - 2016 - Martin Clunes explores some of the lesser-known islands off Australia's coast

Medieval Lives - 2013 - This series takes a look at how people handled life's three major rites of passage in the Middle Ages: birth, marriage, and death.

Monarchy with David Starkey - 2005 - Dr. David Starkey hosts this in-depth series about Britain's kings and queens from the Saxon era to the early 20th century.

Monty Don's Paradise Gardens - 2018 - Gardening expert Monty Don takes us to the Middle East and beyond in search of some of the world's finest "paradise" gardens.

My Welsh Sheepdog - 2016 - BBC presenter Kate Humble travels around Wales with her dog Teg to learn more about the rare Welsh sheepdog breed.

Narnia's Lost Poet: The Secret Lives and Loves of C.S. Lewis - 2013 - C.S. Lewis biographer A.N. Wilson embarks on a journey to find the man behind Narnia. He was incredibly secretive about his private life, and even his best friend (J.R.R. Tolkien) was unaware of his late-in-life marriage to a divorced American woman.

Off the Beaten Track - 2018 - BBC presenter Kate Humble is back with her Welsh sheepdog Teg, this time travelling through some of the wildest bits of Wales.

Penelope Keith's Hidden Coastal Villages - 2018 - Penelope Keith (*The Good Life*) travels the UK, visiting some of the most beautiful coastal villages.

Penelope Keith's Hidden Villages - 2014 to 2016 - Penelope Keith takes us on a tour of the UK's loveliest villages and quirkiest characters.

Penelope Keith's Village of the Year - 2018 - This delightful competition gives us a great deal of insight into what makes some of the UK's most beautiful villages tick. Rather than just looking at the scenery, we get to meet village inhabitants and find out what they love about the places they call home.

Poirot: Super Sleuths - 2006 - David Suchet takes us behind the scenes to look at the enduring appeal of Hercule Poirot. The programme features interviews with cast, crew, and a variety of Agatha Christie experts.

Queen Elizabeth's Battle for Church Music - 2017 - Historian Lucy Worsley takes a look at how Queen Elizabeth I and her siblings handled religious music after the English Reformation.

Rococo Before Bedtime - 2014 - British art historian Waldemar Januszczak examines the history and grandeur of the Rococo period.

Rome: Empire Without Limit - 2016 - Historian Mary Beard takes a look at how a small city like Rome was able to capture an empire - and why it ultimately fell.

Savile Row - 2008 - This fascinating documentary series goes behind the scenes of the iconic Savile Row storefronts most of us will never visit. Here, skilled craftsmen apply their talents to make some of the finest suits in the entire world. Now threatened by chain stores and a decline in appreciation for fine handiwork, we see the shops struggling to stay relevant and pay rent in one of the world's most expensive cities and neighbourhoods.

Scotch! The Story of Whisky - 2017 - This short series takes a look at the history and science of the Scottish whisky industry.

She-Wolves: England's Early Queens - 2012 - Presenter Helen Castor explores the lives of seven of England's early queens and how they managed to challenge male power and rule in a time where women had comparatively few rights.

Shoreline Detectives - 2017 to 2019 - Dr. Tori Herridge and her team of historians and archaeologists explore seabeds and sand banks to find remnants of Britain's history.

Soundbreaking: Stories from the Cutting Edge of Recorded Music - 2016 - Using dozens of interviews and rare studio footage, this eight-part series takes a look at the impact of recorded music on our lives.

Testament - 1988 - Archaeologist John Romer takes a look at the roots of the Bible and what archaeology can tell us about it.

The Art Detectives - 2017 to present - Art experts track down previously-unknown masterpieces by some of the world's greatest artists.

The Big House Reborn - 2015 - This series follows National Trust conservators as they work on restoring The Mount Stewart House.

The Nile: 5000 Years of History - 2018 - Historian Bettany Hughes takes us on a 900-mile adventure along the River Nile, sharing history and landmarks as she goes.

The Real Dr. Zhivago - 2017 - This documentary follows Boris Pasternak's 20-year journey to write his great classic, *Dr. Zhivago*.

The Rise of the Nazi Party - 2014 - This 10-episode series takes a look at how Hitler and his inner circle used economic uncertainty to influence regular people into going along with their genocidal agenda.

The Spy Who Went Into the Cold - 2013 - At the height of the Cold War in 1963, Kim Philby defected to Moscow after 30 years in senior positions in British intelligence offices. This documentary takes a look back at the scandal.

The Story of Math - 2008 - Oxford professor Marcus du Sautoy makes mathematics fun and engaging as he tells the story of how it developed and how it affects our daily lives.

The Story of Women and Power - 2015 - Historian Amanda Vickery takes us on a tour of the 300-year battle for women's equality.

The Yorkshire Vet - 2015 to present - This engaging series follows the staff of Skeldale Veterinary Centre as they work with the animals.

Theatreland - 2010 - This docuseries goes behind the scenes of the Haymarket's production of *Waiting for Godot*, giving us a look at what it takes to make a West End theatre survive and thrive.

Time Team - 1994 to 2014 - A group of archaeologists travel around Britain working on different excavation sites.

Treasure Houses of Britain – 2011 - This series travels around Britain, exploring the history and architecture of some of the island's greatest estates.

Victoria Wood's A Nice Cup of Tea - 2013 - Comedian Victoria Wood travels the globe to investigate Britain's love of tea.

Victorian House of Arts and Crafts - 2019 - Over the course of four episodes, we see a late 1800s Victorian Arts & Crafts commune in the Welsh hills painstakingly brought back to life as a group of six 21st century crafters – three men and three women move in to experience the highs and lows of living and working together as a creative commune. Over their month-long stay, the crafters are set to renovate four of the key spaces in the house.

Vintage Roads: Great and Small - 2018 to present - Christopher Timothy and Peter Davison, stars of All Creatures Great & Small, host this entertaining travelogue about the golden age of motoring. Behind the wheel of a classic car, they explore beautiful backroads and the history of motoring in Britain.

Wainwright Walks - 2007 - Julia Bradbury stars in this outdoor series following some of guidebook author Alfred Wainwright's best walks.

Walks with My Dog - 2017 - British celebrities like John Nettles and Robert Lindsay explore the countryside with their dogs.

Young, Gifted, and Classical: The Making of a Maestro - 2017 - At 17, Sheku Kannah-Mason because the first black winner of the BBC Young Musician competition. This documentary looks at what drives him and his musically-talented family to succeed.

BRITBOX

Website: http://britbox.com

Description: A joint venture between the BBC and ITV, this service focuses exclusively on British programming. In addition to the standard categories, BritBox also offers several soaps, quiz shows, and panel shows, along with a number of live events throughout the year.

Available On: Roku, Fire TV, Apple TV, Apple iPhone & iPad, Chromecast, Android phones and tablets, and computer (via web browser). You can also subscribe via Amazon Prime Video.

Cost: $6.99/month, $69.99/year

Now Streaming

Mysteries & Crime Dramas

15 Days - 2019 - This crime thriller is a mystery told in reverse. It immediately flashes back to 15 days prior to the crime, allowing viewers to watch a family crisis as it festers and develops into something truly terrible. The series is a re-make of the Welsh series *35 Diwrnod*, and even includes some of the same actors.

35 Days - 2014 to 2019 - Each season of this Welsh mystery begins with a murder, then rolls the clock back 35 days to follow the events that led to the murderous conclusion.

A Confession - 2019 - Martin Freeman (*Sherlock*), Siobhan Finneran (*Downton Abbey*), and Imelda Staunton (*Cranford*) star in this drama based on a real-life tragedy. The series dramatises the search for Sian O'Callaghan, a young woman who went missing in Swindon, Wiltshire after a taxi ride.

A Touch of Frost - 1992 to 2010 - Rumpled and slovenly DI Jack Frost follows his instincts to find justice for the underdogs. The gritty series is set in the fictional South Midlands town of Denton, and Sir David

Jason (*Only Fools and Horses*) stars.

Agatha Christie's Evil Under the Sun - 1982 - On the trail of a millionaire's fake diamond, Poirot finds himself at a resort full of rich and famous people – and a murderer. This film was Peter Ustinov's first outing as the Belgian detective, and you'll also see Dames Maggie Smith and Diana Rigg looking quite a bit younger.

Agatha Christie's Marple - 2004 to 2013 - BritBox offers Seasons 1-5 of this delightful mystery adaptation. In the first three, Geraldine McEwan portrays the iconic sleuth, with Julia McKenzie taking over after that.

Agatha Christie's Poirot - 1989 to 2020 - David Suchet portrays the eccentric Belgian Detective Poirot in this long-running series of Agatha Christie mysteries. Acorn TV has seasons 7 and 8, while BritBox has all the others.

Agatha Christie's Seven Dials Mystery - 1981 - Cheryl Campbell (*Breathless*) stars as Lady Eileen "Bundle" Brent, a young and glamorous aristocrat who insinuates herself into all sorts of unsavoury situations...including murder.

Agatha Christie's The Mirror Crack'd - 1980 - This star-studded movie features Angela Lansbury (*Murder, She Wrote*) as Miss Marple, investigating a murder that takes place while a movie films in her quiet village (as if we needed any more evidence that murders follow Angela Lansbury). Supporting actors include Rock Hudson, Tony Curtis, Kim Novak, and Elizabeth Taylor.

Agatha Christie's The Murder of Roger Ackroyd (Radio Play) - 1939 - Orson Welles directs and plays Hercule Poirot in this radio dramatisation of the classic Agatha Christie story. When a woman is found dead of an overdose, a rumour links her to Roger Ackroyd, who is then also found dead. Hercule Poirot is left to unravel the mystery.

Agatha Christie's The Secret Adversary - 1983 - In this Tommy and Tuppence mystery, James Warwick (*Agatha Christie's Partners in Crime*) and Francesca Annis (also in *Agatha Christie's Partners in Crime*) star as two friends who decide to become investigators to get a bit of extra money. What seems like a simple idea quickly becomes quite dangerous. This production immediately preceded the related television series.

Agatha Christie's Why Didn't They Ask Evans? - 1981 - When Agatha Christie was alive, she allowed very few television adaptations of her work because she didn't care for the medium. After her death, daugher Rosalind Hicks relaxed the restrictions - and this was the first major production to move forward as a result. While golfing on the coast of Wales, Bobby Jones hits a stranger whose puzzling last words are, "Why didn't they ask Evans?"

An Inspector Calls - 2015 - Set in 1912, this mystery follows Inspector Goole as he investigates the wealthy Birling family in connection with the suicide of a young woman. Each family member has their own set of dark and intriguing secrets.

The Bay - 2019 to present - Morven Christie (*Grantchester*) plays DS Lisa Armstrong, a family liaison officer who discovers she has a personal connection to a missing persons case. Many have compared this series to *Broadchurch*, and it's been renewed for a second season.

Best in Paradise - 2020 - In this exclusive BritBox interview, cast members Kris Marshall (*Sanditon, Love Actually*), Josephine Jobert, Don Warrington (*Holby City*), and Tobi Bakare (*Kingsman, Silent Witness*) share anecdotes and insights about their favourite episodes of *Death in Paradise*.

The Blake Mysteries: Ghost Stories - 2018 - After her husband Lucien's disappearance, Jean Blake (formerly Beazley) struggles to adapt to life without him. She doesn't get much time to breathe, though, as she's pulled into a murder investigation just eight months after his disappearance.

The Bletchley Circle: San Francisco - 2018 to 2019 - This Bletchley Circle spin-off picks up in 1956 when former colleagues Millie and Jean learn of a set of murders in San Francisco that mimic a murder they saw during the war. They reach out to an American codebreaker they knew during the war, and before too long, they're all solving murders together in the Bay Area.

Blue Murder - 2003 to 2009 - DCI Janine Lewis struggles with the challenge of being a single mom to four kids while leading a team of detectives through homicide investigations. Caroline Quentin (*Jonathan Creek*) stars.

Boon - 1986 to 1992 - After suffering permanent lung damage rescuing a child from a fire, a fireman retires and begins a new life of odd jobs and later, detective work.

Cadfael - 1994 to 1998 - In 12th century Shrewsbury, a monk solves mysteries. Derek Jacobi (*Last Tango in Halifax*) stars.

The City & The City - 2018 - Inspector Borlú investigates a murder in the twin city, which occupies the same space differently. This unusual series blends mystery with science fiction.

Cold Blood - 2005 to 2008 - A notorious murderer is finally placed in prison, but they can't find his last victim. Now, he's playing a ruthless game with the detective who wants what he knows.

The Coroner - 2015 to 2016 - A solicitor returns to her coastal hometown, becomes coroner, and investigates suspicious deaths.

Cracker - 1993 to 2006 - Though he's obnoxious and anti-social, Fitz is a brilliant criminal psychologist and police consultant.

Dalziel & Pascoe - 1996 to 2007 - Two Yorkshire-based police partners with very different personalities find a way to bond as they solve crimes. This series was based on the Dalziel and Pascoe novels by Reginald Hill, and stars Warren Clarke (*Poldark*) and Colin Buchanan (*The Pale Horse*) in the title roles. Colin Buchanan has also narrated a number of Reginald Hill audiobooks.

Dark Heart - 2018 - DI Wagstaffe leads an investigation into a series of attacks on accused pedophiles.

Death in Paradise - 2011 to present - A British inspector who's fundamentally incompatible with island life is sent to investigate murders on a tropical island. This long-running series began with Ben Miller (*The Worst Week of My Life*) in the lead role, but the torch was later passed to Kris Marshall (*Love Actually*), Ardal O'Hanlon (*Father Ted*), and Ralf Little (*The Cafe*).

The Doctor Blake Mysteries - 2013 to 2018 - Dr. Lucien Blake left his Australian home in Ballarat as a young man. Now, he finds himself returning to take over not only his dead father's medical practice, but also his on-call role as the town's police surgeon. Craig McLachlan (*Packed to the Rafters*) stars as Dr. Blake.

Emerald Falls - 2008 - After her divorce, Joni Ferguson and her 15-year-old son move to the Blue Mountains in New South Wales, Australia to open a bed and breakfast. Just six months after starting her new life, the local doctor is found dead in his home. When Joni shows up on the list of suspects, her son Zac sets out to prove her innocence.

The Fall - 2013 to 2016 - Gillian Anderson (*The X-Files*) and Jamie Dornan (*50 Shades of Grey*) star in this series about a senior investigator who goes head-to-head with a serial killer who's attacking young professional women in Belfast.

Father Brown - 1974 - A Catholic priest dips his toe into mysteries in spite of the police warning him off. Kenneth More (*The Forsyte Saga*) stars as Father Brown in this early adaptation of G.K. Chesterson's *Father Brown* stories.

Father Brown - 2013 to present - Based on the mysteries of GK Chesterson, a Catholic priest solves mysteries in his small English village. Mark Williams (*Blandings*) stars as Father Brown in this long-running

adaptation.

From Darkness - 2015 - In Greater Manchester, Officer Claire is disturbed by four bodies that seem linked to her past cases.

The Gil Mayo Mysteries (aka Mayo) - 2006 - Gil Mayo is an eccentric detective with a life full of complications and awkwardness. His ex-love interest is a colleague, and he's raising a teenage girl on his own. Alistair McGowan (*Leonardo*) stars in this light mystery.

Good Cop - 2012 - When his best friend is killed on duty, a good cop wants revenge. Warren Brown (*Luther*) stars as John Paul Rocksavage.

Hetty Wainthropp Investigates - 1996 to 1998 - A tough old pensioner becomes a private detective and investigates crimes with the help of her husband and a teenage boy called Geoffrey. Dame Patricia Routledge (*Keeping Up Appearances*) stars in this cozy mystery.

Hound of the Baskervilles - 1982 - Tom Baker steps into the world of Sherlock Holmes in this faithful adaptation of the classic Sherlock Holmes story.

The Ice House - 1997 - The peaceful lives of three women are shattered when a corpse is discovered in the ice house on their property. Daniel Craig (*James Bond series*) stars.

In Plain Sight - 2016 - This series covers serial killer Peter Manuel's crimes in 1950s Lanarkshire, Scotland. Though it's a dramatisation, it's based on a true story.

In the Dark - 2017 - While dealing with an unexpected pregnancy, DI Weeks returns to her hometown to help a childhood friend after an abduction.

The Inspector Lynley Mysteries - 2001 to 2007 - An Oxford-educated detective pairs up with a working-class partner to investigate mysteries.

Inspector Morse - 1987 to 2000 - Grumpy, classical music-loving Inspector Morse investigates crimes around Oxford with his junior partner Sergeant Lewis. This much-loved British mystery series is based on the books of Colin Dexter, and it later spawned two additional television shows (*Inspector Lewis* and *Endeavour*).

Jonathan Creek - 1997 to 2016 - After meeting a pushy investigative journalist, an eccentric magic trick developer finds himself investigating murders.

The Last Detective - 2003 to 2007 - Because he's decent, old fashioned and a generally good guy, his fellow detectives and his boss don't like him much. Still, DC Davies proves that his style works by constantly solving cases no one else wants.

Lewis (Pilot) - 2006 - Five years after the end of Inspector Morse, his long-time partner, Inspector Lewis, is paired up with DS Hathaway to investigate a murder on the Oxford campus. This pilot was the beginning of the Inspector Lewis series that would end up going on for as many episodes as its predecessor.

Life of Crime - 2013 - Hayley Atwell (*Agent Carter*) stars as Denise Woods, a bright WPC attempting to solve the murders of three possibly connected victims across three decades. Each episode of the series is filmed in a different decade, and she has a different rank in each.

Life on Mars - 2006 to 2007 - DCI Sam Tyler has a car accident in 2006 and wakes up in the 70s. John Simm (*White Dragon*) stars alongside Philip Glenister (*Living the Dream*) in this much-loved series. The series is often cited for its excellent classic rock soundtrack, and it was recently announced that after a long break, it will be coming back with a third season.

Maigret - 1992 to 1993 - Michael Gambon stars as Georges Simenon's iconic French detective in this early-90s adaptation. Each of the 12 episodes is based on a single Maigret novel.

Maigret - 2016 to 2017 - Rowan Atkinson takes on a rare serious role as he fills the role of Maigret in this two series, four episode adaptation. Each of the four episodes are based on a single novel (*Maigret Sets a Trap, Maigret's Dead Man, Maigret at the Crossroads,* and *Inspector Maigret and the Strangled Stripper*).

The Mallorca Files - 2019 - This drama stars Elen Rhys (*Ordinary Lies*) and Julian Looman as a pair of international detectives who solve crimes on the Baleric island of Mallorca. It's a light, action-driven drama with a bit of British and German culture clash between the detectives.

Midsomer Murders - 1998 to present - In Midsomer County, the landscapes are beautiful, the villagers all have secrets, and murder is rampant. This British mystery classic features John Nettles as DCI Tom Barnaby through the first 13 seasons, with Neil Dudgeon as DCI John Barnaby for the later seasons.

Midsomer Murders: 20th Anniversary Documentary - 2019 - John Nettles presents this look back at Midsomer Murders on its 20th anniversary. The hour-long special features appearances by Neil Dudgeon, Nick Hendrix, Daniel Casey, Jason Hughes, Jane Wymark, and more.

Midsomer Murders Favourites - 1998 to 2018 - This collection rounds up the favourite episodes of several Midsomer Murders cast members - Neil Dudgeon, John Nettles, Annette Badland, and Nick Hendrix. Each episode includes commentary from the actor in question.

Miss Marple - 1984 to 1992 - In the small village of St. Mary Mead, Miss Marple helps her community by solving murders. In this collection of Christie tales, Joan Hickson takes the title role.

The Moonstone - 1972 to 1973 - In this Hugh Leonard adaptation, a man goes on a quest to find a stolen but cursed stone that's said to bring ill fortune to all who possess it. This series is based on the Wilkie Collins novel of the same name.

The Moonstone - 2016 - This updated adaptation of the Wilkie Collins novel stars Joshua Silver as Franklin Blake alongside Terenia Edwards (*On Chesil Beach*) as Rachel Verinder.

The Mrs. Bradley Mysteries - 1998 - Diana Rigg (*The Avengers*) stars as Mrs. Bradley, a sort of edgy Miss Marple who solves mysteries with the assistance of her devoted chauffeur George Moody (Neil Dudgeon, *Midsomer Murders*).

New Blood - 2016 - Two young investigators are brought together by cases that initially appear unrelated.

Prime Suspect - 1991 to 2006 - Helen Mirren stars as Detective Jane Tennison, battling crime as well as sexism on the job.

Quirke - 2014 - Gabe Byrne plays a pathologist in 1950s Dublin.

Rebus - 2000 to 2004 - Based on the novels of Scottish author Ian Rankin, Inspector Rebus is an old-fashioned detective in every sense of the word. He smokes, drinks, and doesn't have a lot of luck with his personal life.

River - 2015 - Stellan Skarsgård, Nicola Walker, and Lesley Manville star in this series about a brilliant police officer haunted by guilt.

Rosemary & Thyme - 2003 to 2008 - Former policewoman Laura and a horticulture professor Rosemary are brought together by a love of gardening, but murder seems to follow them. Felicity Kendal (*The Good Life*) and Pam Ferris (*Call the Midwife*) star in this quaint mystery series.

The Ruth Rendell Mysteries: Next Chapters (aka Ruth Rendell Mysteries) - 1994 to 2000 - This collection includes a variety of suspenseful tales adapted from the novels of author Ruth Rendell.

Scott & Bailey - 2011 to 2016 - Two very different female police detectives enjoy a close friendship and productive partnership.

Shakespeare & Hathaway - 2018 to present - In beautiful Stratford-Upon-Avon, an unlikely pair of private investigators solves crimes together.

Sherlock Holmes - 1984 to 1994 - Jeremy Brett and David Burke star in this set of Sherlock Holmes adventures.

Sherlock Holmes & the Case of the Silk Stocking - 2004 - Rupert Everett (*An Ideal Husband*) stars as Sherlock Holmes in this television movie in which a serial killer is stalking and kidnapping young daughters of the aristocracy. The disappearances bring Sherlock Holmes and Watson out of retirement to seek the perpetrator. Neil Dudgeon (*Midsomer Murders*) plays Lestrade, and Ian Hart (*The Last Kingdom*) plays Dr. Watson.

Shetland - 2013 to present - In the remote island community of Shetland, DI Jimmy Perez and his team investigate threats to the peace of their village. This series is based on the Shetland novels by Ann Cleeves.

Silent Witness - 1996 to present - A team of pathologists investigates crimes based on evidence gleaned from autopsies.

Stonemouth - 2015 - A man returns to his small Scottish hometown in hopes of finding out the truth about his friend's murder.

The Suspicions of Mr. Whicher: Beyond the Pale - 2014 - Whicher is hired to investigate threats made to the son of an important government employee, leading him to some of the most dangerous parts of Victorian London. Paddy Considine (*Informer*) stars.

The Suspicions of Mr. Whicher: The Murder at Road Hill House - 2011 - Based on Kate Summerscale's best-selling novel, this series sees DI Whicher pursuing the murderer of a three-year-old boy. Paddy Considine (*Informer*) stars.

The Suspicions of Mr. Whicher: The Murder in Angel Lane - 2013 - Whicher investigates the death of a young girl, pitting him against some of London's wealthiest and most powerful individuals. Paddy Considine (*Informer*) stars.

The Suspicions of Mr. Whicher: The Ties That Bind - 2014 - This entry sees Whicher taking on what appears to be a simple infidelity case, but it soon turns much darker. Paddy Considine (*Informer*) stars.

Taggart - 1983 to 2010 - This long-running crime series revolves around a group of detectives in Scotland. Initially set in the Maryhill CID of Strathclyde Police, many later storylines were set and shot in other parts of Greater Glasgow and other areas of Scotland.

Thorne: Scaredy Cat - 2010 - Thorne is working with a new team to tackle a tough double murder case, but it's not long before he's hunting down two different serial killers.

Thorne: Sleepyhead - 2010 - DI Thorne (David Morrissey, *Men Behaving Badly*) is in a race against time to find a serial killer who enjoys making unusual attacks on young women.

Vera - 2011 to present - DCI Vera Stanhope investigates murders in the Northumberland countryside. Brenda Blethyn (*Chance in a Million*) stars in this long-running crime drama based on Ann Cleeves' *Vera* novels. This series is split between Acorn TV and BritBox, with BritBox having seasons 3, 4, 5, 8, 9, and 10.

Vera Postmortem - 2018 - This BritBox exclusive includes interviews with Brenda Blethyn (Vera herself) and author Ann Cleeves. They discuss what it's like making the series, along with some of their favourite moments.

Waking the Dead - 2000 to 2011 - Using new forensic technology, DS Boyd and his team open unsolved cases.

Wallander - 2008 to 2016 - This English-language, Sweden-based mystery series is an adaptation of Henning Mankell's novels about Kurt Wallander, a highly empathetic detective.

What Remains - 2013 - When a young couple moves into an apartment, they find a dead body and it kicks off an investigation into a young woman's disappearance two years prior.

Without Motive - 2000 to 2001 - A detective attempts to solve a series of murders that seemingly lack motive.

Wycliffe - 1993 to 1998 - Based on W.J. Burley's novels, this Cornwall-based series features DS Charles Wycliffe, a man who investigates murders with a unique level of determination and accuracy.

Zen - 2011 - A handsome detective works to bring integrity and justice to Roman streets.

BRITBOX

Dramas

A Christmas Carol - 1977 - Michael Hordern (*The Wind in the Willows*) stars as Ebenezer Scrooge in this adaptation of Dickens' classic Christmas story of greed and redemption.

The Alchemists - 1999 - Grant Show (*Melrose Place*) stars in this thriller set in the world of genetic engineering. The series was based on Peter James' 1996 novel, *Alchemist*.

A Song for Jenny - 2015 - Based on real events, this film tells the story of a mother struggling after her daughter was killed in the 2005 London bombings.

Against the Law - 2017 - When Peter Wildeblood and Edward McNally fell in love in 1952, it was still a crime in Britain. This film takes a look at the devastating consequences for each of the two men.

Age Before Beauty - 2018 - This contemporary drama is set in a struggling family-owned beauty salon in Manchester.

An Adventure in Space & Time - 2013 - This television movie is a dramatisation of how Doctor Who was brought to our televisions back in 1963.

Aristocrats - 1999 - This miniseries follows the lives of four aristocratic sisters through 1700s England.

Armadillo - 2001 - When loss adjuster Lorimer Black goes out on a routine appointment, he finds a hanged man. This three-part miniseries is based on William Boyd's 1998 novel of the same name.

Ballykissangel - *Ireland* - 1996 to 2001 - A young English priest adjusts to the pace of life in a small Irish village. Stephen Tompkinson (*DCI Banks*) stars as Father Peter Clifford.

Bancroft - 2017 to present - DS Elizabeth Bancroft is a brilliant officer, but the questionable tactics she employed in the past are coming back to haunt her

Banished - 2015 - When British convicts are sent to Australia to pay for their crimes, they and the soldiers who guard them have to adapt to the new world.

The Baron - 1966 to 1967 - American Steve Forrest (*S.W.A.T.*) plays John Mannering, an antiques dealer who dabbles in undercover work for the British Diplomatic Intelligence. It was the first ITC Entertainment programme made in full colour without marionettes, and it was based on the Baron series by Anthony Morton.

Bleak House - 2005 - This classic BBC adaptation is based on the Dickens legal drama of the same name. The miniseries features an all-star cast that includes Gillian Anderson (*The Fall*), Timothy West (*Great Canal Journeys*), Carey Mulligan (*Collateral*), Alun Armstrong (*New Tricks*), Sheila Hancock (*Edie*), Catherine Tate (*Doctor Who*), and Hugo Speer (*The Full Monty*).

Bramwell - 1995 to 1998 - Set in 1895, Eleanor Bramwell works first under a doctor's supervision and then opens her own infirmary.

Brideshead Revisited - 1981 - Jeremy Irons and Anthony Andrews star in this adaptation of Evelyn Waugh's novel by the same name. *The Telegraph* awarded it the top position in its list of greatest television adaptations of all time.

Broken - 2017 - Sean Bean stars as Father Michael, a flawed but good-hearted Catholic priest in Northern England.

Campion - 1989 to 1990 - An aristocrat in the 1930s adopts a fake name and

29

investigates mysteries with help from his servant. Peter Davison (*Doctor Who*) stars as Albert Campion, with Brian Glover (*Rumble*) as his manservant. The series was based on the Albert Campion mystery novels written by Margery Allingham.

Casualty - 1986 to present - This *Holby City* spinoff takes place in the A&E (Accidents and Emergency) department of the fictional Holby City Hospital.

Casualty 1900s: London Hospital - 2006 to 2009 - This medical period drama was inspired by the *Holby City* spinoff *Casualty*, but is otherwise unrelated. It takes place in the receiving room of the London Hospital in London's East End, and each case is based on the writings and memoirs of real doctors and nurses from the time period.

The Champions - 1968 to 1969 - After a plane crash in the Himalayas, three secret agents are rescued by members of an advanced civilisation living secretly in the mountains. In the course of the rescue, they grant the three agents a set of supernatural abilities. Now, they use those special talents in service of a mysterious international agency called Nemesis.

Charles II: The Power and the Passion - 2003 - Rufus Sewell (*The Pale Horse*) stars in this four-part drama about the life of Charles II.

Christopher and His Kind - 2011 - This BBC television film tells the story of novelist Christopher Isherwood's youthful experiences as a young gay man living in Berlin in the 1930s. Matt Smith (*Doctor Who*) and Toby Jones (*Detectorists*) star.

Churchill: The Darkest Hour - 2013 - This docu-drama takes a look at Winston Churchill's experiences during World War I.

Coalition - 2015 - This tense political TV movie follows David Cameron, Nick Clegg, and Gordon Brown in the aftermath of the 2010 UK general election.

Cold Feet - 1998 to 2003 - This long-running dramedy follows the lives of six thirtysomething friends living in Manchester, England as they do their best to get their lives sorted.

Cold Feet: The New Years - 2016 to 2020 - Nearly 15 years after the original series ended, it returned for another set of episodes focusing on the Manchester-based friends, now in their 50s. Though 2020 marked the last set of episodes for this run, there's been talk of an additional series when the group is facing the next big phase of life.

Coronation Street - 1960 to present - Running since 1960, and there are more than 9400 episodes of this daytime drama classic. The show is set in the fictional area of Wetherfield, where residents walk cobbled streets among terraced houses and the ever-present Rovers Return pub. No service currently offers all 9000+ episodes, but BritBox maintains a running set of the most recent episodes.

Cranford - 2007 to 2009 - *Cranford* tells the story of women in a small, fictional market town at the dawn of the Industrial Revolution. Dame Judi Dench (*As Time Goes By*) stars in this modern adaptation of Elizabeth Gaskell's novellas.

Crime Story - 1992 to 1993 - This series features dramatic reenacts of some of Britain's most heinous and notorious crimes. Among them are the tale of Erwin van Haarlem, the story of Graham Young, and a case in which a young man's body was found by divers in a Lancashire quarry.

Daleks' Invasion Earth 2150 A.D. - 1966 - This theatrical adaptation of "The Dalek Invasion of Earth" sees Peter Cushing reprising his role as Dr. Who, an inventor who created the Tardis to travel through time.

David Copperfield - 1999 - Daniel Radcliffe (*Harry Potter*) stars as young David in this adaptation of the Dickens novel.

Desperate Romantics – 2009 - In 1851 London, a group of artists lead colorful lives amidst the chaos of the Industrial Revolution.

Dickensian - 2015 to 2016 - This ambitious miniseries is set in the world of Charles Dickens's novels, bringing together a variety of characters in 19th century London.

Dirk Gently - 2010 to 2012 - An unusual detective looks to the universe for holistic solutions to mysteries. Stephen Mangan (*Bliss*) stars in this adaptation of the popular Douglas Adams novels.

Classic Doctor Who - 1963 to 1989 - *Doctor Who* originally ran for 26 seasons between 1963 and 1989. Though some episodes of the British sci-fi classic no longer exist, those that are available are included on BritBox.

Doctor Who Specials - 1991 to 2013 - This collection features some of the less common *Classic Doctor Who* specials, including the un-aired pilot and reunion episode.

Doctor Who: The Doctors Revisited - 2013 - This series introduces the first seven doctors from Doctor Who. It includes classic footage and interviews from cast and crew members.

Doctor Zhivago - 2002 - Kiera Knightley (*Pride and Prejudice*) and Hans Matheson (*The Tudors*) star in this miniseries adaptation of Boris Pasternak's classic 1957 novel.

Dr. Who and the Daleks - 1965 - This feature length adaptation of "The Daleks" stars Peter Cushing as Dr. Who, a man who invented a device to travel across time and space with his granddaughters.

Dunkirk - 2004 - Benedict Cumberbatch (*Sherlock*) stars in this docudrama about the Dunkirk evacuation during World War II. The series uses a mixture of eyewitness accounts, archive footage, and newly-dramatised sequences to bring the story to life.

EastEnders - 1985 to present - Known for its diversity and modern storylines, EastEnders is set in the fictional London borough of Walford around a Victorian square that includes a pub (The Queen Vic), a market, a launderette, and a cafe. As with a number of British soaps, BritBox typically keeps a running set of the most recent episodes.

Elizabeth R - 1971 - Brenda Jackson (*Women in Love*) stars as Elizabeth I in this series about the "Virgin Queen". She won two Emmys for the performance.

Emma - 2009 - Romola Garai (*The Hour*) stars as Emma Woodhouse in this four-part adaptation of Jane Austen's classic novel. Jonny Lee Miller (*Elementary*) plays her dear friend Mr. Knightley.

Emmerdale - 1972 to present - Originally known as *Emmerdale Farm*, this series was originally set in a village called Beckindale. In the 90s, the show rebranded and began to focus on the entire village of Emmerdale. Now, storylines are bigger, sexier, and more dramatic than ever.

Extremely Dangerous - 1999 - Sean Bean (*Game of Thrones*) stars as a former MI-5 agent seeking vengeance after being wrongfully convicted of his family's murder.

Father and Son - 2009 - Michael O'Connor may have been one of the toughest gangsters around, but he thinks he's left that behind when he moves to Ireland to start over. When his son Séan is accused of a murder he didn't commit, Michael must return to Manchester and face his past.

Fields of Gold - 2002 - Benedict Cumberbatch (*Sherlock*) and Anna Friel (*Marcella*) star in this two-part thriller about genetically modified food.

Five by Five - 2017 - Idris Elba (*Luther*) stars in this series of five intertwining short films about random encounters in London.

Florence Nightingale - 2008 - This hour-long film tells the story of Florence Nightingale's defining moments after the Crimean War, and how those moment would shape the impact she would come to have on medicine.

Frankie - 2013 - Eve Myles (*Keeping Faith*) stars as the head nurse on a traveling nursing team.

Gideon's Daughter - 2006 - Emily Blunt (*The Devil Wears Prada*), Tom Hardy (*The Dark Night Rises*), and Bill Nighy (*Love Actually*) star in this film about a public relations guru who rethinks his life as his daughter goes off to study at the University of Edinburgh and he goes through a series of personal changes. The series is set in the late 90s against the backdrop of Princess Diana's death and the development of the Millennium Dome.

Great Expectations - 1999 - Ioan Gruffudd (*Harrow*) stars as Pip in this dark and unsentimental retelling of Dickens' classic novel.

Heartbeat - 1992 to 2010 - This Yorkshire-based period crime drama ran for 18 seasons and 372 episodes, focusing on the lives of characters in a small village. Initially, it focused on a central couple, PC Nick Rowan and Dr. Kate Rowan, but as time went on, it branched out to include storylines all over the village. The series is based on the "Constable" novels written by Peter N. Walker under the pseudonym Nicholas Rhea.

Hearts and Bones - 2000 to 2001 - Damian Lewis (*Band of Brothers*), Dervla Kirwan (*Ballykissangel*), Hugo Speer (*London Kills*) and Sarah Parish (*Bancroft*) star in this drama about a group of young adults who move from Coventry to London together.

The Heist at Hatton Garden - 2019 - Also known as The Heist at Hatton Garden, this series is based on the true story of a spectacular diamond heist carried out in London by a group of elderly criminals. The all-star cast includes Timothy Spall (*Blandings*), Alex Norton (*Taggart*), David Hayman (*The Paradise*), and Kenneth Cranham (*The White Princess*).

Him - 2016 - Fionn Whitehead (*Dunkirk*) stars as a character known only as HIM. Set in suburban London, the series follows as he struggles to adjust to telekinetic powers inherited from his grandfather.

Holby City - 1999 to present - This medical soap follows the lives of those working on the wards of Holby City Hospital. This series is a spin-off from *Casualty*, and it's set in the same hospital with occasional cross-over characters and plots. It was designed to offer a look at what happened to people taken from the A&E (emergency room) to the other departments within the hospital.

Homefront - 2012 to 2014 - This six-episode miniseries follows the lives of four army wives in the UK while their husbands are serving in Afghanistan.

Isolation Stories - 2020 - Filmed remotely during the COVID-19 pandemic of 2020, this limited dramatic series taps into the feelings different people experience during lockdown.

Jane Eyre - 2006 - Ruth Wilson (*Luther*) stars as Jane Eyre in this mildly steamy adaptation of Charlotte Brontë's classic novel.

Jekyll & Hyde - 1990 - Michael Caine (*The Dark Knight*) stars as Dr. Henry Jekyll (and Mr. Edward Hyde) in this chilling feature-length adaptation of the classic Victorian horror story.

The Jury - 2002 to 2011 - When the killing of a 15-year-old boy rocks the nation, 12 jurors find themselves under intense pressure to make the right decision. The second season is entirely unconnected to the first, and sees a set of jurors called up to handle the controversial retrial of a convicted murderer.

Justice - 2011 - Robert Pugh (*Game of Thrones*) and Jodie Comer (*Killing Eve*) star in this short-lived dramatic series about a judge sworking in the Public Justice Centre

in Dovefield, Liverpool. It's a rough area, and it's no easy task bringing a bit of law and order to the area.

K9 & Company: A Girl's Best Friend - 1981 - This single-episode television pilot was intended as a spin-off of Doctor Who, featuring series regular Sarah Jane Smith (Elisabeth Sladen) and K9, a dog robot voiced by John Leeson. It sees Sarah Jane searching for her missing aunt in a quiet Gloucestershire village.

Kat & Alfie: Redwater - 2017 - 32 years after giving her son up for adoption, Kat moves to the town of Redwater in an attempt to find him.

Kavanagh QC - 1995 to 2001 - John Thaw (*Inspector Morse*) stars as James Kavanagh QC, a barrister with a working-class background and a strong sense of right and wrong. It was one of Thaw's final roles before he died of cancer at the age of 60. Pay close attention to the guest stars in this one, as it's loaded with actors who went on to well-known roles, including Lesley Manville (*Mum*), Larry Lamb (*Gavin & Stacey*), Barry Jackson (*Midsomer Murders*), Phyllis Logan (*Downton Abbey*), Bill Night (*Love Actually*), and Julian Fellowes (*Downton Abbey*).

Killed By My Debt - 2018 - This programme tells the story of Jerome, a young man whose small debt and poor prospects led him to kill himself. Chance Perdomo (*Chilling Adventures of Sabrina*) stars.

Lark Rise to Candleford - 2008 to 2011 - Set in the late 19th century in the small Oxfordshire hamlet of Lark Rise and the nearby market town of Candleford, this period drama follows a young woman who moves towns to work in a post office. The series is based on Flora Thompson's semi-autobiographical novels about living in the English countryside.

Line of Duty - 2012 to present - This series focuses on a group of officers in the ACU (Anti-Corruption Unit), a team that investigates the wrongdoings of its fellow officers.

Little Boy Blue - 2017 - This ITV series is a dramatisation of the real-life murder of 11-year-old Rhys Jones during a wave of gang violence in Liverpool in 2007.

London Road - 2015 - Olivia Colman (*Broadchurch*) and Tom Hardy (*Peaky Blinders*) star in this film adaptation of the musical of the same name (which is based on a series of interviews about the Suffolk Strangler).

Lost in Austen - 2008 - A bored young *Pride and Prejudice* fan is changed forever when Elizabeth Bennet stumbles into her modern bathroom. This miniseries includes Hugh Bonneville (*Downton Abbey*) as Mr. Bennet, Morven Christie (*Grantchester*) as Jane Bennet, and Jemima Rooper (*Gold Digger*) as lead Amanda Price.

Margaret - 2009 - Lindsay Duncan (*Rome*) stars as Margaret Thatcher in this drama about her fall from power.

MI-5 (aka Spooks) - 2002 to 2011 - This dramatic series follows top secret missions of the MI-5, the UK's elite domestic security and counter-intelligence agency. Matthew Macfadyen (*Pride & Prejudice*), Keeley Hawes (*Bodyguard*), Hermione Norris (*Cold Feet*), and Richard Armitage (*North & South*) are among the stars of this long-running series.

Miss Austen Regrets - 2008 - This feature-length drama is based on Jane Austen's life and collected letters. Olivia Williams (*An Education*) plays Jane Austen.

Mo - 2010 - Julie Walters (*Dinnerladies*) stars in this biopic about the life of Mo Mowlam, a controversial Labour Party politician in Northern Ireland.

The Moorside - 2017 - This two-part television drama is based on the 2008 disappearance of 9-year-old Shannon Matthews in Dewsbury, West Yorkshire. The cast includes Sheridan Smith (*Gavin & Stacey*), Gemma Whelan (*Game of Thrones*), Sian Brooke (*Doctor Foster*), and Sibhan Finneran (*Downton Abbey*).

Mother's Day - 2018 - Based on a true story, this film follows two mothers, one English and one Irish, as they pave the way for peace in the aftermath of an IRA attack in Warrington, England.

Moving On – 2009 to 2016 - This anthology series gives us stories of people preparing to move on to something new in their lives.

Mrs. Brown - 1997 - Dame Judi Dench stars in this film about Queen Victoria and her unusual friendship with servant John Brown (Billy Connolly). Her portrayal of the scandalous relationship earned an Academy Award nomination.

Murdered by My Boyfriend - 2014 - This dramatisation of a true story tells of a young woman who falls in love with the wrong man. The adaptation was commissioned to help educate young viewers about the dangers of relationship abuse.

Murdered by My Father - 2016 - This one-off drama tells the story of a young British Asian Muslim girl who was killed by her father for loving the wrong man.

Murdered for Being Different - 2017 - Based on the real 2007 murder of Sophie Lancaster, this film sees two young goths attacked for being different.

My Boy Jack - 2007 - Daniel Radcliffe (*Harry Potter*), Carey Mulligan (*Pride and Prejudice*), and Kim Cattrall (*Sex and the City*) star in this WWI drama about Rudyard Kipling and his son John. The name of the film is taken from Kipling's poem, "My Boy Jack".

NW - 2016 - Based on Zadie Smith's award-winning novel, this series follows two friends from a northwest London housing estate as they reunite during a challenging time.

Oliver Twist - 2007 - Morven Christie (*Grantchester*), Tom Hardy (*Peaky Blinders*), and Sarah Lancashire (*Happy Valley*) all appear in this star-studded adaptation of the Dickens classic.

One Night - 2012 - In one night, the lives of four people are linked by a single event.

Ordinary Lies - 2015 to 2016 - Each series of this show is set in a perfectly ordinary location, but the people have dark secrets. Series 1 takes place at a car dealership in Warrington, while Series 2 is set in a sporting goods company.

Our Friends in the North - 1996 - This series follows a group of four friends from Newcastle as their lives unfold over a period of 31 years. Daniel Craig (*Quantum of Solace*) and Christopher Eccleston (*Doctor Who*) are among the stars.

Our Girl - 2013 to present - This series follows a young woman from East London as she embarks on her career as an army medic. Lacey Turner (*EastEnders*) stars as Molly Dawes, with Michelle Keegan (*Brassic*) entering later as Georgie Lane.

The Passing Bells - 2014 - This British-Polish drama tells the story of two teens, one British and one German, who sign up to fight in WWI.

Poldark - 1996 - John Bowe (*Prime Suspect*)

and Ioan Gruffudd (*Harrow*) star in this feature-length adaptation of the Poldark story.

Pride & Prejudice - 1995 - Jennifer Ehle and Colin Firth star in this much-loved adaptation of Jane Austen's classic novel that starts with "a single man in possession of a good fortune".

The Quatermass Experiment - 2005 - Based on the 1950s sci-fi classic, this film focuses on the sole survivor of a rocket crash, and the Professor who must stop him. David Tennant (*Doctor Who*) appears as Dr. Gordon Briscoe.

Reg - 2016 - Tim Roth (*Reservoir Dogs*) stars as Reg Keys in this political drama about a bereaved military father who took on Tony Blair in the 2005 elections.

The Royal - 2003 to 2011 - This *Heartbeat* spinoff is set in the 1960s and focuses on an NHS hospital serving the seaside Yorkshire town of Elsinby.

Royal Celebration - 1993 - Keira Knightley (*Pride & Prejudice*) and Minnie Driver (*Good Will Hunting*) star in this drama about the wedding of Prince Charles and Lady Diana.

The Royal Today - 2008 - This follow-up to *The Royal* takes place in the same Yorkshire hospital, but 40 years later.

The Sandbaggers - 1978 to 1980 - This spy drama follows the men and woman on the front lines of the Cold War. Based in Leeds, it starred Roy Marsden (Adam Dalgliesh in the P.D. James adaptations).

Sharpe - 1993 to 2010 - Sean Bean (*Game of Thrones*) stars in this 19th century period drama set during the Napoleonic Wars in Spain. It's based on the *Sharpe* novels by Bernard Cornwell.

Single Father - 2010 - David Tennant stars in this drama about a regular guy trying to raise his family after the death of his wife.

The Six Wives of Henry VIII - 1971 - This collection of television plays focuses on the wives of Henry VIII, with each play telling the story of one woman. Second Doctor Patrick Troughton (*Doctor Who*) is among the stars.

Small Island - 2009 - Based on the 2004 novel of the same title by Andrea Levy, this film sees Naomie Harris (*28 Days Later*) and Ruth Wilson (*Mrs. Wilson*) playing two women who struggle to achieve their dreams in World War II London. Benedict Cumberbatch (*Sherlock*) and David Oyelowo (*Spooks/MI-5*) also appear.

Sticks and Stones - 2019 - After a sales pitch goes terribly wrong, Thomas Benson begins to feel his colleagues have turned against him. Desperate to fix things, he resorts to extreme measures to get back on top. Ben Miller (*Death in Paradise*) is among the stars of this psychological thriller.

The Street - 2006 to 2009 - Each episode takes a look at what's going on with a different family on one street.

The Sweeney - 1975 to 1978 - Before John Thaw played Inspector Morse, and before Dennis Waterman appeared on *New Tricks*, they co-starred in The Sweeney. Groundbreaking at the time, this was one of the first TV portrayals to show British police as ruthless, rule-bending, and fallible. Thaw and Waterman play two members of the Flying Squad, a branch of police that handle armed robbery and violent crimes in London.

That Day We Sang - 2014 - Based on the Victoria Wood musical of the same name, this television adaptation starring Imelda Staunton (*A Confession*) is based in 1969 with flashbacks to 1929. It tells the story of a middle-aged couple that finds love when they meet on a television programme about a choir they were once in.

Three Girls - 2017 - Authorities ignore the trafficking of young girls by British Pakistani men.

Tina & Bobby - 2017 - This miniseries follows the relationship of Tina Dean and her West Ham United footballer husband, Bobby Moore.

Tipping the Velvet - 2002 - This period drama tells the story of a love affair between two music hall women in the 1890s. Rachael Stirling (*Detectorists*) and Keeley Hawes (*Bodyguard*) star. The series is based on Sarah Waters' best-selling 1998 debut novel of the same name.

Trauma - 2018 - This thriller shows how two fathers' lives collide when one man's son dies at the hands of the other.

Tutankhamun - 2016 - This adventure miniseries is based on Howard Carter's discovery of King Tut's tomb.

Upstairs Downstairs - 1971 to 1977 - This drama follows the aristocratic Bellamy family and the servants who live downstairs. The series is set between the years of 1903 and 1930, showing the gradual decline of the aristocratic class in Britain.

Upstairs Downstairs - 2010 to 2012 - This series picks up the Upstairs Downstairs saga shortly after the original series. Covering 1936 to 1939, it tells the story of the new owners of 165 Eaton Place, ending with the outbreak of World War II. Ed Stoppard (*Home Fires*) and Keeley Hawes (*Bodyguard*) play new owners Sir Hallam Holland and Lady Agnes Holland.

The Victim - 2019 - This four-part Scottish miniseries tells the story of Anna Dean (Kelly MacDonald, *Boardwalk Empire*), a mother whose young son was murdered more than a decade prior. She's been accused of sharing information about the man she believes to be guilty, damaging his reputation and causing him to be attacked. The series focuses on the trial and a mother's unrelenting search for the truth.

The Village - 2013 to 2014 - Written by Peter Moffat (*Cambridge Spies*), this series is set in a Derbyshire village between 1914 and the mid-1920s. Originally envisioned as a 42-hour epic televised drama, it lasted just two seasons. It tells the story of life and history through the eyes of Bert Middleton and his fellow villagers.

White Heat - 2012 - Claire Foy (*The Crown*) stars in this epic drama about the lives of seven students who meet in a London flatshare during the 1960s. Some have compared it to a more female-friendly version of *Our Friends in the North*. Each of the six episodes take place in a different year: 1965, 1967, 1973, 1979, 1982, and 1990.

Wild Bill - 2019 - Rob Lowe stars as Chief Constable Bill Hixon in this dramedy about a widowed American police chief who moves to Lincolnshire with his daughter after he's sacked for assaulting a boy who shared inappropriate images of his daughter online. Rachael Stirling (*The Bletchley Circle, Detectorists*) stars as Lady Mary Harborough, a local judge who becomes well-acquainted with Hixon.

WPC 56 - 2013 to 2015 - This period crime drama follows Gina Dawson, the first woman police constable in her West Midlands hometown. The first two seasons focus on Gina's struggles to gain acceptance in a male-dominated work environment, while the third season follows her successor at the station.

The Shakespeare Collection

This collection was added to BritBox in early 2020.

A Midsummer Night's Dream (1981)

A Midsummer Night's Dream (2016)

A Winter's Tale (1981)

All's Well That Ends Well (1981)

Antony and Cleopatra (1981)

As You Like It (1978)

The Comedy of Errors (1983)

Cymbeline (1982)

Hamlet, Prince of Denmark (1980)

Henry IV: Parts 1 and 2 (1979)

Henry V (1979)

Henry VI: Parts 1-3 (1983)

Henry VIII (1979)

Julius Caesar (1979)

King Lear (1982)

The Life and Death of King John (1984)

Love's Labour's Lost (1985)

Macbeth (1983)

Measure for Measure (1979)

The Merchant of Venice (1980)

The Merry Wives of Windsor (1982)

Much Ado About Nothing (1984)

Othello (1981)

Pericles, Prince of Tyre (1984)

Richard II (1979)

Romeo and Juliet (1978)

The Taming of the Shrew (1980)

The Tempest (1980)

Timon of Athens (1981)

Titus Andronicus (1985)

The Tragedy of Coriolanus (1984)

The Tragedy of Richard III (1983)

Troilus and Cressida (1981)

Twelfth Night (1980)

The Two Gentlemen of Verona (1983)

Comedies

300 Years of French and Saunders - 2017 - This special brings much-loved comedy team Jennifer Saunders and Dawn French back together for another set of hilarious sketches.

8 Out of 10 Cats - 2019 - This quirky panel show comes up with unusual questions and then polls the general public to get their take on the issues.

8 Out of 10 Cats Does Countdown - 2012 to present - This show is a mash-up of *8 Out of 10 Cats* and the more intellectually-challenging *Countdown*. Initially created as a special, it proved quite popular and it's now been running since 2012.

A Bit of Fry & Laurie - 1987 to 1989 - This sketch show is an important piece of British comedy history, and it was responsible for turning Stephen Fry (*Kingdom*) and Hugh Laurie (*House*) into household names.

A Child's Christmases in Wales - 2009 - Michael Sheen narrates this nostalgic comedy about a series of Christmases in the life of a South Wales family during the 1980s.

Absolutely Fabulous - 1992 to 2012 - In this groundbreaking classic, two wild women do everything but act their age. The series was based on a sketch comedy called "Modern Mother and Daughter" by Dawn French (*Vicar of Dibley*) and Jennifer Saunders (Edina Monsoon in *Absolutely Fabulous*). Joanna Lumley stars alongside Saunders as Patsy Stone, and Julia Sawalha plays Edina's daughter Saffron.

Alan Davies: As Yet Untitled - 2014 to 2015 - Alan Davies (*Jonathan Creek*) hosts this discussion show featuring a mix of famous and soon-to-be famous faces. Topics of discussion include everything from the US military to giant rabbits to Bob Mortimer's unusually high backside.

Alfresco - 1983 to 1984 - This early-80s variety show is packed with now-famous actors like Emma Thompson, Robbie Coltrane, Hugh Laurie, and Stephen Fry.

All Creatures Great and Small - 1978 to 1980 - Set in the lovely Yorkshire Dales, this classic comedy is based on the books of James Herriot (pen name to James Alfred Wight). It follows the adventures of a country veterinarian in 1930s England.

Are You Being Served? - 1972 to 1985 - At the Grace Brothers Department Store, fine fashions are served with a healthy side of mischief.

Are You Being Served? - 2016 - In this one-off reboot of the original series, a young Mr. Grace is determined to bring the store into the 1980s...in 1988. It was poorly reviewed, and no further episodes were made.

Are You Being Served? Again! - 1982 to 1993 - When the Grace Brothers store is closed, the staff takes over managing a manor house in the countryside.

As Time Goes By - 1992 to 2002 - Separated by a lost letter during the war, lovers Lionel and Jean are reunited by chance many years later. Dame Judi Dench stars opposite Geoffrey Palmer in this charming light comedy.

At Last the 1948 Show - 1967 - A must for *Monty Python* fans, this quirky 1967 comedy sketch series features future MP collaborators John Cleese and Graham Chapman.

BBC's Lost Sitcoms - 2016 - This collection features re-enactments of three lost sitcom episodes from iconic BBC sitcoms: *Steptoe & Son, Hancock's Half Hour*, and *Till Death Us Do Part*.

Benidorm - 2007 to 2018 - In this delightfully tacky comedy, a parade of British holidaymakers try to get their money's worth at an all-inclusive resort in Benidorm. If you enjoy spotting well-known British actors in guest roles, this is a great one to check out. It includes guest appearances from Mark Heap (*Friday Night Dinner*), Nigel Havers (*Coronation Street*), Una Stubbs (*Sherlock*), Wendy Richard (*Are You Being Served?*), and Kate O'Mara (*Doctor Who*), among others.

Bill - 2015 - This quirky take on Shakespeare's rise to fame comes to us from the same folks who made Horrible Histories. Mathew Baynton (aka Deano in *Gavin & Stacey*) portrays Shakespeare as a hopeless young lute player heading to London with big dreams.

Billionaire Boy - 2016 - When Joe's father Len invents a new sort of toilet roll, they become overnight billionaires. Now, Joe can have anything money can buy - but he soon learns it can't buy everything.

Blackadder - 1983 to 1989 - Rowan Atkinson stars as antihero Edmund Blackadder, accompanied by Sir Tony Robinson as his sidekick Baldrick. Each series of this quirky comedy is set in a different period within British history, and Edmund carries different titles throughout. The "essence" of each character remains largely the same in each series, though.

Blandings - 2013 to 2014 - A nobleman struggles to keep his stately home and strange family in line so he can spend more time with his beloved pig. The series was based on P.G. Wodehouse's *Blandings Castle* stories, and it's one of a relatively small number of scripted programmes filmed on location in Northern Ireland (mostly at Crom Castle in County Fermanagh).

Bliss - 2018 - Stephen Mangan plays a man living an exhausting double life in this family sitcom.

Boy Meets Girl - 2015 to 2016 - This romantic comedy combines a transgender romance with age gap love, pairing a 40-something transgender woman with a 26-year-old man.

Bucket - 2017 - When free-spirited Mim tells her daughter she's dying, they go on a road trip together. Miriam Margolyes (*Miss Fisher's Murder Mysteries*) stars alongside Frog Stone (*No Offence*).

Rowan Atkinson Presents: Canned Laughter - 1979 - This short comedy tells the story of a dinner date gone terribly wrong. It's often considered an early inspiration for Atkinson's Mr. Bean character.

Clash of the Santas - 2008 - This follow-up to Northern Lights sees Robson Green (*Grantchester*) and Mark Benton (*Shakespeare & Hathaway*) reprising their roles as bickering friends Colin and Howie. In this outing, they're off to the World Santa Championships in Lithuania.

Click and Collect - 2018 - Stephen Merchant (*Hello Ladies*) stars as Andrew, a man on a desperate Christmas mission to purchase the elusive Sparklehoof the Unicorn Princess for his daughter.

Cruise of the Gods - 2002 - Steve Coogan, David Walliams, and Rob Brydon star in this feature-length comedy about a group of 1980s sci-fi programme actors reuniting to attend a cruise arranged by the show's fan club.

Damned - 2016 to 2018 - Alan Davies (*Jonathan Creek*) and Jo Brand (*Getting On*) star in this series about workers dealing with endless bureacracy in a social services department.

Edge of Heaven - 2014 - In the seaside town of Margate, a close-knit but quirky family runs a 1980s-themed guest house.

Father Ted - 1995 to 1998 - Father Ted lives with two other very strange priests on the not-so-quiet Craggy Island in Ireland.

Fawlty Towers - 1975 to 1979 - John Cleese and Prunella Scales star in this classic British comedy about a very poorly managed hotel. Though it only lasted 12 episodes, it's considered one of the great British comedy classics.

Gavin & Stacey - 2007 to 2019 - After months of chatting, Gavin and Stacey leave their homes in Essex and Wales to meet for the first time in London. This much-loved comedy classic features a number of British acting favourites including Larry Lamb, Ruth Jones, Alison Steadman, Rob Brydon, and James Corden.

Hold the Sunset - 2018 to 2019 - Two mature neighbors are anxious to start a new life together, but they're interrupted when Edith's adult son arrives on her doorstep. Alison Steadman (*Gavin & Stacey*) and John Cleese (*Fawlty Towers*) star, and Jason Watkins (*The Crown*) plays Edith's adult son Roger.

Horrible Histories: Formidable Florence Nightingale - 2018 - Florence Nightingale gets the *Horrible Histories* treatment, and we follow her as she embarks on her journey to help soldiers during the Crimean War.

Insert Name Here - 2017 to 2018 - This comedy panel show focuses on people with one thing in common. They all have the same name. Sue Perkins hosts, and Josh Widdecombe and Richard Osman act as team captains.

Inside No. 9 - 2014 to 2020 - Dark humor, crime, drama, and horror are showcased in this anthology series. Every episode incorporates the number nine in some way, so keep an eye out as you watch.

Keeping Up Appearances - 1990 to 2002 - Dame Patricia Routledge stars as Hyacinth Bucket, a woman in perpetual denial of her working-class roots.

Last of the Summer Wine - 1973 to 2010 - The world's longest-running sitcom features grandpas gone wild in rural Yorkshire.

Living the Dream - 2017 to present - When a Yorkshire family buys an RV park in Florida and moves to pursue the American dream, they end up with a serious case of culture shock.

Mapp and Lucia - 1985 to 1986 - Based on E.F. Benson's novels, this series is set in the fictional coastal Sussex town of Tilling-on-Sea during the 1920s and 30s. Prunella Scales (*Fawlty Towers*) and Geraldine McEwan (*Marple*) star.

Mapp and Lucia - 2014 - Steve Pemberton (*Inside No. 9*) wrote this later adaptation of E.F. Benson's novels, with Miranda Richardson (*Blackadder*) and Anna Chancellor (*Spooks*, aka *MI-5*) starring. Like the first adaptation, this one was also filmed largely in Rye, East Sussex.

Marley's Ghosts - 2015 to 2016 - After an accident, Marley (Sarah Alexander, *Coupling*) is haunted by the ghosts of her husband, her lover, and a local vicar.

Mock the Week - 2005 to present - This satirical celebrity panel show is hosted by Dara Ó Briain and sees two temas of comedians tackling news and world events, often with improvised funny answers.

Mr. Stink - 2012 - This hour-long television adaptation is based on David Walliams' novel of the same name. It follows 12-year-old Chloe Crumb as she befriends an unusual homeless man named Mr. Stink.

Mr. Bean - 1992 to 1995 - Bumbling Mr. Bean rarely speaks and has some very peculiar ways of doing things, but it usually works out for him. Rowan Atkinson (*Maigret*) stars as the iconic British character.

Mrs. Brown's Boys - 2011 to 2020 - Brendan O'Carroll stars as Agnes Brown (in drag), powerful Irish matriarch. She's loud, nosy, and fiercely proud of her substantial brood.

Mum - 2016 to 2019 - After her husband dies, a woman tries to rebuild her life amidst all manner of problems from family and friends.

Newzoids - 2015 to 2016 - This unusual sketch show features animated puppets tackling current events and pop culture. Often compared to *Spitting Image*, the series has poked fun at public figures like Nigel Farage, Prince George, Donald Trump, and Boris Johnson.

Northern Lights - 2006 to 2007 - Robson Green and Mark Benton are Colin and Howie, best friends with a deep affection for one another...and an intense rivalry. The two work at the same transport depot, they're married to sisters, and they live on the same street.

Not Safe for Work - 2015 - When budget cuts move Katherine's civil servant job to Northampton, she reluctantly goes along with the relocation.

Not the Nine O'Clock News - 1995 - This vintage sketch news comedy features Mel Smith (*Alas Smith and Jones*) and Rowan Atkinson (*Mr. Bean*).

The Office - 2001 to 2003 - Before there was Michael Scott in the US, there was David Brent in Slough, England. Written by Ricky Gervais (*After Life*) and Stephen Merchant (*Hello Ladies*), this mockumentary-style programme takes place in the office of the fictional Wernham Hogg paper company. Mackenzie Crook (*Detectorists*) and Martin Freeman (*Sherlock*) are also among the stars.

One Foot in the Grave - 1990 to 1992 - Victor Meldrew (Richard Wilson, *Merlin*) may be a pensioner, but he still has plenty to say about what goes on in the world. The series follows his misadventures - mostly of his own creation - as he attempts to keep himself busy in retirement. It was created and written by David Renwick, also known for *Jonathan Creek*.

Only Fools and Horses - 1981 to 2003 - This classic comedy follows a couple of dodgy brothers always out for the big score.

Porridge - 1974 to 1977 - This prison comedy features a man trying to do his time honestly and stay out of trouble. Ronnie Barker (*Open All Hours*) stars as habitual criminal Fletch, and Richard Beckinsale (*The Lovers*) stars as Lennie Godber, the new cellmate he decides to mentor.

Porridge - 2016 to 2017 - This modern reboot sees Fletch's grandson Nigel Fletcher navigating his way through Wakeley Prison.

Psychoville - 2009 to 2011 - This award-winning comedy is a mash-up of everything from horror to thriller to mystery to black comedy, and it sees Reece Shearsmith and Steve Pemberton (both of *Inside No. 9*) playing a number of characters. In the series, five different characters around England have received threatening letters stating, "I know what you did..."

Puppy Love - 2014 - This heartwarming sitcom sees two women doing their best to handle cute dogs and challenging families. Joanna Scanlan (*No Offence*) and Vicki Pepperdine (*Getting On*) star.

QI - Stephen Fry and Sandi Toksvig star in this entertaining quiz show where contestants are more amply rewarded for interesting answers.

Red Dwarf - 1988 to 2020 - In the far future, the last human lives aboard a spaceship with a highly evolved cat-man.

Rev. - 2010 to 2014 - This smart sitcom follows the adventures of an Anglican vicar, his wife, and his run-down inner-city parish. Olivia Colman (*Broadchurch*) and Tom Hollander (*Baptiste*) star.

Ripping Yarns - 1976 to 1979 - Monty Python comedians Michael Palin and Terry Jones star in this anthology series that both parodied and celebrated pre-WWII schoolboy literature. Early episodes were directed by Terry Hughes, a BAFTA-winner who would later go on to direct *The Golden Girls* and *3rd Rock from the Sun*.

Scarborough - 2019 - In the coastal town of Scarborough, North Yorkshire, a group of locals live, work, and love, punctuated by frequent trips to the pub for karaoke. The series was written by *Benidorm* writer Darren Litten, but it was not commissioned for a second series.

Spitting Image - 1984 to 1988 - Major public figures are turned into puppets to satirize British life.

Susan Calman's Fringe Benefits - 2019 - Scottish comedian Susan Calman hosts this chat series from the Edinburgh Fringe Festival in 2019.

The Darling Buds of May - 1991 to 1993 - Based on the 1958 H.E. Bates novel of the same name, this series is set in rural 1950s Kent and follows the Larkin family as they go about their daily lives. This early 90s dramedy was a breakout role for Welsh actress Catherine Zeta-Jones.

The Edinburgh Show - 2019 - This series broadcasts from the Edinburgh Fringe Festival, highlighting some of the best acts and most interesting people in attendance.

The Hitchhiker's Guide to the Galaxy - 1981 - Arthur Dent is one of the last surviving members of the human race. Still in his dressing gown, he's dragged through an intergalactic portal and sent on an adventure through the universe. The series is based on Douglas Adams' novel of the same name, and he also wrote the TV adaptation.

The Job Lot - 2013 to 2016 - In a Midlands job centre, it's hard to tell if anyone actually works. Sarah Hadland (*Miranda*) stars.

The League of Gentlemen - 1999 to 2002 - In the fictional Northern England town of Royston Vasey, strange characters exist with interweaving storylines.

The Thick of It - 2005 to 2012 - This political satire follows government officials who lie, cheat, and generally do whatever it takes to keep their jobs.

The Thin Blue Line - 1995 to 1996 - Rowan Atkinson (*Mr. Bean*) stars as Inspector Fowler, an arrogant but ethical uniformed cop who's constantly being shown up by the plain-clothes detectives. This comedy is set in the fictional English town of Gasforth.

The Vicar of Dibley - 1994 to 2015 - When the 100-year-old Vicar of Dibley is replaced by a woman, some villagers are less than pleased. Dawn French (*The Trouble With Maggie Cole*) stars.

There She Goes - 2018 to present - David Tennant (*Doctor Who*) stars in this dramedy about a family dealing with the challenges of their daughter's chromosomal disorder. The series was based on the real-life experiences of writer and creator Shaun Pye. Miley Locke plays the young Rosie Yates.

Up the Women - 2013 to 2015 - Set in 1910, this comedy takes place among the women of the Banbury Intricate Craft Circle as they participate in the women's suffrage movement. To support their efforts, they form a league called Banbury Intricate Craft Circle Politely Requests Women's Suffrage (BICCPRWS).

Upstart Crow - 2016 to 2018 - This sitcom gives us William Shakespeare, before he was famous.

Waiting for God - 1990 to 1992 - Two grumpy pensioners fall in love while biding their time in a retirement home.

Would I Lie to You? - This comedy panel show sees contestants bluffing about their deepest and darkest secrets whilst the other team attempts to figure out what's true.

Yes, Minister - 1980 to 1984 - James is a Cabinet Minister who thinks he's finally in a position to get things done.

Yes, Prime Minister - 1986 to 1988 - This follow-up to Yes Minister continues with the same cast but a new address on Downing Street.

Young Hyacinth - 2016 - *Keeping Up Appearances* writer Roy Clarke returned to create this prequel to the original series. Kerry Howard (*Him & Her*) stars as young Hyacinth Bucket (then Walton) in this 1950s-based period comedy.

Documentary & Lifestyle

24 Hours in Police Custody - 2014 to 2019 - This dramatic docu-series follows police detectives around the clock as they work to build cases against suspects in custody before running out of time.

7 Up & Me - 2019 - This special takes a look at how "The Up Series" has impacted popular culture over the years it's been produced.

70 Glorious Years - 1996 - Take a look back on Queen Elizabeth II's life as she celebrates her 70th birthday.

A History of Ancient Britain - 2011 to 2012 - Scottish archaeologist Neil Oliver looks back at thousands of years of ancient history to tell the story of how Britain came to be.

A Queen is Crowned - 1953 - This feature-length documentary is narrated by Sir Laurence Olivier and offers a Technicolor look at Queen Elizabeth II's 1953 coronation.

A Very British Murder with Lucy Worsley - 2013 - Historian Lucy Worsley takes a look at the British fascination with murder and mystery, along with some of the famous murders of 19th century Britain.

Africa & Britain: A Forgotten History - 2016 - Historian David Olusoga takes a look at the enduring and occasionally difficult relationship between Great Britain and Africa.

All Aboard! - 2015 to 2016 - This series takes us on several slow, uninterrupted journeys around Britain. Whether moving by bus, canal boat, or sled, there are no interruptions for talking, just the scenery of the journey with a few facts imposed over parts of the landscape.

Ancient Rome: The Rise and Fall of an

Empire - 2006 - This dramatised documentary gives us greater insight into how the Roman Empire was built and destroyed by excessive greed, lust, and ambition.

Anthem for Doomed Youth: The War Poets - 2015 - Poet Wilfred Owen was killed in action in France during World War I. Using his diaries, letters, and poems, Peter Florence tells his story.

Antiques Roadshow - 1979 to present - Filmed at a variety of stately homes around the country, this series allows members of the public to bring in cherished items for expert appraisal.

The Aristocrats - 2011 to 2012 - This series takes a look at four of the families that make up modern-day British high society. These are the individuals who, through no skill, talent, or hard work of their own, have been fortunate enough to inherit titles, incredible opportunities, and grand estates.

Around the World in 80 Faiths - 2009 - Pete Owen Jones takes us on a journey around the world, taking a look at how people worship in six continents.

Autumnwatch - 2019 - This edition of the popular nature series takes us to the Cairngorms in Scotland to see how autumn is unfolding out in the wild.

The BBC at War - 2015 - Presenter Jonathan Dimbleby shows us how the BBC helped out in the fight against Hitler and fascism, and how it's helped to shape the British government over time.

Brexitcast - 2019 to 2020 - Some of the BBC's best political commentators explain Brexit, talk about what's happening in Westminster, and generally have a laugh about the state of things.

Britain's Biggest Adventures with Bear Grylls - 2015 - Bear Grylls combines history and adrenaline as he visits North Wales, the Yorkshire Dales, and the Scottish Highlands in search of Britain's biggest adventures.

Britain's Royal Weddings - 2011 - This series takes a look back at some of the grandest royal weddings in Britain's history.

Britain's Secret Treasures - 2012 to 2013 - Presenter Michael Buerk and historian Bettany Hughes take a look at 50 of the greatest treasures ever discovered by members of the public in the UK.

Britain's Tudor Treasure - 2015 - Historian Lucy Worsley celebrates the 500th anniversary of one of the finest surviving Tudor structures, Hampton Court.

The Britannia Awards - 2018 to 2019 - This Los Angeles-based British award show is presented by BAFTA. In this particular round of awards, honorees included Emilia Clarke, Cate Blanchett, and Jim Carrey.

Cameraman to the Queen - 2015 - For nearly 20 years, Peter Wilkinson has enjoyed a high level of royal access as he captured both state events and personal moments. This short documentary is a tribute to the effort, discretion, and loyalty involved in his work.

Caroline Quentin's National Parks - 2013 - Caroline Quentin takes us on trips to three of Great Britain's most beautiful national parks - the New Forest, Local Lomond, and Snowdonia.

Charles & Diana: Wedding of the Century - 2011 - This documentary takes a look back at the wedding of Prince Charles and Lady Diana Spencer, examining its impact on both participants and viewers.

Civilisation - 1969 - Art historian Sir Kenneth Clark offers his thoughts on the ideas and values that have influenced the evolution of western civilisation over the years. Though more than 50 years old, many continue to count the series among the greatest documentaries in existence.

Classic Doctor Who Comic Con Panel - 2017 - Colin Baker, Peter Davison, and Sophie Aldred come together to discuss fan questions during Comic Con 2017.

Coast - 2005 to present - This series mixes history, nature, and great scenery as they travel around the coastline of the UK and surrounding areas.

Code Blue: Murder - 2019 - Detectives from the South Wales Police Major Crime team investigate murders and seek justice for those who are grieving.

Codebreakers: The Secret Geniuses of World War II - 2011 - This documentary takes a look at how two men hacked into Hitler's super-code machine, ultimately turning the Battle of Kursk and powering the D-Day landings.

Corrie at Christmas - 2019 - Celebrate some of the best *Coronation Street* Christmas moments from the last six decades.

Countryfile Autumn Diaries - 2019 - Enjoy the countryside around Oxford, England as autumn sets in. You can almost feel the cool, crisp air through the screen.

Countryfile Spring Diaries - 2019 - Few things are more beautiful than the British countryside coming back to life after a long winter. This series takes a look at the flora and fauna as spring arrives in the country.

David Suchet on the Orient Express - 2010 - The quintessential Poirot, David Suchet, sets off on a journey to find out why the Orient Express is so famous around the world.

Days of Majesty - 1993 - This film was made to mark the 40th anniversary of Queen Elizabeth II's coronation, and it offers a look back at a variety of royal celebrations over the years.

Dead Good Job - 2012 - This series takes a look at the different ways Brits choose to say their final goodbyes to friends and loved ones.

Decoding the Future - 2019 - This BritBox production sits down to talk with a couple of women who worked as codebreakers during World War 2.

Funny is Funny: A Conversation with Normal Lear - 2018 - Emmy award-winning television pioneer Norman Lear sits down to reflect on his lengthy career.

Gardeners' World - 1968 to present - This long-running gardening series offers ideas, expert advice, and lovely scenery.

Gentlemen, The Queen - 1953 - This vintage film provides an up-close look at the early years of Queen Elizabeth II's life, including King George VI's coronation, her first broadcast, the war years, and her engagement.

Girls with Autism - 2015 - Because autistic girls and women are often better at masking their unique traits, they've gone largely overlooked in studies of autism. At the Limpsfield Grange boarding school, they're doing their best to change perceptions and help autistic girls lead better lives.

Good Morning Britain - 2020 - Each day, Susanna Reid and Pierce Morgan share the latest in news, pop culture, sports, and weather.

Great Escape: The Untold Story - 2001 - During World War II, 76 men attempted escape from the Stalag Luft III prisoner of war camp in Germany. Of those men, 3 made it home, 73 were captured, and 50 were shot on Hitler's instruction. This documentary tells their story.

Hairy Bikers Everyday Gourmets - 2013 - The Hairy Bikers show us how to prepare impressive feasts on very average budgets.

Hairy Bikers' Bakeation - 2012 - Hairy Bikers Si and Dave take a 5000-mile road trip around Europe, sampling the best baked goods on the continent.

Hidden: World's Best Monster Mystery - Loch Ness - 2001 - For centuries, there's been rumour of a monster hiding in the murky depths of Scotland's Loch Ness. This programme takes a look at those who claim to have seen it, and those who spend their lives looking for it. **Fun fact**: Naturalist and Nessie expert Adrian Shine (along with his lovely wife Maralyn) helped IHeartBritishTV.com's co-editors get engaged in Drumnadrochit last year.

Home Away from Home - 2014 - This series sees families swapping homes for a change of pace. On each swap, homeowners leave packets of information and activities for the new inhabitants of their homes.

Inside Claridges - 2012 - Over the course of three episodes, we go behind the scenes at one of Britain's poshest hotels, looking at what it takes to deliver five-star services with an emphasis on tradition.

Kirstie's Vintage Home - 2012 - Kirstie Allsopp helps viewers learn to add stylish vintage touches to their homes. This show blends DIY, upcycling, and bit of mid-century inspiration.

Licence to Thrill: Paul Hollywood Meets Aston Martin - 2015 - Though better known for his baking skills, this series sees Paul Hollywood exploring the world of Aston Martin cars. In addition to meeting with the latest company boss, he also trains up to race.

Looking for Victoria - 2003 - Prunella Scales (*Fawlty Towers*) takes a look back at Queen Victoria, the monarch she's been portraying in a one-woman show for roughly 20 years.

Louis Theroux - 2007 to 2016 - This series sees British documentarian Louis Theroux tackling a variety of controversial topics including American religious extremists, Miami prisons, and an American school for austistic individuals.

Marco's Great British Feast - 2008 - Chef Marco Pierre White travels around Britain sourcing some of the best and most unique local ingredients (including gull eggs).

Mary Berry's Absolute Favourites - 2014 to 2015 - Britain's favourite home cook shares some of her absolute favourite recipes from a lifetime of cooking.

Mary Berry's Country House Secrets - 2017 - In this series, Mary Berry travels to some of the grandest homes in Great Britain to see what goes on in their kitchen. It includes visits to Highclere Castle, Scone Palace, Powderham Castle, and Goodwood House.

Meghan & Harry: A Revolutionary Romance - 2018 - This series takes a look at the excitement some had ahead of the wedding of Meghan Markle and the former Prince Harry. It offers a look back at the different backgrounds of the two, with speculation about what brought them together.

Monumental Challenge - 2010 - Visit some of the world's greatest landmarks and learn about the specialist teams that maintain, repair, and expand them. The series visits the Eiffel Tower, the Sydney Harbour Bridge, Big Ben, Santiago Di Compostela, the Taj Mahal, and The Bund (China's Wall Street).

Murder, Mystery, and My Family - 2018 to present - This true crime series pairs the relatives of convicted killers with talented criminal barristers, allowing for a new examination of evidence using modern forensic techniques.

Nigellissima - 2012 - Nigella Lawson shows

viewers how to bring a bit of Italy into their kitchens, even without access to specialty Italian grocery stores.

Our Cops in the North - 2019 - Meet the detectives, emergency response officers, and command centres of the Northumbrian Police Force as they struggle to maintain the peace and catch the guilty in their little corner of the world.

Panorama: Fighting Coronavirus - The Scientific Battle - 2020 - This series offers reports from the scientific frontline, offering insights into what experts are doing to combat the virus that's gripped the world.

Paul O'Grady: For the Love of Dogs - 2012 - Comedian Paul O'Grady explores the bond between man and dog, Much of the series takes place at the Battersea Dogs & Cats Home.

Pompeii: The Last Day - 2003 - In AD79. Mount Vesuvius erupted, obliterating a number of Roman cities (including Pompeii). It's said to have released 100,000 times the thermal energy of the Hiroshima-Nagasaki bombings. This documentary attempts to dramatise that last day, giving us a better idea of what happened before the eruption.

Prime Minister's Questions - 2013 to present - In the House of Commons, MPs put their questions to Prime Minister Boris Johnson.

Question Time - 2019 to 2020 - This debate show sees politicians and media figures answering questions from the general public.

Rachel Khoo's Kitchen Notebook: London - 2014 - London-born chef Rachel Khoo goes back to London to explore the food scene and offer tips on how to create great British meals at home.

Rachels' Coastal Cooking - 2015 - Chef Rachel Allen hits the road to track down local food and ingredients around the Irish coast.

Royal Babies - 2013 - Filmed shortly before the birth of Prince George, this short documentary takes a look back at royal history and traditions pertaining to pregnancy, birth, and new babies.

The Royal Edinburgh Military Tattoo - 2019 - Each year, this incredible variety show is performed against the backdrop of Edinburgh Castle. It features bagpipes, military bands, dancers, and more.

The Royal Variety Performance - 2019 - Join Prince William and Catherine, Duchess of Cambridge for a night of variety entertainment at the London Palladium.

Secrets from the Sky - 2014 - Using drones, historian Bettany Hughes takes a look at Britain's historic sites from the air.

Seven Wonders of the Commonwealth - 2014 - Several presenters travel the globe to see the people and the natural wonders of nations in the Commonwealth.

Shakespeare in Italy - 2012 - Shakespeare placed a number of his most famous plays in cities around Italy. This series sees Francesco da Mosto and a variety of special guests (including Emma Thompson) travelling around the country and visiting Shakespearean locations like Padua, Verona, and Venice.

Springwatch - 2005 to present - Along with *Autumnwatch* and *Winterwatch*, this series follows British flora and fauna through the changing of the seasons each year.

Suffragettes - 2018 - Lucy Worsley presents this documentary about a group of working-class women working towards the right to vote.

Supermarket Secrets - 2013 to 2014 - Go behind the scenes of some of Britain's biggest supermarket chains to learn how they bring us fresh food on a truly massive scale. Learn how they forecast demand, develop new products, and automate increasingly large portions of what they do.

Swingin' Christmas - 2010 - Michael Parkinson hosts this festive, musical Christmas special. The programme features special guest Seth MacFarlane and music led by conductor John Wilson.

Tales from Northumberland with Robson Green - 2016 - *Grantchester* actor Robson Green returns to his home county to walk viewers through a part of the country he knows well.

Tales from the Coast with Robson Green - 2017 - Follow Robson Green on a trip around the British coast, visiting North Devon, Wales, the Outer Hebrides, Essex, and Suffolk.

The Coronavirus Newscast - 2020 - The *Brexitcast* team takes on COVID-19 and post-Brexit politics.

The Great British Countryside - 2012 -

Hugh Dennis (*Outnumbered*) and Julia Bradbury (*Countryfile*) lead us through four very different but equally stunning British landscapes. The series visits Cornwall and Devon, Yorkshire, the South Downs, and the Scottish Highlands.

The Great Chelsea Garden Challenge - 2015 - Six amateurs compete for a change to design and build a garden for display on Man Avenue at the 2015 RHS Chelsea Flower Show.

The Hairy Biker's Christmas Party - 2011 - Hairy Bikers Dave Myers and Si King show us how to make the perfect festive finger foods for a Christmas party with friends.

The Instant Gardener - 2015 - Danny Clark, garden designer extraordinaire, renovates the gardens of deserving members of the public.

The Lights Before Christmas - 2019 - Enjoy 90 minutes of unhurried footage of some of Britain's best Christmas lights.

The Lights Before Christmas: Luminous London - 2018 - Follow a hop-on, hop-off tour of London's best Christmas lights.

The Monarchy - 1992 - This early 90s series takes a closer look at the British monarchy - the allure, their purpose, and how much they cost the British taxpayer.

The Mystery of Mary Magdalene - 2013 - Melvyn Bragg takes a closer look at the questions surrounding Mary Magdalene, a highly controversial biblical figure.

The Shard: Hotel in the Clouds - 2014 - The Shard is a London hotel that promises the ultimate in luxury. This documentary takes a look at what goes on behind the scenes.

The Story of Luxury - 2011 - This two-part docuseries takes a look at the things we've valued over the years, with a particular emphasis on luxury in the Classical and Medieval time periods.

The Up Series - 1964 to 2013 - This series represents the world's longest-running documentary, following a group of Britons as they pass through life's stages. The series began with 14 individuals back in 1964, and they do follow-up interviews every seven years.

The Women of World War One - 2014 - Kate Adie takes a look at the impact women had on the outcome of WWI. Though not on the front lines, women contributed to the war effort in many ways.

This Farming Life - 2016 to 2019 - This dramatic docuseries gives us an often unromantic look at the highs and lows of modern farm life in Britain.

Unfinished Portrait: The Life of Agatha Christie - 1990 - Based on the notoriously private Christie's personal correspondence, this biographical programme takes a look at why a proper English lady might spend so much time imagining grisly murders.

Vincent Van Gogh: Painted with Words - 2010 - Benedict Cumberbatch (*Sherlock*) takes on the role of the iconic Dutch post-impressionist. Though dramatised, the dialogue is sourced from Van Gogh's own words.

Virgin Atlantic: Up in the Air - 2015 - Virgin Atlantic may be hip, but that hasn't translated to a stable financial situation. This programme follows CEO Craig Keeger as he attempts to turn things around.

WED Talks - 2018 - This programme counts down to the wedding of Meghan and Harry, looking at the preparations and traditions that go along with royal weddings.

Winterwatch - 2005 to present - Filming in the Scottish Highlands, the *Winterwatch* team looks at what's going on with the local wildlife, along with a bit on how all of Britain's wildlife is doing.

PBS MASTERPIECE

Website: http://amazon.com/channels/masterpiece

Description: Only available via Amazon, this PBS channel offers a wide variety of British programmes, particularly period dramas and mysteries. It also offers a number of foreign-language "Walter Presents" shows.

Available On: Roku, Amazon Fire TV, Android devices, iPad, desktop, Chromecast, and most smart TVs.

Cost: $5.99/month

Now Streaming

Anne of Green Gables: Fire and Dew - *Canada* - 2018 - This adaptation of L.M. Montgomery's Anne of Green Gables world has Anne growing up and heading off to college in the city.

Apple Tree Yard – 2017 - This miniseries is based on Louise Doughty's novel by the same name, and it's a suspenseful combination of sex and murder. When a woman gets an intriguing proposition, it excites her – until she realizes it may not be quite what it seemed. Emily Watson and Ben Chaplin star.

A Room with a View - 2007 - Elaine Cassidy (*No Offence*) stars alongside Rafe Spall (*Desperate Romantics*) in this story about a young Englishwoman in 1912 who finds love on a trip to Italy.

Arthur and George - 2015 - Martin Clunes (*Doc Martin*) stars as Sir Arthur Conan Doyle. When he finds himself outraged at an injustice against an Anglo-Indian solicitor, he uses his own fictional detective's methods to get justice for the man.

Baptiste - 2019 - This spinoff from the series *The Missing* sees Tchéky Karyo returning as Julien Baptiste, a clever

detective who agrees to help the Dutch police look for a missing sex worker in Amsterdam. Tom Hollander (*Rev*) and Jessica Raine (*Call the Midwife*) also star.

Beecham House - 2019 - Set in 1795, this period drama follows a former East India Company soldier determined to create a safe home in Delhi for his family. Critics have dubbed it "The Dehli Downton". Tom Bateman (*Vanity Fair*) and Lesley Nicol (*Downton Abbey*) star.

The Best of Men - 2014 - This docudrama tells the story of Dr. Ludwig Guttman, a doctor who arrived at England's Stoke Mandeville hospital during WWII and revolutionised the care of paraplegics.

The Bletchley Circle - 2012 to 2014 - In 1952, four former Bletchley Park codebreakers from WWII come together to track a killer.

Breathless - 2013 - Set in early 1960s England, this series looks at the lives of hospital staff who perform illegal off-site abortions in their spare time.

The Child in Time - 2018 - Benedict Cumberbatch (*Sherlock*) stars in this film about a man struggling to find purpose after the disappearance of his daughter. It's based on a novel by Ian McEwan.

Collision – 2009 - After a multi-car accident, a group of relative strangers see their secrets unfold around that single event that ties them together. This short series was written by Anthony Horowitz of *Midsomer Murders* fame, and *Shetland* fans will notice Douglas Henshall as DI John Tolin.

The Crimson Field - 2014 to 2015 - At a busy WWI hospital, Kitty tries to escape her past.

Dancing on the Edge – 2013 - In early 1930s London, a black jazz group is coming up in the world. Unfortunately, tragedy strikes before they can fully appreciate their success. This six-episode series features a mixture of British high society and the much uglier underbelly of racism and poverty in London at the time.

Death Comes to Pemberley – 2014 - Three episodes pay homage to Jane Austen's *Pride and Prejudice*, bringing us into the home of Elizabeth and Darcy after six years of marriage. As they prepare for their annual ball, tragedy brings the festivities to a halt.

Deep Water - 2019 - Anna Friel (*Marcella*) stars in this miniseries about three mothers struggling with challenging moral and ethical problems.

Elizabeth I: The Virgin Queen – 2005 - Anne-Marie Duff stars in this miniseries about Queen Elizabeth I, the enigmatic and long-reigning queen who never took a husband. Tom Hardy stars as her dear friend and possible lover Robert Dudley, 1st Earl of Leicester, and Emilia Fox takes on the role of Dudley's wife.

Endeavour – 2012 to present - In this prequel to *Inspector Morse*, a young Endeavour works with Sergeant Thursday to develop his investigative skills. Shaun Evans stars as Morse during this 1960s period mystery.

The Escape Artist – 2014 - David Tennant stars in this three-episode series about a junior barrister whose specialty is getting clients out of very tough spots. Unfortunately, this means his hands aren't entirely clean when those clients re-offend. Sophie Okonedo (*Mayday*) stars as his courtroom rival, Maggie Gardner.

Excalibur: Behind the Movie - 2020 - The 1981 film *Excalibur* is still considered by some to be one of the finest adaptations of the Arthurian legend. It also launched the careers of several well-known Irish and British actors including Ciarán Hinds, Liam Neeson, Sir Patrick Stewart, Helen Mirren, and Gabriel Byrne. This documentary takes a look back at the masterpiece.

Exile – 2011 - John Simm (*Life on Mars*) stars in this mystery-thriller about a man who returns home after his life falls apart – only to find a different kind of trouble there.

Far From the Madding Crowd - 1998 - This television movie is an adaptation of Thomas Hardy's novel of the same name, this time starring Paloma Baeza (*A Touch of Frost*) and Nathaniel Parker (*Inspector Lynley Mysteries*). Set against the backdrop of rural southwest England during Victorian times, it follows the life of Bathsheba Everdene and the people she knows in her small farming community.

The Forsyte Saga – This 2002 adaptation of John Galsworthy's novel follows the life of an English family over 34 years stretching from Victorian England to World War 1.

Frankie Drake Mysteries – *Canada* - 2018 to present - Set in 1920s Toronto, Frankie Drake is a great series for anyone who loved *Miss Fisher's Murder Mysteries*. Ms. Drake is a female detective whose Drake Detective Agency takes on the cases police don't want. Along with her trusty partner Trudy, they get into all manner of trouble.

Grantchester – 2014 to present - In the village of Grantchester, a clever vicar assists a local police detective with his investigations. James Norton (*Happy*

Valley) stars as vicar Sidney Chambers, and Robson Green (*Wire in the Blood*) plays DI Geordie Keating. Later in the series, Tom Brittany takes over for him in the role of Reverend Will Davenport, a former inner-city chaplain.

The Great Fire - 2015 - This four-part series is a dramatisation of 1666's Great Fire of London. The fire went on for four days, leaving nearly 90% of the city's population homeless.

Great Houses with Julian Fellowes - 2015 - This two-part series sees Julian Fellowes (*Downton Abbey*) guide us on a tour of two of Britain's great homes, Burghley House and Goodwood House.

Great Performances: Macbeth - 2010 - Sir Patrick Stewart stars in this acclaimed adaptation of Shakespeare's "Scottish Play".

Henry and Anne: The Lovers Who Changed History - 2014 - Historian Dr. Suzannah Lipscomb tells the story of the love affair between Henry VIII and Anne Boleyn.

Henry IX: Lost King - 2017 - Many have called Henry Frederick, Prince of Wales the best king England never had. Though bright and promising, he died at the age of 18 from typhoid fever. This documentary looks at the achievements in his short life, along with what might of been, had he lived.

Inside the Court of Henry VIII - 2015 - This documentary takes a look at why things were so terribly chaotic and brutal inside the court of Henry VIII.

Inspector Lewis - 2006 to 2015 - Inspector Lewis was a lovely parting gift after the departure of Inspector Morse. In Lewis, Kevin Whately returns to play Morse's former sidekick once more – except this time, he's the DI and his sidekick is DS James Hathaway.

Jamestown – 2017 to 2019 - This series goes 400 years back in time to follow a group of English settlers in 1619 Virginia. When it opens, it's a little more than a decade since a group of men settled Virginia, and a group of woman is arriving to marry the men who settled

the area and paid their way over.

The Jewel in the Crown - 1984 - This award-winning television serial is set during the final days of the British Raj in India during and after World War II. The series is based on Paul Scott's *Raj Quartet* novels.

Les Misérables – 2018 - Victor Hugo's epic tale of love and poverty in war-torn France returns to the screen in this 2018 adaptation starring Olivia Colman, Dominic West, and Lily Collins. The 6-episode miniseries takes a deeper dive into some characters who have traditionally gotten a bit less screentime (like Fantine), making the progression slower and more grueling – but also much more dramatic.

Lovejoy - 1986 to 1994 - Ian McShane (*Deadwood*) stars as Lovejoy, the slightly shady antiques dealer and part-time detective. *Downton Abbey* fans will be delighted to see a young Phyllis Logan (aka Mrs. Hughes) in this early role.

Lucy Worsley's Royal Myths and Secrets - 2020 - This three-part series sees historian Lucy Worsley travelling across Europe in search of places central to royal history.

Lucy Worsley's 12 Days of Tudor Christmas - 2019 - Lucy Worsley takes us on a fun and educational stroll through Tudor Christmas festivities.

The Making of a Lady - 2012 - This film follows Emily, an educated but penniless woman who goes into service as a lady's companion.

Man in an Orange Shirt - 2018 - This two-part series tells two separate love stories set 60 years apart. One, a forbidden relationship, takes place during WWII, while the other is modern.

Mansfield Park - 2007 - Billie Piper (*Doctor Who*) stars in this television movie adaptation of Jane Austen's third novel. It's about a young woman sent to live with wealthier relatives, who later falls in love with her sensitive cousin.

Margaret: The Rebel Princess - 2019 - A controversial figure in her time, Princess Margaret was a reflection of many of the societal changes going on during her time. This series takes a look at her life and influence.

Masterpiece: The Chaperone - 2018 - With a screenplay by Julian Fellowes (*Downton Abbey*), this period drama focuses on Norma Carlisle, a middle-aged woman charged with chaperoning the teenage Louise Brooks, not yet a flapper icon and sex symbol.

Masterpiece: Wind in the Willows - 2007 - Matt Lucas (*Little Britain*) stars as Mr. Toad in this feature-length adaptation of Kenneth Grahame's classic tale.

The Miniaturist – This 2017 BBC miniseries is an adaptation of Jessie Burton's novel by the same name. In 17th century Amsterdam, a woman moves in with her new husband and his sister. Oddly, the husband gives her a mysterious dollhouse to occupy her time.

Mr. Selfridge - 2013 to 2016 - Jeremy Piven (*Entourage*) stars as the American Harry Gordon Selfridge, a man who revolutionised British retail.

Mrs. Wilson – 2018 - Mrs. Wilson is fascinating because it's not just a true story, it's a true story about the grandmother of Ruth Wilson (*Luther*), the actress playing the title role. Alison Wilson was widowed in 1963, only to realize her husband had been leading a secret life. Iain Glen (*Jack Taylor*) plays her departed husband, a foreign intelligence officer with more than one "Mrs. Wilson" in his life.

Murder on the Homefront - 2014 - This crime drama is set during the London Blitz of 1940, where the worst criminals could use blackouts and destruction to hide their terrible crimes. It premiered with a feature length pilot broken into two parts, but further episodes were not commissioned.

Nicholas and Alexandra: The Letters - 2019 - Dr. Suzannah Lipscomb presents this two-part docudrama about the love story between Tsar Nicholas II and his wife Alexandra.

Northanger Abbey - 2007 - Felicity Jones (*Brideshead Revisited*) stars in this adaptation of Jane Austen's classic parody of Gothic fiction. She plays seventeen-year-old tomboy Catherine Morland, a young woman with a wild imagination and love of Gothic novels.

Pie in the Sky - 1994 to 1997 - When DI Crabbe leaves the police force to open a restaurant, they continue to pull him back in for part-time crime-solving.

Pollyanna - 2016 - Pam Ferris (*Rosemary & Thyme*), Kenneth Cranham, and Tom Ellis (*Miranda*) are among the stars of this television movie based on the *Pollyanna* novels of American author Eleanor H. Porter. Georgina Terry (*William and Mary*) stars as Pollyanna.

Poldark Revealed - 2016 - This programme goes on set to get a look at what makes Poldark such an enduring favourite.

Press - 2019 - This series follows the rivalry between two major newspapers, taking a hard look at some of the awful things they do to get a scoop. David Suchet (*Poirot*) appears.

Prince Charles at 70 - 2019 - This documentary takes a look at Prince Charles' ongoing charity work and his likely future role as monarch of the United Kingdom.

Queen and Country - 2012 - Trevor McDonald walks us through some of the British monarchy's greatest traditions and institutions.

The Queen at War - 2020 - This documentary takes a look at how Queen Elizabeth II served her country during WWII, and how the war shaped her.

Queen Elizabeth's Secret Agents - 2018 - This docuseries takes a look at the incredible father-and-son team that kept Queen Elizabeth I safe.

Rebecca – 1997 - Emilia Fox and Charles Dance star as the new Mr. and Mrs. Maxim de Winter in this adaptation of Daphne du Maurier's classic gothic suspense novel. Diana Rigg plays Mrs. Danvers, the housekeeper still loyal to her dead mistress, Rebecca.

Reilly, Ace of Spies – 1983 - In this series, we get a glimpse at the life of Sidney Reilly, the spy who inspired James Bond.

Remember Me – 2014 - Michael Palin (*Monty Python, Great Railway Journeys*), Jodie Comer (*Killing Eve*), and Mark Addy (*The*

Syndicate) star in this sublimely creepy three-part mystery about a series of unfortunate events that unfold around an unhappy pensioner who fakes a fall in order to be moved to a care home. The scenery is perfectly bleak and atmospheric, and the cast is outstanding.

Royal Paintbox - 2014 - Hosted by Prince Charles himself, this documentary takes a look at rarely seen art created by British royals from the past and present.

Royal Wives at War - 2016 - This documentary uses dramatised monologues to give us a closer look at the 1936 abdication crisis through the eyes of the two women most deeply involved - Elizabeth the Queen Mother and American Wallis Simpson.

Rumpole of the Bailey – 1978 to 1992 – Leo McKern starred as Horace Rumpole, a defense barrister who often took on underdog clients.

Sanditon - 2019 - Prior to her early death at the age of 41, Jane Austen began a new and different sort of work. It was the story of Sanditon, a fledgling seaside resort town along the southern coast of England. It was never finished. In this miniseries, screenwriter Andrew Davies (*Mr. Selfridge, Pride & Prejudice*) finishes her final masterpiece. Rose Williams (*Curfew*) stars as Charlotte Heywood, and Theo James plays the outrageous Sidney Parker. Anne Reid (*Last Tango in Halifax*) and Kris Marshall (*Death in Paradise*) also appear.

Secrets of Britain - 2014 - This series takes a look at the secrets behind some of Britain's most notable landmarks and institutions. It covers the Tower of London, Selfridges, Scotland Yard, the London Underground, Her Majesty's Secret Service, and Westminster.

Secrets of Britain's Great Cathedrals - 2019 - Though many travel shows visit the great cathedrals, few of them offer as much detail as this eight-part series. It covers York Minster, Canterbury Cathedral, St. Paul's Cathedral, Westminster Abbey, Salisbury Cathedral, Wells Cathedral, Bath Abbey, Gloucester Cathedral, Durham Cathedral, Lincoln Cathedral, Worcester Cathedral, Tewkesbury Abbey, St. David's, Brecon, St. Asaph, Bangor Cathedral, Ely Cathedral, Peterborough Cathedral, and King's College Cambridge.

Secrets of Highclere Castle - 2013 - This hour-long documentary takes a look at the stately home made famous by *Downton Abbey*.

Secrets of Iconic British Estates - 2013 - This lovely British tour series takes us to Hampton Court, Althorp, and Chatsworth.

Secrets of the Manor House - 2012 - While life may have seemed glamorous in Britain's stately homes, this series looks at the real challenges faced by owners of these massive estates.

Secrets of the Six Wives - 2017 - Historian Dr. Lucy Worsley hosts this series about the most dramatic moments in the lives of Henry VIII and his many wives.

Spying on the Royals - 2018 - In the late 1930s, King Edward VIII and his American lover were considered a significant security risk to the country. This documentary looks at the controversial espionage operation that kept tabs on the pair.

Tales from the Royal Wardrobe - 2015 - Historian Dr. Lucy Worsley takes a look at the phenomenon of watching royal attire, offering evidence that it's not just a modern behaviour.

Three Sovereigns for Sarah - 1986 - Vanessa Redgrave (*Mrs. Dalloway*) stars in this historic drama about the Salem witch trials.

Tudor Monastery Farm at Christmas – 2013 - Historians and archaeologists look at how the Tudors celebrated the 12 days of Christmas.

Unforgotten – 2015 to present - Cassie and Sunny use modern technology to get to the bottom of very cold cases. This recent crime drama is based in London and stars Nicola Walker and Sanjeev Bhaskar as Cassie and Sunny.

Vicious - 2013 to 2016 - Sir Ian McKellen and Sir Derek Jacobi star as an aging gay couple with a hilariously snarky love/hate relationship. The two live together in a Covent Garden flat, entertaining frequent guests, hoping for Freddie's big acting break, and checking to make sure their elderly dog is still alive.

Victoria - 2016 to present - This series stars Jenna Coleman (*Doctor Who*) as Victoria and Tom Hughes (*The Game*) as Prince Albert, along with Peter Bowles (*To the Manor Born, Executive Stress*) as the

Duke of Wellington. Much like *The Crown* is to Queen Elizabeth II, *Victoria* follows Queen Victoria as she progresses through her lengthy reign.

Victoria and Albert: The Wedding - 2019 - Historian Lucy Worsley re-stages the wedding of Queen Victoria and Prince Albert, using historic documents, diary entries, and archives to pull together all the necessary details. More than just a re-enactment, she also talks about how the wedding changed history and created new traditions.

Vienna Blood - 2019 - Set in 1900s Vienna, this three-part drama follows brilliant English doctor Max Liebermann as he studies under Sigmund Freud. When Liebermann encounters Austrian detective Oskar Rheinhardt, they forge a partnership to take on some of Vienna's most deadly and disturbing cases.

What the Durrells Did Next - 2019 - Hosted by *Durrells* star Keeley Hawes, this special takes a look at what happened to the real-life Durrell family after they left Corfu.

The Widower - 2015 - Reece Shearsmith (*Inside No. 9*) and Sheridan Smith (*Gavin & Stacey*) star in this miniseries about Malcolm Webster, a man who worked as a nurse and also happened to be a serial killer.

The Windermere Children - 2020 - This movie tells the true story of child survivors of the Holocaust and their rehabilitation in the Lake District in England.

The Windermere Children: In Their Own Words - 2020 - This documentary talks with some of the children whose new, post-Holocaust lives began along the shore of Lake Windermere in England.

The Windsors: A Royal Family - 2018 - This four-part documentary offers an in-depth look at Britain's current royal family, including interviews with friends, aides, and family members.

Wolf Hall - 2015 - This historical drama charts Thomas Cromwell's rise in the Tudor Court as he moved from a poor blacksmith's son to the closest advisor of Henry VIII. The series is based on Hilary Mantel's award-winning novel.

The Woman in White – 2018 - This BBC miniseries adaptation of Wilkie Collins' famous book of the same name includes Jessie Buckley, Ben Hardy, and Olivia Vinall. This classic gothic tale begins when a man meets a mysterious woman in white before heading to Limmeridge House to tutor his nieces. He's told it's a woman who escaped from an asylum, but already, a mystery has begun to unfold around him.

World on Fire - 2019 - This miniseries follows ordinary people from Poland, France, Germany, and the United Kingdom during the early years of World War II. The large and talented cast includes Helen Hunt (*Mad About You*), Lesley Manville (*Mum*), and Sean Bean (*Game of Thrones*)

The Worricker Trilogy - 2014 - An analyst in the British intelligence forces want to find out why the PM had his friend killed. Bill Night (*Love Actually*) stars.

Wuthering Heights - 2009 - Charlotte Riley (*Press*) and Andrew Lincoln (*The Walking Dead*) star in this two-part adaptation of Emily Brontë's classic novel.

INSIDE OUTSIDE

Website: https://www.inside-outside.tv/

Description: This subscription service offers a selection of the best British home and garden television shows. Though the total amount of programming is relatively low, you may still feel it's worth it to subscribe occasionally.

Available On: Roku, Amazon Fire TV, Apple TV, Apple iPhone & iPad, Android TV, Android phones and tablets, computer (via web browser). You can also subscribe via Amazon Prime Video.

Cost: $5.99/month

Now Streaming

Big Dreams Small Spaces, Series 1-3 - Monty Don joins amateur gardeners to help them realise the big dreams they have for their small gardens.

Great Interior Design Challenge, Series 1-4 - Amateur designers attempt to transform inside spaces.

The Secret History of the British Garden - Monty Don takes us through the history and evolution of the British garden. The series is made up of four hour-long episodes, each one covering a century of gardening history.

Garden Rescue, Series 1-2 - Charlie Dimmock and the Rich brothers compete to design garden spaces for people around Great Britain.

Gardeners' World - 1968 to present - This long-running series offers support, ideas, and guidance for gardeners all over the UK - and the world.

Secret Removers - This series follows individuals as they arrange secret moves for friends and family members.

Kevin McCloud's Escape to the Wild, Series 1 - In this series, Kevin McCloud travels the globe to meet people who've moved to remote and challenging places. From the Arctic Circle to the jungles of Central America, this is a show about

people in search of a simpler life.

Jimmy Doherty's Escape to the Wild, Series 2 - This series follows British families who've given up on the rat race and relocated to remote parts of the world. Locations covered in this series include Indonesia, Uganda, and the Yukon.

Love Your Garden, Series 1 & 3 - Alan Titchmarsh and his team travel the country, educating viewers and helping guests find ways to get more from their gardens.

The Garden Pantry - This New Zealand-based series focuses on edible gardening, with loads of great scenery from around the country. Some episodes also get into food prep and preserving.

Discovering Korean Food with Gizzi Erskine - Gizze Erskine is a food writer for The Independent, and this series has her leading us around Korea in search of the best Korean food - while educating viewers about the different types of Korean dishes.

Get Growing - In this series, the Get Growing team travels to different locations around the British countryside, helping families solve their toughest backyard gardening problems.

The Autistic Gardener - This fun series sees a team of autistic gardeners - led by an award-winning autistic gardener - as they remodel garden spaces for a variety of individuals around the UK. Aside from gardening knowledge, you'll also learn a thing or two about the unique skills and challenges of people on the autism spectrum.

Food Glorious Food - This series travels around the UK, checking out some of the best food on offer in different regions. Areas visited include Malvern, Harrogate, Brighton, Yorkshire, and Knebworth.

Beat My Build - This series sees small property developers around the UK going head-to-head in a competition to see who can complete their projects effectively, quickly, and at a profit.

Market Kitchen - This fun British series focuses on using local markets to get seasonal produce - then preparing dishes based on those finds.

Paul Hollywood Pies & Puds - This series features mostly savoury dishes by Paul Hollywood (of the *Great British Bake Off*). Dishes include Corned Beef Hash Pie, Paul's Cream Tea Pudding, Meat & Two Potato Pie, Thai Chicken Pie, Paul's Luxury Fish Pie, Traditional Mutton Scotch Pies, Goats Herd Pie, and more.

How to Haggle for a House - In this series, financial expert George Harrigan-Brown goes face-to-face to negotiate with property vendors to help buyers get better deals. He doesn't reveal the deal until after they've seen the house. Episodes featured include Eastbourne, London, Bath, Edinburgh, and Kendal/Lake District.

Operation Homefront - This series sees ex-British soldiers putting their skills to work in a variety of community projects around the UK. Among the projects are an Oxfordshire Scout Hut, a Glasgow community centre, and a Southampton Boathouse.

Homes Under the Hammer, Series 4 & 5 - This long-running British auction series follows property auctions that frequently require a large amount of refurbishment or development. The series follows properties from auction to refurbishment, though not every project is seen through to completion.

You Deserve This House - This heartwarming series seeks out deserving homeowners in desperate need of renovation. From a retired nurse to a speech therapist to an ex-firefighter, you'll see good people getting some much-needed kindness from their fellow Brits.

Hoarder SOS - This series sees professional organizers helping people living in extreme clutter. With a bit of help, they're able to get a new start on life without all the baggage.

Royal Upstairs Downstairs - This 20-episode series travels in the footsteps of Queen Victoria, visiting and exploring the stately homes she visited during her reign. The series begins with Chatsworth, moving on to Shugborough, Harewood, Holkham, Brighton, Scone, Walmer, Wimpole, Belvoir, Blair, Burghley, Hatfield, Castle Howard, Stoneleigh, Warwick, Penryhn, Floors Castle, Hughenden, and Waddesdon,

House Swap - This four-part series follows people who've decided they would rather trade houses than attempt to buy and sell them.

Damned Designs: Don't Demolish My Home - In this series, we see individuals whose building projects have somehow broken local rules that put their project at risk. Whether it's an off-grid retreat they built or a home they imported and assembled without proper planning permissions, they fight to get on the good side of local authorities so they can save their homes.

Clarissa & the King's Cookbook - This brief documentary sees medieval foodie Clarissa Dickson Wright tracking down Britain's oldest-known cookbook, The Forme of Cury. Though brief, it's fascinating to see her recreate recipes from the 700-year-old scroll.

Hoarders, Get Your House in Order - This is another show that takes a look at Brits whose collections and obsessions have gotten a bit out of control. They've crossed the line between healthy collecting and real quality of life issues, and the series is aimed at helping them make changes for the better.

Kitchen Criminals - This amusing series sees top chefs John Burton Race and Angela Hartnett traveling around the US looking for its absolute worst cooks. They visit every region of the UK, from England to Wales to Scotland and Northern Ireland.

BEST OF BRITISH TV

Now Streaming

2000 Tattoos But Don't Judge Me - 2015 - This four-part series takes a look at some of Britain's most extreme body modifiers as they embark on new phases of their lives.

Air Farce New Year's Eve Special - 2009 to 2017 - This annual special features a popular Canadian comedy troupe, Air Farce.

All Creatures Great & Stuffed - 2015 - This short documentary takes a look at the "taxidermy as art" craze.

Allotment Wars - 2013 - It's easy to romanticise allotments as a beautiful, peaceful part of English life. This series shows a different reality, though, where it's harvest-or-lose-out, and neighbours battle over plots of land.

Angry Britain - 2014 - Rage seems to be increasing in Britain, and this series takes a look at some of the most egregious examples, along with the possible reasons for the shift.

The Bank - 2015 - Go behind the scenes in a British bank to learn how money moves around in modern Britain.

The Betrayal - 2014 - This short programme tells the stories of people who've been betrayed by those they loved and trusted.

Big Star's Little Star - 2013 to present - This game show sees celebrities pairing up with their children to answer questions and win money for charity.

Britain on Call - 2013 - This documentary takes a look at night workers in Manchester and the strange things they have to deal with.

Britain's Poshest Nannies - 2014 - Take a look behind the scenes at Norland College, a school that's been training nannies for the rich and famous since the reign of Queen Victoria.

Britain's Secret Homes - 2013 - Some of Britain's most popular actors and television presenters explore the secrets of great homes around the country. From Twiggy to Mark Williams to Michael Portillo to Sir David Jason, it's an interesting trip through history in five parts.

Brits Behind Bars - 2015 - As more and more Brits travel the world, there's been an increase in those who find themselves on the wrong side of the legal system in other countries. This series demonstrates how a simple holiday can turn ugly.

Call Security - 2015 - This documentary takes a look at the rapidly growing business of private security.

Come Dine With Me Couples - 2014 - Couples attempt to host the perfect dinner party, each hoping to score the most points and win a cash prize.

Diary of a Teenage Virgin - 2013 - This series explores what it's like to be a teenage virgin in a modern era of social media and largely unrestricted access to pornography.

Dinner Party Wars - 2013 - This Canadian series sees a chef and a style expert judging the best dinner party efforts of its contestants.

Elizabeth: Queen, Wife, Mother - 2012 - In the wake of her Diamond Jubilee, this programme looks at Queen Elizabeth from the eyes of those who know her well.

Escorts - 2015 - Triple-BAFTA winner Dan Reed explores the modern world of high-class prostitution.

Farewell Tina - 2015 - Michelle Keegan was one of Coronation Street's favourite stars, and this programme takes a look back at her time in the role of Tina.

The Fried Chicken Shop: Life in a Day - 2013 - This fly-on-the-wall docuseries follows the goings on in a single South London fried chicken shop.

From Russia With Cash - 2015 - A significant part of London's property boom has been fueled by overseas buyers laundering money. This series sees an undercover reporter pretend to be a corrupt Russian property buyer looking to buy a property with his mistress.

Frontline Police - 2012 - Ex-cop Rav Wilding teams up with the Essex Police's Special Ops team, giving us a peek at what this elite unit does to stay prepared for the challenges that come their way.

Gibraltar: Britain in the Sun - 2013 - Follow the lives of British ex-pats living in the sunny British Overseas Territory of Gibraltar between Africa and Spain.

Girls to Men - 2015 - Three young Brits prepare to transform themselves into men.

Great Night Out - 2013 - Four friends attempt to help each other through a variety of life problems, but they nearly always make things worse. This comedy follows their efforts to fix things while never straying too far from their local pub.

Harbour Lives - 2014 - Ben Fogle returns to his home area of Poole, Britain's largest natural harbour. Here, he takes a look at the way people live their lives along the Dorset coast.

Hotel of Mum and Dad - 2013 - Young couples still living at home get a chance to test out their independence in temporary housing. Will they succeed, or will they rush back to the "Hotel of Mum and Dad"?

Hot Tub Britain - 2014 - The hot tub has taken off in Britain, and this documentary takes a closer look at the craze.

In-Law Wedding Wars - 2011 - Engaged couples allow one of their mothers to plan their weddings.

Inside Claridges - 2012 - Over the course of three episodes, we go behind the scenes at one of Britain's poshest hotels, looking at what it takes to deliver five-star services with an emphasis on tradition.

The Jonathan Ross Show, Season 9 - 2011 to present - This British comedy chat show normally airs on Saturday evenings in the UK, featuring a variety of celebrities and performers.

The Kumars - 2014 - This revival of *The Kumars at No. 42* features a shortened name and more of a chat show format. In the new series, Sanjeev is divorced and living with his family in a flat behind their Hounslow gift shop. Interviewed celebrities include Daniel Radcliffe, Olivia Colman, Jenny Agutter, James Corden, and Hugh Jackman.

My Transgender Kid - 2015 - This programme follows ordinary British families whose children feel they were born with the wrong gender.

Outnumbered - 2007 to 2014 - Hugh Dennis and Claire Skinner star in this sitcom about a couple who are outnumbered by their three children.

Our Lives: I'm a Teenage Grandmother - 2015 - Young Zara is only 16, but she suffers from lipodystrophy, which causes her to look and sound much older than she really is.

Our Lives: The Men With Many Wives - 2014 - Though illegal in the UK, polygamy is on the rise, particularly in Muslim communities. This documentary talks with some of the people involved in polygamy.

Revenge Porn - 2015 - This short film takes a look at what happens when intimate photos fall into the wrong hands.

Rita & Me - 2015 - This hour-long tribute celebrates Barbara Knox, the woman who played Rita on Coronation Street for 50 years.

The Royal Bodyguard - 2011 to 2012 - Follow the exploits of Captain Guy Hubble, a fictional ex-guardsman who now works as a Royal Bodyguard after saving the queen's life on the day of the State Opening of Parliament. Sir David Jason stars.

Royal Variety Performance - 2015 - Stars of stage and screen come together for one night of entertainment.

Secret Life of the Human Pups - 2016 - Learn what goes on in the human "puppy play" community where grown men crave doggy treats and squeaky toys.

Secrets of the Gay Sauna - 2015 - Enter the secretive world of gay saunas, places where men go to meet strangers for sex.

Seven Dwarves: The Wedding - 2012 - The housemates from *Seven Dwarves* return to find out what's been going on since they all lived together.

Seventy With a Six-Pack - 2016 - Today's senior citizens aren't all tea and biscuits and outings to stately homes. This programme takes a look at some of the British pensioners preparing for the World Bodybuilding Finals in Miami.

The Shard: Hotel in the Clouds - 2014 - The Shard is a London hotel that promises the ultimate in luxury. This documentary takes a look at what goes on behind the scenes.

Strippers - 2014 - Filmed over five months in the Scottish cities of Edinburgh, Glasgow, and Aberdeen, this series takes a look at what's leading young women to become erotic dancers.

Sunday Night at the Palladium (aka Tonight at the London Palladium)- 1955 to 2017 - This long-running entertainment series has been re-vamped and re-booted numerous times over the years, and episodes feature acts like Simply Red, David Gray, Deacon Blue, Josh Groban, and numerous less well-known performers.

Up All Night: The Minicab Office - 2013 - In the clubbing destination of Norwich, Courtesy Taxis is at the eye of the drunken storm. This series takes a look at what happens after last call when people start looking for taxis.

Wedding Town - 2016 - Historically, Gretna Green, Scotland was a place where English couples could dash off to get married to get married under more lenient marriage laws (and without parental consent). Today, couples are still heading there to tie the knot, and this series takes a look at some of those weddings.

The Week the Women Came - 2013 - This short programme follows psychosexual therapist Trudy Hannington as she tries to help two women get their sex lives back on track.

White Van Man - 2011 - Will Mellor (*No Offence*) and Georgia Moffett (*The Bill*) are among the stars of this sitcom about a terribly incompetent handyman and his assistant.

Whose Line is it Anyway: Australia - 2016 - Improvisation is the name of the game in this 10-part game show.

The Woman Who Ate Her House - 2016 - This documentary follows people with pica, a rare condition that compels them to eat unusual substances not generally intended for consumption.

The Worst Week of My Life -2004 to 2006 - Ben Miller (*Death in Paradise*), Sarah Alexander (*Marley's Ghosts*), and Alison Steadman (*Gavin & Stacey*) are among the stars of this quirky sitcom about a man with a terrible tendency to get himself in unusual and embarrassing predicaments.

You, Me, & Them - 2013 - Anthony Head (*Buffy the Vampire Slayer*) and Eve Myles (*Keeping Faith*) star in this light sitcom about a May-December romance and an overly involved family.

PRIME VIDEO

Website: http://amazon.com

Description: As part of their Amazon Prime membership, Amazon offers thousands of shows and movies you can view at no additional cost. It's also possible to purchase a Prime Video membership without the free shipping benefits (at a slightly lower monthly cost).

Available On: Roku, Amazon Fire TV, Android devices, iPad, desktop, Chromecast, and most smart TVs.

Cost: $12.99/month or $119/year for Prime, $8.99/month for just Prime Video

Now Streaming

Mysteries & Crime Dramas

Agatha Christie's Ordeal by Innocence – 2018 - When a wealthy woman is murdered, her adopted son is arrested in spite of his claims of innocence. Later, his guilt is thrown into doubt and the family scrambles to figure out who killed her.

Amber – *Ireland* – 2014 - This Irish miniseries explores the circumstances surrounding the disappearance of a 14-year-old girl.

Amnesia – 2004 - Detective Stone struggles mightily to unravel and come to terms with the disappearance of his wife.

Appropriate Adult – 2011 - A woman finds herself involved in a serial killer case as the "appropriate adult" who helps vulnerable adults facing criminal charges.

Bedlam – 2011 to 2012 - When a haunted former asylum is turned into a high-end apartment building, it has unexpected consequences for the new tenants.

The Bench – 2001 to 2002 - This legal drama takes place in a busy Welsh magistrates court. It follows the challenges they face in court, along with the pressures of working on a high-profile legal team.

Black Widows - *Finland* - 2016 to 2017 - Three best friends are going through a mid-life crisis and think that life will be better if their husbands are dead. Unfortunately for them, it's not as easy as they had imagined.

Blood Ties - *Canada* - 2007 - When a Toronto detective begins losing her eyesight, she becomes a PI and teams up with a 470-year-old vampire (who is also the illegitimate son of Henry VIII). The series is an adaptation of author Tanya Huff's *Blood* novels.

The Blue Rose - *New Zealand* - 2013 - This investigative drama sees a group of law firm employees joining together to figure out what happened in the mysterious death of a co-worker.

Bounty Hunters – 2019 - Jack Whitehall and Rosie Perez star in this series about a sheltered Brit and a tough Brooklynite who must work together to help save his family's business after a dodgy antiques deal involving looted treasures.

The Brief – 2004 to 2005 - This legal series comes from the creators of *Inspector Morse* and *Kavanagh QC*, and it stars Alan Davies

(*Jonathan Creek*) as a criminal lawyer with a penchant for gambling.

The Broker's Man – 1997 to 1998 - A former detective investigates insurance claims while trying to hold his family life together. Features Kevin Whately (*Inspector Morse*) in the lead.

Cadfael - 1994 to 1998 - In 12th century Shrewsbury, a monk solves mysteries. Derek Jacobi (*Last Tango in Halifax*) stars.

Charlie Jade – *Canada/South Africa* – 2005 - This sci-fi mystery series focuses on a detective trapped in our parallel universe.

Chiller – 1995 - Martin Clunes and Nigel Havers star in this horror series about friends who receive prophecies during a seance in the basement of a London cafe.

The City & the City – 2018 - David Morrissey stars in this BBC sci-fi/mystery production about an inspector in the Extreme Crime Squad of the fictional European city-state of Beszel. When a student is murdered in Beszel's twin city of UI Qoman, he investigates.

City of Vice – 2008 - This historical crime drama is set in Georgian London and executed with incredible attention to detail.

Cold Squad – *Canada* – 1998 to 2005 - This long-running Canadian series follows a team that works on cold cases ranging from 5 to 50 or more years old.

Colonel March of Scotland Yard – 1956 - This vintage detective series offers 26 episodes of classic 1950s British mystery.

Crownies – *Australia* – 2011 - Marta Dusseldorp (*A Place to Call Home*) stars in this series about young solicitors who act as primary points of contact for police, witnesses, and victims.

Cuffs – 2015 - In quirky coastal Brighton, police officers are over-stretched and under-resourced, but they do the best they can with what they've got.

Dark Angel – 2017 - *Downton Abbey*'s Joanne Froggatt plays the Victorian poisoner Mary Ann Cotton, a woman who murdered her husbands and children.

DCI Banks – 2010 to 2016 - Stephen Tomkinson (*Ballykissangel, Wild at Heart*) stars as DCI Alan Banks, a skilled but stubborn Yorkshire-based investigator.

A Difficult Woman – *Australia* – 1998 - A woman with a brilliant career and promising relationship sees everything derailed when a close friend is murdered. As she gets more information, it leads her well out of her comfort zone as she pursues the killer.

Donovan – 2004 - This psychological thriller follows Joe Donovan, a forensics expert turned author who investigates some of the most evil crimes. Some of them hit a little too close to home.

Durham County – *Canada* – 2007 to 2010 - A man moves his family in hopes of a new start, then a local serial killer throws a wrench in that peaceful new beginning.

Endeavour – 2012 to present - In this prequel to Inspector Morse, a young Endeavour works with Sergeant Thursday to develop his investigative skills. Shaun Evans stars as Morse during this 1960s period mystery.

The Fall - 2013 to 2016 - Gillian Anderson (*The X-Files*) and Jamie Dornan (*50 Shades of Grey*) star in this series about a senior investigator who goes head-to-head with a serial killer who's attacking young professional women in Belfast.

The Field of Blood - 2011 to 2013 - Set in early 1980s Glasgow, a young woman skillfully solves murders on a police force full of men. Unfortunately, her dedication to the truth also puts her in danger. The series stars BAFTA winner Jayd Johnson (*River City*) as Paddy Meehan, working alongside Peter Capaldi (*Doctor Who*) and David Morrissey (*The Missing*).

The Gentle Touch - 1980 - Jill Gascoine stars as Britain's first female police detective. Within hours of her promotion to Detective Inspector, she learns her husband has been gunned down.

Gracepoint – 2014 - David Tennant stars in this American remake of *Broadchurch*.

Grantchester – 2014 to present - In the village of Grantchester, a clever vicar assists a local police detective with his investigations. James Norton (*Happy Valley*) stars as vicar Sidney Chambers, and Robson Green (*Wire in the Blood*) plays DI Geordie Keating. Later in the series, Tom Brittany takes over for him in the role of Reverend Will Davenport.

The Guilty – 1992 - Michael Kitchen (*Foyle's War*) and Caroline Catz (*Doc Martin*) star in this series where a young man gets in over his head during a search for his real father.

Half Moon Investigations – 2009 - This comedy-mystery series for kids was filmed in North Lanarkshire, Scotland, and follows young investigator Fletcher Moon as he goes on stakeouts and undercover operations with his partner, Red Sharkey.

Hamish Macbeth - 1995 to 1997 - Hamish Macbeth (Robert Carlyle, *The Full Monty*) is a talented but unambitious Highlands constable who doesn't always follow the rules. The series was filmed in the lovely Highland village of Plockton on the shores of Loch Carron, and it's a great watch for those who enjoy good scenery.

Hammer House of Horror – 1980 - This classic anthology series tells tales of mystery, suspense, and horror.

Intruders – 2014 - John Simm (*Life on Mars*) stars as an ex-cop whose wife goes missing. The ensuing investigation leads him to Seattle, and a secret society dedicated to chasing immortality by hiding in the bodies of others. Based on Michael Marshall Smith's novel.

The Jury – 2002 to 2011 - This series follows the men and women brought together to act as jurors in a high-profile case involving a young Sikh student.

Kavanagh QC - 1995 to 2001 - John Thaw (*Inspector Morse*) stars as James Kavanagh QC, a barrister with a working-class background and a strong sense of right and wrong. It was one of Thaw's final roles before he died of cancer at the age of 60. It's loaded with actors who went on to well-known roles, including Lesley Manville (*Mum*), Larry Lamb (*Gavin & Stacey*), Barry Jackson (*Midsomer Murders*), Phyllis Logan (*Downton Abbey*), Bill Night (*Love Actually*), and Julian Fellowes (*Downton Abbey*).

The Kettering Incident – *Australia* - 2016 - The show begins when Dr. Anna Macy returns to the small Tasmania town of Kettering 15 years after the mysterious disappearance of her friend. When another little girl disappears, things get interesting.

Lanester - *France* - 2018 - In France, three strange murders have been committed, each left with a strange display. Detective Eric Lanester loses his sight during the investigation, but carries on.

Line of Duty – 2012 to present - This suspenseful British police series is set in the fictional "anti-corruption unit" AC-12, where the police police the police. Yes, we know that sentence is a bit weird. The series is great, though. Lennie James, Vicky McClure, Martin Compston, and Adrian Dunbar all feature.

Liverpool 1 - 1998 to 1999 - This gritty, Liverpool-based police drama dives into the city's underworld. We follow the vice squad at Bridewell as they fight drug dealers, paeodophiles, pimps, and porn peddlers in this rough-around-the-edges port city. Samantha Womack stars as DC Isobel de Pauli.

The Living & the Dead – 2016 - When a man inherits his family estate in Somerset, strange things begin to happen.

Luther – 2010 to 2019 - Idris Elba stars as a brilliant London detective who frequently gets into trouble because of his passion for the job.

The Missing – 2014 to 2017 - James Nesbitt (*Cold Feet*) stars in this drama about the disappearance of a 5-year-old and the manhunt that follows.

The Mixer – 1992 - Though technically a French and German production, this series is set in 1930s London. It focuses on a penniless nobleman who robs thieves of their stolen property with the help of his trusty valet.

Mom P.I. – *Canada* – 1990 to 1991 - Rosemary Dunsmore stars as Sally Sullivan, a widowed mother who teams up with PI Bernie Fox (Stuart Margolin) to solve mysteries and bring down criminals.

Murder City - 2004 to 2006 - DI Susan Alembic (Amanda Donohoe) and DS Luke Stone (Kris Marshall) are opposites, but they're very effective at working together to solve tough crimes.

Murphy's Law – 2003 to 2007 - James Nesbitt stars as DS Tommy Murphy, a maverick cop with a dark personal history. When given a final chance to prove his suitability for duty, he takes on a dangerous undercover assignment.

New Tricks – 2003 to 2015 - This long-running series focuses on a group of police who come out of retirement to work unsolved cases.

The Night Manager – 2016 - Based on John le Carre's novel focuses on an ex-British soldier recruited to join MI-6 and infiltrate a group of arms dealers.

The Nightmare World of HG Wells – 2016 - This four-part series dramatizes several of

Wells' short stories.

The Pale Horse - 2020 - This two-part adaptation of Agatha Christie's story by the same name was written and executive produced by Sarah Phelps. Written in 1961, the original story is a creepy tale about what happens after a list of names is found in the shoe of a dead woman.

Paradox – 2009 - This sci-fi police drama focuses on a group of investigators who seek out evidence for crimes that haven't yet occurred.

Parents - 2012 - A businesswoman finds out her husband has lost their life savings on the day she loses her job, and they have to go live with her parents.

Picnic at Hanging Rock – *Australia* – 2018 - In the year 1900, three schoolgirls and their governess disappeared. From there, the mystery deepens.

Prey – 2014 to 2015 - Manchester detective Marcus Farrow (played by John Simm) is on the run, accused of a crime and desperate to prove his innocence. All the while, his former friends and colleagues do their best to hunt him down. This series reunites Philip Glenister and John Simm, who also appeared together in *Life on Mars*.

Prime Suspect: Tennison – 2017 - Set in the 1970s, this series is a prequel to the Helen Mirren classic, Prime Suspect.

Proof – 2004 - This thriller dives into the world of European high finance, beginning when a number of illegal Eastern European immigrants are found dead in a cargo container in Dublin.

River - 2015 - Stellan Skarsgård, Nicola Walker, and Lesley Manville star in this series about a brilliant police officer haunted by guilt.

The Ruth Rendell Mysteries - 1994 to 2000 - This collection includes a variety of suspenseful tales adapted from the novels of author Ruth Rendell.

The Saint - 1962 to 1969 - Roger Moore stars as Simon Templar, a wealthy adventurer who travels the world solving crimes and engaging in all manner of secret agent hijinks. Though the settings are occasionally exotic, nearly every episode was filmed at a studio in Hertfordshire using "blue-screen" technology. The series was based on the Simon Templar novels by Leslie Charteris.

Sapphire and Steel – 1979 to 1982 - Interdimensional operatives save the world from evil forces on a regular basis. Stars Joanna Lumley and David McCallum.

Scott & Bailey - 2011 to 2016 - Two very different female police detectives enjoy a close friendship and productive partnership.

Secrets and Lies – *Australia* – 2015 to 2016 - A regular suburban family guy finds the body of a young child and promptly becomes the leading suspect.

Second Sight – 2001 - Clive Owen stars in this series about an ambitious detective who is slowly but surely losing his sight.

The Secret of Crickley Hall – 2012 - Suranne Jones and Tom Ellis star in this supernatural miniseries about a family that relocates to a grand old estate up north after the disappearance of their young son.

Sherlock Holmes: Incident at Victoria Falls – 1992 - Sherlock Holmes steps out of retirement to help transport a valuable diamond from Africa to London.

Sherlock Holmes and the Leading Lady – 1991 - Sherlock Holmes pauses his retirement to help track down a stolen prototype for a bomb detonator.

The Silence – 2010 - While struggling to integrate into the hearing world, a young girl with a new cochlear implant witnesses the murder of a police officer. Douglas Henshall (*Shetland*) is among the stars of this miniseries.

Silent Witness - 1996 to present - A team of pathologists investigates crimes based on evidence gleaned from autopsies.

State of Mind - 2003 - After discovering her husband has been unfaithful, Grace takes her son Adam and moves back home with her mother, a busy GP. Niamh Cusack, Rowena Cooper, and Andrew Lincoln star.

Tales of the Unexpected – 1979 to 1985 - Though not a traditional mystery series, this Roald Dahl-created show features a variety of unusual and bizarre stories.

Thirteen – 2016 - This BBC Three series centers around a 26-year-old woman who manages to escape from a cellar she's been trapped in for 13 years.

Thriller – 1973 to 1976 - This long-running 1970s anthology series includes a few supernatural tales, but mostly a lot of suspense and mystery. It also includes a surprising number of American guest stars.

Tin Star – 2017 to 2019 - A former British detective moves to the Canadian Rockies and fights crime near a massive new oil refinery.

Touching Evil – 1997 to 1999 - Robson Green (*Grantchester*) and Nicola Walker (*River*) star in this series about a police officer with a special ability to detect criminals.

Trust - 2000 - Caroline Goodall (*Schindler's List*) stars as Anne, a successful young woman in what seems like a happy marriage. Unfortunately, there's something quite dark on the horizon.

The Tunnel – 2016 to 2018 - This British-French show focuses on two teams of detectives who work together on cross-channel investigations.

Undercover – 2016 - This series tells the story of Maya, a barrister about to become the first black director of public prosecutions as her personal life suffers.

Unforgotten – 2015 to present - Cassie and Sunny use modern technology to get to the bottom of very cold cases. This recent crime drama is based in London and stars Nicola Walker and Sanjeev Bhaskar as Cassie and Sunny.

Vexed – 2010 to 2012 - A young male and female detective team frustrate each other with their different attitudes and complicated personal lives.

The Vice – 1999 to 2003 - Inspector Chappel leads the Metropolitan Vice Squad, investigating cases of prostitution and pornography in London.

Whitechapel - 2009 to 2013 - An inspector, a detective sergeant, and a historical

homicide expert look at crimes that may have connections to the Whitechapel district.

White Dragon – 2019 - John Simm stars in this tense mystery about a man who starts to notice highly suspicious things after his wife is killed in a car accident in Hong Kong.

The Widow - 2019 - Kate Beckinsale stars in this drama about a woman who believes herself to be a widow, only to find that her husband did not actually die in a plane crash. While watching a news story on unrest in the Congo, she sees a man who looks like her husband and sets off to figure out what happened.

Wolcott – 1981 - Warren Clarke (*Dalziel & Pascoe*) and George Harris (*Casualty*) star in this miniseries about a black policeman promoted to the CID in London's East End.

The Worricker Trilogy - 2014 - An analyst in the British intelligence forces want to find out why the PM had his friend killed. Bill Night (*Love Actually*) stars.

WPC 56 - 2013 to 2015 - This period crime drama follows Gina Dawson, the first woman police constable in her West Midlands hometown. The first two seasons focus on Gina's struggles to gain acceptance in a male-dominated work environment, while the third season follows her successor at the station.

Wycliffe - 1993 to 1998 - Based on W.J. Burley's novels, this Cornwall-based series features DS Charles Wycliffe, a man who investigates murders with a unique level of determination and accuracy.

Young Lions – *Australia* – 2002 - This Australian police drama follows the personal and professional lives of a group of young detective senior constables.

Period Dramas

A Family At War - 1970 - In this classic family saga, we follow the daily life of the Ashtons, a working-class family in Liverpool during the time of WWII.

The Aristocrats – 1999 - This 18th century period drama follows the lives of the Lennox sisters, four aristocratic women hoping to find happiness.

A Tale of Two Cities - 1980 - Paul Shelley and Ralph Michael star in this classic

Dickens story of love and sacrifice amidst the French Revolution.

Banished – 2015 - In 1787, Britain sent its unwanted citizens to Australia. This series is about that new society.

Beau Geste – 1982 - Three British brothers join the French Foreign Legion in this 1982 miniseries. Based on the novel by PC Wren.

Bleak House – 1985 - This adaptation of the classic Dickens novel features Diana

Rigg as Lady Honoria Dedlock.

The Bleak Old Shop of Stuff - 2012 - As proprietor of The Old Shop of Stuff, Jedrington Secret-Past sells all manner of unusual items. Unfortunately, Malifax Skulkingworm wants to make his life miserable. Robert Webb (*Peep Show*), Stephen Fry (*Kingdom*), and Katherine Parkison (*The IT Crowd*) star.

Body and Soul - 1993 - Kristin Scott Thomas stars as Sister Gabriel, a nun forced to leave the convent when her brother dies and her family needs her help to save their mill. This miniseries is based on Marcell Bernstein's novel.

Bramwell – 1995 to 1998 - In 1895, Dr. Eleanor Bramwell does her best to improve public health in Victorian London.

Britannia – 2018 - This US-UK co-production shows the Roman invasion in 43AD Britannia.

The Buccaneers – 1995 - Four American women secure wealthy British husbands, only to find it's not all it's cracked up to be.

Crime and Punishment – 2002 - John Simm (*Life on Mars*) stars as Raskolnikov in this BBC production of the classic Dostoesvsky novel.

Daniel Deronda – 2002 - This adaptation of George Eliot's final novel focuses on a Victorian man torn between the love of two women.

David Copperfield – 1986 - Simon Callow makes an appearance in this adaptation of the classic Dickens novel.

David Copperfield – 1999 - Daniel Radcliffe (*Harry Potter*) stars as young David in this adaptation of the Dickens novel.

Desperate Romantics – 2009 - In 1851 London, a group of artists lead colorful lives amidst the chaos of the Industrial Revolution.

The Devil's Mistress – 2008 - During the English Civil War, a young woman exploits a country in crisis for her own self-preservation. The follow-up to this series is called *New Worlds*.

Dickensian – 2015 to 2016 - This ambitious miniseries is set in the world of Charles Dickens' novels, bringing together a variety of characters in 19th century London.

Doctor Thorne – 2016 - This series tells the story of penniless Mary Thorne and her relationship with a wealthy family nearby.

Dombey and Son – 1983 - This 1983 Charles Dickens adaptation reminds us that money can't protect you from the heartbreak of life.

Dombey and Son – 2015 - This 2015 miniseries chronicles the life of a man who desperately wants a son to carry on his work.

Downton Abbey - 2010 to 2015 - This period drama follows the lives of the Crawley family and their servants during the early 1900s.

Drovers' Gold – 1997 - In 1843 Wales, an English drover refuses to give a widow a fair price for her cattle, so she sends her son to take the herd to market in London.

The Durrells in Corfu – 2016 to 2019 - This popular British series tells the story of a widow who moves her family out of 1930s England in search of a better life.

Elizabeth I – 2014 - This two-part series focuses on the controversial scandals surrounding Elizabeth I, including alleged lovers and espionage.

Enemy at the Door – 1978 - This drama focuses on life in the British Channel Islands during the German occupation in WWII.

Fanny by Gaslight – 1981 - This BBC miniseries is an adaptation of Michael Sadleir's novel of the same name. It tells the story of a young woman who is orphaned in Victorian London, facing great hardship. The story has romance, scandal, prostitution, perversion, and blackmail.

From There to Here – 2014 - In 1996, England took on Scotland at the European Championship. At the same time, three men are caught up in an IRA explosion at a local pub, changing their lives forever.

Great Expectations – 1981 - This is the 1981 BBC adaptation of the classic Dickens novel.

Great Expectations - 1999 - Clive Russell and Charlotte Rampling star in this adaptation of the Dickens classic.

The Great Train Robbery - 2013 - This two-part series tells the story of 1963's Great Train Robbery from two perspectives - the side of the robbers, and the side of the cops. Martin Compston (*Line of Duty*), Luke Evans (*The Girl on the Train*), and Jim Broadbent (*Iris*) star.

Hard Times – 1977 - This adaptation of the Dickens novel contrasts seriousness and materialism against the magic of life.

Heat of the Sun – 1998 - This series was filmed on location in Africa, and set in 1930s high society Kenya. It follows a policeman working within the close-knit community of expats – many of whom harbour dark secrets.

Home Fires – 2015 to 2017 - In WWII-era Britain, a group of women get by in a small village.

Howards End – 2018 - This miniseries is based on the E.M. Forster novel, and it examines class differences in 1900s England through the lens of three families.

Island at War – 2004 - This miniseries depicts life under Nazi occupation on St. Gregory Island (a fictionalized version of the Channel Islands – see *The Guernsey Literary and Potato Peel Pie Society* on Netflix for something similar).

Ivanhoe – 1997 - This is the BBC adaptation of the classic Sir Walter Scott novel.

Jane Eyre – 1983 - This adaptation of Brontë's classic stars Timothy Dalton and Zelah Clarke as Jane and Mr. Rochester.

Jane Eyre – 2006 - Anne Reid, Aidan McArdle, and Andrew Buchan star in this BBC adaptation of the Charlotte Brontë classic.

Jessica – *Australia* – 2003 - In Australia, a young girl is placed in an asylum on false pretenses, and her only hope is a less-than-promising lawyer.

King Lear – 2018 - This Prime Original stars Anthony Hopkins as King Lear.

The Last Post – 2017 - In 1965, British soldiers fight a Yemeni insurgency in British-controlled Aden. This series focuses heavily on the women and children who came with them.

Life in Squares – 2015 - This series dramatizes the lives of those in the Bloomsbury group, a set of influential artists, writers, and intellectuals in England.

Lillie - 1978 - This period drama tells the story of Lillie Langtry, a beautiful woman who managed to woo tons of wealthy men and become a well-known actress. Francesca Annis (*Reckless*) and Peter Egan (*Downton Abbey*) star.

Little Dorrit – 2008 - Claire Foy and Matthew Macfayden star in this adaptation of Dickens's story of struggle in 1820s London.

Lorna Doone – 2000 - When a man falls in love with a woman from the same clan that killed his father, he's horrified.

Love in a Cold Climate – 2001 - Between 1929 and 1940, three young women search for love.

Madame Bovary – 2000 - In Flaubert's classic, a woman marries a doctor in hopes of escaping a boring provincial life. It doesn't work.

Mansfield Park - 1983 - Sylvestra Le Touzel stars as Fanny Price in this miniseries adaptation of Jane Austen's third novel. It's about a young woman sent to live with wealthier relatives, who later falls in love with her sensitive cousin.

Martin Chuzzlewit - 1994 - When a wealthy old man nears death, everyone comes out of the woodwork to try to get their piece of his riches. This miniseries is based on the Dickens novel of the same name.

Masterpiece: Indian Summers – 2015 - This drama dives into live in a social club during the final years of British colonial rule of India.

Merlin - 2009 to 2013 - Colin Morgan (*The Fall*) stars as a young Merlin in his days as a mere servant to Prince Arthur of Camelot. In this version of Camelot, magic is banned and Merlin is forced to keep his talent hidden away.

Middlemarch – 1994 - Robert Hardy, Rufus Sewell, Pam Ferris, and Dame Judi Dench all appear in this adaptation of the classic George Eliot novel.

The Mill - 2013 to 2014 - This period drama is based on the real stories of textile mill workers in 1830s England. Set in Cheshire, it depicts the harsh realities of the Industrial Revolution that transformed England.

Miss Austen Regrets - 2008 - This feature-length drama is based on Jane Austen's life and collected letters. Olivia Williams (*An Education*) plays Jane Austen.

Moby Dick - 1998 - Sir Patrick Stewart stars as Captain Ahab in this adaptation of Herman Melville's novel.

Moby Dick – 2011 - This British, Australian,

and American co-production tells Herman Melville's story of Captain Ahab and the great white whale, Moby Dick.

The Moonstone - 2016 - This updated adaptation of the Wilkie Collins novel stars Joshua Silver as Franklin Blake alongside Terenia Edwards (*On Chesil Beach*) as Rachel Verinder.

My Mother & Other Strangers – 2017 - This period drama is set in 1940s Northern Ireland, documenting the culture clash that occurred when American servicemen were stationed along the Ards Peninsula.

My Uncle Silas – 2001 - Based on stories by H.E. Bates, this series follows a boisterous Bedfordshire uncle as he cares for his nephew over the summer in turn-of-the-century England. Stars Sue Johnston and Albert Finney.

The Nativity - 2010 - Writer Tony Jordan adapts the classic tale of Mary and Joseph and baby Jesus. Peter Capaldi (*Doctor Who*) and Tatiana Maslany (*Orphan Black*) are among the stars.

Neverland – 2011 - In turn-of-the-century London, a couple of pickpockets discover a portal to Neverland.

Oliver Twist – 1985 - This is the 1985 BBC adaptation of the classic Dickens tale with Ben Rodska as Oliver Twist. Keep an eye out for Frank Middlemaas (*As Time Goes By*) and Miriam Margolyes (*Miss Fisher's Murder Mysteries*) as Mr. Brownlow and Mrs. Bumble.

Oliver Twist – 2007 - In this 2007 adaptation of the Dickens classic, we see appearances from Morven Christie, Tom Hardy, and Sarah Lancashire, among others. The story focuses on the difficult life of a young orphan after he's sold into an apprenticeship with an undertaker.

Our Mutual Friend – 1998 - This adaptation of Dickens's last completed novel contrasts money and poverty in Victorian London.

The Palace – 2008 - A fictional British royal family deals with all manner of upper class problems.

The Paradise - 2012 to 2013 - In this period drama, a young and ambitious woman heads to the city to make her way working in a department store

The Passing Bells – 2014 - This BBC period drama takes place between 1914 and 1918, following two young men, one British and one German, as World War I takes a heavy toll on their lives.

The Pickwick Papers – 1985 - Nigel Stock and Clive Swift star in this adaptation of Dickens' great comic masterpiece.

Pinocchio – 2010 - Robbie Kay plays Pinocchio alongside Bob Hoskins as Geppetto.

Poldark - 1996 - John Bowe (*Prime Suspect*) and Ioan Gruffudd (*Harrow*) star in this feature-length adaptation of the Poldark story.

Poldark – 2015 to 2019 - Ross Poldark returns home to Cornwall after fighting in the American Revolution, only to find his fortune in ruins and the woman he loves promised to another man. Aidan Turner stars in this adaptation of the classic story.

Pride and Prejudice - 1980 - Elizabeth Garvie and David Rintoul star in this television adaptation of Austen's classic.

The Prisoner of Zenda – 1984 - An Englishman poses as Ruritania's monarch when the real king is abducted.

The Rainbow - 1988 - This three-part series is an adaptation of D.H. Lawrence's novel about a young woman emerging into adulthood. The story's frank treatment of sexual desire and same-sex relations caused it to be banned in Britain for 11 years.

Robin Hood – 2006 - After fighting in the Crusades, Robin Hood returns home to find a corrupt, changed Nottingham.

Sense and Sensibility – 2008 - This BBC production is based on the Jane Austen novel of the same name.

Sinbad – 2012 - This BBC production tells the story of Sinbad, a man whose life falls apart after he unintentionally kills another man.

Spies of Warsaw - 2013 - David Tennant stars in this story set across three Euopean cities ahead of World War II. The series is based on Alan Furst's spy novel of the same name.

Stranded - 2002 - Roger Allam (*Endeavour*) stars in this retelling of the classic Swiss Family Robinson.

The Talisman – 1980 - Based on the story by Sir Walter Scott, this miniseries tells the story of a brave Scottish knight who foils

Richard the Lionheart's assassins during the Crusades.

The Tenant of Wildfell Hall – 1996 - In a remote Yorkshire village, a widow and her son move into the creepy, crumbling Wildfell Hall. Based on the classic story by Anne Brontë.

Tess of the D'Urbervilles - 2008 - In this miniseries based on the Thomas Hardy work, Tess Durbeyfield is a poor country girl with connections to nobility.

Thomas & Sarah – 1979 - This spin-off of Upstairs, Downstairs follows Thomas, the chauffeur, and Sarah the house and nursery maid after they leave Eaton Place.

Tom Jones – 1997 - In Georgian England, Tom Jones finds no shortage of trouble or romance.

To the Ends of the Earth – 2005 - This BBC series is based on William Golding's novels of a sea journey to Australia from England in 1812-13. Benedict Cumberbatch (*Sherlock*) stars.

United – 2011 - David Tennant stars in this sports period drama about the 1958 Munich air crash that claimed 8 of Manchester United's members.

Vanity Fair – 1987 - This adaptation of Thackeray's Napoleonic War-era tale starred Eve Matheson, Rebecca Saire, James Saxon, and Simon Dormandy in the lead roles.

Vanity Fair – 1998 - This BBC adaptation of Thackeray's novel featured a screenplay by Andrew Davies, with Natasha Little in the role of Becky Sharp.

Vanity Fair – 2018 - This ITV production of Thackeray's classic includes performances by Michael Palin, Olivia Cooke, Suranne Jones, and Martin Clunes.

A Very English Scandal – 2018 - Hugh Grant stars as the first British politician to stand trial for conspiracy to murder.

Victoria – 2016 to present - This ITV drama features Jenna Coleman as a young Queen Victoria during her early years on the throne.

The Way We Live Now - 2001 - Based on Anthony Trollope's novel, this miniseries tells a Victorian tale of power, corruption, love, greed, and progress. It features appearances by Matthew Macfadyen, Cillian Murphy, Rob Brydon, Jim Carter, David Suchet, and more.

We'll Meet Again – 1982 - Set in 1943, this series shows us what happens in a small East Anglian town when war-weary Brits play host to American troops.

Wish Me Luck - 1988 to 1990 - This series follows brave female undercover agents as they crossed enemy lines to get valuable intelligence during WWII.

Women in Love – 2011 - Rosamund Pike and Rachael Stirling star in this adaptation of DH Lawrence's classic. It was originally written as a sequel to *The Rainbow*.

Other Dramas

Always Greener – *Australia* – 2001 to 2003 - This dramedy tells the story of two families who joke about swapping places, then actually do it. The series takes place in rural Inverness and suburban Sydney.

At Home With the Braithwaites – 2000 to 2003 - With an all-star cast that includes Amanda Redman, Peter Davison, and Julia Graham, this drama follows the life of Aliston Braithwaite and her family. She wins 38 million pounds in the lottery, only to hide it from her family in favour of setting up a secret charity to do good things with the money.

Banana – 2015 - This Channel 4 miniseries follows 8 gay couples through a variety of relationship dramas.

Band of Gold – 1995 to 1997 - Geraldine James stars in this Bradford-based series about desperate streetwalkers trying to make their way through hard times in Northern England.

Bed of Roses - *Australia* - 2008 to 2011 - A mother and daughter struggle after the death of their husband and father.

Being Erica – *Canada* – 2009 to 2011 - A young woman participates in a strange form of therapy that involves time travel.

Being Human – 2008 to 2013 - A vampire,

werewolf, and ghost try to coexist as roommates.

Big Sky – *Australia* – 1997 to 1999 - This soap-y drama follows the employees at Big Sky Aviation as they form friendships and fly high over the Australian landscape.

Bonekickers – 2008 - Archaeologists piece together mysteries and find themselves in dangerous situations.

Boy Meets Girl - 2009 - After a freak accident, a man and woman find themselves trapped in each other's bodies. Martin Freeman (*Sherlock*) and Rachael Stirling (*Detectorists*) star in this ITV dramedy. This is not to be confused with the other *Boy Meets Girl* on BritBox.

Captain Scarlet & the Mysterons – 1967 - This 1960s series followed an unkillable agent in charge of the fight against extraterrestrial terrorists.

Chancer – 1990 to 1991 - Clive Owen plays Stephen Crane, a schemer who takes advantage of opportunities using manipulation and misdirection. As a young business analyst/con man in London, he's called in to help save a struggling motor company.

Clink - 2019 - This drama is set in the fictional BPS Bridewell women's prison, and focuses on the women who live there, and the woman who runs the place. Many have compared it to British prison series Bad Girls, and at least one cast member, Alicya Eyo (who plays new Governor Dominique Darby), was also in Bad Girls.

Cold Feet - 1998 to 2003 - This long-running dramedy follows the lives of six thirtysomething friends living in Manchester, England as they do their best to get their lives sorted.

Danger Man, aka Secret Agent – 1961 to 1968 - Patrick McGoohan (*The Prisoner*) stars as John Drake, a special operative for NATO specialising in security assignments involving threats to world peace.

The Darling Buds of May - 1991 to 1993 - Based on the 1958 H.E. Bates novel of the same name, this series is set in rural 1950s Kent and follows the Larkin family as they go about their daily lives. This early 90s dramedy was a breakout role for Welsh actress Catherine Zeta-Jones.

The Deep - 2010 - James Nesbitt (*Cold Feet*) and Minnie Driver (*Good Will Hunting*) star in this series about oceanographers who become stranded in the Arctic while looking for new forms of life beneath the ice.

Desi Rascals – 2015 - This series follows young adult members of the British-Asian community.

Do or Die – 2001 - This two part UK drama is set over seven years in London and Sydney. When a couple's child is diagnosed with leukaemia and in need of a perfect blood match, they decide it's time to trace relatives down in Australia.

Emmerdale - 1972 to present - Originally known as Emmerdale Farm, this series was originally set in a village called Beckindale. In the 90s, the show rebranded and began to focus on the entire village of Emmerdale. Now, storylines are bigger, sexier, and more dramatic than ever.

The Fades – 2011 - A young man is haunted by dreams he can't explain, and he begins to see spirits around him – some of them malicious.

Flood – 2008 - An engineer must rush to save millions of Londoners when floods threaten the city.

Foreign Exchange – *Australia/Ireland* – 2004 - When two children from Ireland and Australia discover a portal between the two countries, they're able to travel between the two countries and have adventures along the way.

Good Omens – 2019 - David Tennant and Michael Sheen star in this adaptation of Neil Gaiman and Terry Pratchett's novel by the same name. In it, two angels have grown quite fond of the human world, and they plan to do everything in their power to stop it from ending in accordance with the Divine Plan.

Grafters - 1998 to 1999 - Robson Green (*Grantchester*) and Stephen Tompkinson (*DCI Banks*) star in this series about two brothers who work together as builders and have terribly dysfunctional family lives.

Hearts & Bones – 2000 to 2001 - This drama follows a group of 20 and 30-something friends who move to London and transition into proper adult lives.

The Hitchhiker's Guide to the Galaxy - 1981 - Arthur Dent is one of the last surviving members of the human race. Still in his dressing gown, he's dragged through an intergalactic portal and sent on an adventure through the universe. The series is based on Douglas Adams' novel of the same name, and he also wrote the TV adaptation.

Home & Away – *Australia* – 1988 to 1989 - This soap opera follows the residents of Summer Bay, a coastal town near Sydney in Australia.

Humans – 2015 to 2018 - In a parallel modern world, everyone has a robotic servant.

Hustle - 2004 to 2012 - This series follows a group of talented con artists who prefer to operate long cons on the greedy and corrupt of London.

The Indian Doctor - 2010 to 2013 - An Indian doctor and his wife move to a small Welsh mining village during the 1960s. They have to adjust to culture shock, and Dr. Sharma must win the trust of the locals as their GP.

In the Flesh – 2013 to 2014 - After a zombie war, scientists work to cure and rehabilitate ex-zombies.

Jackson's Wharf – *New Zealand* – 1999 to 2000 - Set in a fictional coastal town, this series revolves around the rivalry between two brothers: cop Frank and lawyer Ben.

Joe 90 – 1968 - Another marionette-based programme, this one follows the adventures of a pre-teen secret agent who can almost instantly have any skills loaded into his brain.

Love/Hate – 2010 to 2014 - When a young man returns to Dublin after a year away, he wants to stay clean, but circumstances drag him into the world of Irish gangs.

Love Lies Bleeding – 2006 - A self-made millionaire finds himself caught up in a strange and deadly conspiracy after an old friend shows up.

Mobile – 2007 - Michael Kitchen (*Foyle's War*) appears in this miniseries about a fictional mobile phone conglomerate and a conspiracy tied into a gangland shooting.

Mount Royal – *Canada* – 1988 - This drama brings to mind shows like Dallas or Dynasty, but it's set against the cosmopolitan backdrop of 1980s Montreal.

Moving On – 2009 to 2016 - This anthology series gives us stories of people preparing to move on to something new in their lives.

Murder Call – *Australia* – 1997 to 2000 - This fun late 90s mystery series mixes

action, suspense, mystery, comedy, and a bit of romance.

Our Girl – 2014 to 2020 - This series follows a teenage girl who gets drunk on her 18th birthday, vomiting in the doorway of an army recruitment office. Strangely drawn to the office, she joins up and serves as an army medic.

Party Tricks - *Australia* - 2014 - This Australian series follows Kate Ballard (Asher Keddie, *X-Men Origins: Wolverine*), a woman facing her first election for State Premier. Victory seems guaranteed until the opposition brings in a new shock candidate – David McLeod (Rodger Corser, *The Heart Guy*). McLeod is a popular media figure, but more concerning is the fact that she had a secret affair with him years earlier.

Peak Practice – 1993 to 2002 - This long-running series follows the doctors at a GP surgery in Cardale, Derbyshire.

The Prisoner –1967 - Patrick McGoohan stars in this surprisingly well-aged series about a secret agent who's abducted and taken to a mysterious prison dressed up as an idyllic seaside village.

Prisoners' Wives – 2012 to 2013 - This dramatic series takes a look at the women involved with men who've been sent to prison.

The Protectors – 1972 to 1974 - Robert Vaughn stars in this 1970s series about a worldwide crime-fighting team that strives to protect the innocent and apprehend the guilty.

Public Enemies – 2012 - Released from prison after a 10 year sentence for murder, a man attempts to adjust to life on the outside. Anna Friel stars alongside Daniel Mays.

Rake - *Australia* - 2011 to 2018 - Defense lawyer Cleaver Greene makes a career out of hopeless cases, perhaps because his own personal life is troubled enough to help him relate.

Red Rock – *Ireland* – 2015 to 2020 - Two feuding families battle it out in this Irish soap.

Republic of Doyle – *Canada* – 2010 to 2014 - Jake Doyle and his father Malachy work together as private investigators with a lot of rough edges. Even if it doesn't sound like your kind of show, you might love it for the scenery.

PRIME VIDEO

Rocket's Island – 2012 to 2015 - Filmed on location on the Isle of Man, this young adult fantasy drama follows foster children who go on magical adventures.

Roman Mysteries – 2007 to 2008 - This young adult series follows four kids in Ancient Rome as they go on quests and solve mysteries.

The Royals - *United States* - 2015 to 2108 - Though American, this prime-time soap stars Elizabeth Hurley and a largely British cast. It tells the story of a fictional British royal family and the power struggles within their ranks.

Run - 2013 - Olivia Colman and Lennie James star in this four-part miniseries about four seemingly unconnected people whose lives intersect after a random act of violence.

The Secret Life of Us – *Australia* – 2001 to 2006 - In an apartment block near Melbourne, residents navigate life's challenges with the help of their friends.

Secret Smile – 2005 - David Tennant stars as a smooth and manipulative spurned lover seeking revenge.

Silk – 2011 to 2014 - This series focuses on the challenges modern-day barristers face in their careers.

The Smoke – 2014 - When a fire fighter is badly injured on the job, he spends nearly a year in recovery. On return, he realises he may not be quite as ready as he thinks.

Soldier Soldier – 1991 to 1997 - Robson Green and Jerome Flynn star in this military drama about soldiers in the King's Own Fusiliers regiment.

Spirit Breaker - 2018 - Dave (Liam Noble, *Peep Show*) wants nothing more than to spend all his time in the pub, and he's not going to let anyone get in the way of his goal. Produced by Dan Summers (*MumDem*), this series never made it beyond the pilot.

Stingray – 1964 - This 1960s marionette-based series focused on the missions of the World Aquanaut Security Patrol.

The Street – 2009 - This drama features a number of familiar faces as they go on about their lives in a rough-around-the-edges Northern English town. Amazon offers Season 3 for viewing by Prime members, and since it's an anthology series, it's not a problem to skip Series 1 and 2.

The Syndicate – 2013 - Each season of this series looks at what happens after a group of people wins the lottery. Amazon offers Season 2 only (the one that takes place among hospital workers).

Terry Pratchett's Hogfather – 2006 - The Hogfather has gone missing on Hogswatch, and Death must take his place.

Thunderbirds – 1966 - This 1960s TV series used marionettes to tell the story of the 21st century Tracy family, who operated a private emergency response service.

The Time of Our Lives - *Australia* - 2013 to 2014 - This drama follows the lives of an extended family in inner-city Melbourne as they build families, pursue careers, and work on their relationships.

Train 48 – *Canada* – 2003 to 2005 - This Canadian drama takes place on a Toronto commuter train, and the format was based on a similar Australian series called *Going Home*.

Truckers - 2013 - Stephen Tompkinson (*DCI Banks*) stars in this drama about a group of truck drivers in Nottinghamshire.

Underbelly – *Australia* – 2011 to 2013 - Each season of this Australian series focuses on the rise and fall of a different underworld figure. While not all seasons are available on Prime, you can enjoy Series 6, about Leslie Squizzy Taylor, and Series 4, about two Australian crime queens.

Where the Heart Is – 1997 to 2004 - Pam Ferris and Sarah Lancashire star in this Yorkshire-based UK drama. It follows a group of dedicated nurses and their community.

The Wild Roses – *Canada* – 2009 - In Alberta, a woman and her daughters own the land an oil firm sits on.

William & Mary – 2003 to 2005 - Martin Clunes and Julie Graham star in this dramedy about an odd couple – a woman who welcomes people into the world, and a man who guides them out of it.

Wired – 2008 - Jodie Whittaker stars alongside Riz Ahmed, Laurence Fox, Charlie Brooks, and Toby Stephens in this suspenseful London-based thriller about a young woman whose high-profile promotion carries unexpected costs. She's quickly pushed into a criminal underworld she had no desire to be a part of.

Wolfblood - 2013 - Wolfblood teenagers have a number of heightened abilities, but their powers also bring danger and a need for secrecy.

Wonderland – *Australia* – 2014 to 2015 - This relationship drama takes place in a Sydney apartment building where most of the characters live.

Young Dracula - 2006 to 2014 - Count Dracula is a single father, and he's moved his kids Vlad and Ingrid to modern-day Britain. Now, little Vlad wants nothing more than to be a normal British kid and fit in with his friends.

Comedies

Absolutely Fabulous - 1992 to 2012 - In this groundbreaking classic, two wild women do everything but act their age. The series was based on a sketch comedy called "Modern Mother and Daughter" by Dawn French (*Vicar of Dibley*) and Jennifer Saunders (Edina Monsoon in *Absolutely Fabulous*). Joanna Lumley stars alongside Saunders as Patsy Stone, and Julia Sawalha plays Edina's daughter Saffron.

After Hours – 2019 - Ardal O'Hanlon appears in this family comedy about a young man named Willow living in Northern England and feeling pretty low about his achievement level in comparison to his friends. Meanwhile, his dad is struggling to find work. Life changes when he meets two new friends who host a popular internet radio show.

'Allo 'Allo - 1982 to 1992 - This classic British comedy is set in a French café during WWII.

Asylum - 2015 - Two men are trapped together in a London embassy in order to avoid extradition.

Atlantis High – *New Zealand* – 2001 - This teen show is set in a school believed to be build atop the Lost City of Atlantis.

A Touch of Cloth - 2012 to 2014 - This series is part mystery, part comedy, and definitely not for the faint of heart or easily offended. John Hannah and Suranne Jones play two detectives in a very unusual police department. The name of the series is based on the euphemism "touching cloth". It is a state of needing to defecate so badly that one's feces begins to protrude and "touch cloth".

Beaver Falls – 2011 to 2012 - Three British friends decide to have one last crazy summer working in an American summer camp.

A Bit of Fry & Laurie - 1987 to 1989 - This sketch show is an important piece of British comedy history, and it was responsible for turning Stephen Fry (*Kingdom*) and Hugh Laurie (*House*) into household names.

A Very British Coup - 1988 - When a radical Labour Party politician becomes Prime Minister, he quickly finds he has a lot of enemies.

Blackadder - 1983 to 1989 - Rowan Atkinson stars as antihero Edmund Blackadder, accompanied by Sir Tony Robinson as his sidekick Baldrick. Each series of this quirky comedy is set in a different period within British history, and Edmund carries different titles throughout. The "essence" of each character remains largely the same in each series, though.

Black Books – 2000 to 2004 - Bernard Black runs a bookshop, but he's not particularly good at dealing with customers.

Blandings – 2013 to 2014 - This fun period comedy follows an eccentric aristocratic family and their crumbling ancestral home. It's based on the writings of PG Wodehouse, and stars Timothy Spall and Jennifer Saunders.

Bridget & Eamon – 2016 to 2019 - Bridget and Eamon are an Irish couple living with an unknown number of children in the Midlands in the 1980s.

Catastophe – 2015 to present - This Prime Original tells the story of an unintended pregnancy between an American ad man and a British teacher.

Coupling – 2000 to 2004 - Six young adults in London navigate the work, love, and the transition into responsible adulthood. Many have called this "the British Friends".

Crackanory - 2013 to 2017 - Inspired by the popular children's series Jackanory, this series brings the same quirky style of storytelling to adults. Episodes include performances from popular British comedians like Sally Phillips (*Miranda*), Stephen Mangan (*Hang Ups*), Ben Miller (*Death in Paradise*), Sharon Horgan (*Catastrophe*), and Katherine Parkinson (*Doc Martin*).

Crims – 2015 - Two teenage boys with no street smarts end up together in a young offender's institute in the UK.

Dead Boss – 2012 - Helen Stephens has been wrongly convicted of killing her boss, and while she hopes she'll be cleared soon, everyone she knows seems to want her in prison.

The Delivery Man – 2015 - Former police officer Matthew begins work as a midwife. He's the first male midwife to hit the unit, and he hopes his new career will give him more satisfaction than his previous work.

Detectorists - 2014 to 2017 - Two quirky friends scan the fields of England with metal detectors, hoping for the big find that will finally let them do the gold dance.

Drifters – 2013 to 2016 - Meg, Bunny, and Laura share a flat in Leeds and face the ups and downs of post-university life.

Family Tree – 2013 - This hilarious series follows one man's efforts to track down long-lost members of his family tree.

Father Ted – 1995 to 1998 - This classic Britcom follows a group of zany priests on the fictional Craggy Island in Ireland.

Fix Her Up – *Australia* – 2018 - In an all-female office, four women work towards love, happiness, and career success.

Fleabag – 2016 to 2019 - Phoebe Waller-Bridge stars as Fleabag, a comically troubled young woman who's experienced a great personal tragedy.

Flickers – 1980 - During the early days of silent film, a lovable Cockney tries to make his fortune in the industry.

Fresh Meat – 2011 to 2016 - Six young friends go off to university.

Friday Night Dinner – 2001 to present - Each Friday night, a Jewish British family meets for dinner. It never goes smoothly (and it always includes a visit from eccentric neighbour Jim).

Gavin & Stacey - 2007 to 2019 - After months of chatting, Gavin and Stacey leave their homes in Essex and Wales to meet for the first time in London. This much-loved comedy classic features a number of British acting favourites including Larry Lamb, Ruth Jones, Alison Steadman, Rob Brydon, and James Corden.

Getting On - 2009 to 2012 - This dark comedy follows the residents and staff in a geriatric ward.

Go Girls – *New Zealand* – 2009 to 2013 - Three twentysomething women realize they've made little progress towards their life goals, and vow to achieve their respective goals of being married, rich, and famous within a year.

Green Wing – 2004 to 2007 - This zany medical comedy features a largely incompetent staff that does very little actual medical work. Among the stars are Tamsin Greig (*Friday Night Dinner*), Mark Heap (*Friday Night Dinner*), Olivia Colman (*Broadchurch*), and Stephen Mangan (*Hang-Ups, Episodes*).

The Kennedys – 2015 - Katherine Parkinson (*The IT Crowd*) stars in this comedy about a family moving from a housing estate to a home, eager to move up the social ladder.

King Gary - 2020 - Gary and Terri King are childhood sweethearts living in suburban East London. Though he's a grown man with his own family, Gary is constantly trying to get out of the shadow of his father.

Laid – *Australia* – 2011 to 2012 - When she realizes all her former lovers are dying in unusual ways, a young woman tries to save the remaining men.

Last Contact – 2014 - This low budget Sussex-based production concerns a team of university researchers seeking out novel ways to communicate with aliens.

Little Devil - 2007 - When his parents won't stop arguing, a little boy decides to try being as good as possible. When that doesn't work, he takes a different approach.

London Irish – 2013 - This occasionally off-colour comedy focuses on a group of Northern Irish ex-pats in the city of London. The series was written by Lisa McGee, best known as the writer and creator of *Derry Girls*.

Lunch Monkeys – 2009 to 2011 - This comedy focuses on the administrative staff at a British law firm.

Market Forces – *New Zealand* – 1998 - This satirical comedy revolves around a group of government employees in New Zealand.

Mind Your Language – 1977 to 1979 - This series follows Jerry Brown, an eager young teacher who takes a job teaching English to students from all over the world.

Mr. Bean - 1992 to 1995 - Bumbling Mr. Bean rarely speaks and has some very peculiar ways of doing things, but it usually works out for him. Rowan Atkinson (*Maigret*) stars as the iconic British character.

MumDem – 2016 - A group of young men born and raised in Cardiff dream of making it big in fashion.

Only When I Laugh – 1979 to 1982 - A group of patients constantly attempt to one-up each other, driving hospital staff crazy.

Outnumbered - 2007 to 2014 - Hugh Dennis and Claire Skinner star in this sitcom about a couple who are outnumbered by their three children.

Pramface – 2012 to 2013 - In Edinburgh, a young woman sleeps with an even younger man and finds herself pregnant.

Peep Show – 2003 to 2015 - Two dysfunctional and very different friends share a flat in London and attempt (rather poorly) to grow up.

Pete vs. Life - 2010 to 2011 - Journalist Pete is a pretty normal guy, except that he's constantly observed and analysed by a couple of sports commentators.

Plus One - 2009 - When a man is invited to his ex-girlfriend's wedding to a pop star, he needs a plus one. Miranda Raison (*Silks*) and Daniel Mays (*Good Omens*) star.

Pompidou – 2015 - This unusual Matt Lucas comedy sees a down-on-his-luck aristocrat living in a caravan outside his crumbling estate, with only his faithful butler and dog to keep him company.

Rovers – 2016 - This working class comedy centers around the people who spend time at the Redbridge Rovers Football Club.

The Royle Family - 1998 to 2012 - This sitcom features a scruffy, argumentative, telly-obsessed family in Manchester. Ralf

Little (*Death in Paradise*) is among its stars.

Sam's Game - 2001 - This short-lived comedy starred TV presenter Davina McCall as Sam, a single woman living in a London flat over a High Street shop. To help pay the rent, she illegally sublets to Alex (comedian Ed Byrne), an Irishman who seems to find no end of troubles.

Some Girls - 2012 to 2014 - This sitcom follows a group of teenage girls who live on the same inner city housing estate.

Still Standing – *Canada* – Comedian Jonny Harris embarks on a road trip around Canada, finding the humor in small and remote towns.

Switch – 2012 - In this short-lived supernatural comedy, a group of young witches lives it up in the big city.

Terry Pratchett's Going Postal - 2010 - This adaptation of Pratchett's novel sees con man Moist von Lipwig (Richard Coyle, *Chilling Adventures of Sabrina*) caught by the law and given two choices: suffer a painful death, or take over a derelict post office. Also starring David Suchet (*Poirot*), Charles Dance (*Game of Thrones*), and Claire Foy (*The Crown*).

That's My Boy – 1981 to 1986 - Mollie Sugden (*Are You Being Served?*) visits an employment agency and quickly finds herself under the employ of the son she gave up for adoption years earlier.

The Thick of It – 2005 to 2012 - This political satire takes place among the team at the Department of Social Affairs and Citizenship, where everything seems to be one giant farce.

Tiny Plastic Men – *Canada* – 2013 to 2018 - Three men test toy and game prototypes in a large toy company.

Trivia - *Ireland* - 2011 to 2012 - A highly-dedicated quiz team leader in Ireland knows everything but how to deal with other people.

Two's Company – 1975 to 1979 - This sitcom follows the relationship between an American woman and a British gentleman.

Uncle - 2014 to 2017 - Nick Helm stars as Andy, a 30-something slacker who's left to care for his nephew in spite of the fact that he's utterly unsuited to the task.

Very British Problems – 2015 to 2016 - This hilarious program interviews celebrities about the cultural quirks of being British.

Warren – 2019 - In this offbeat Lancashire-based comedy, Martin Clunes (*Doc Martin*) stars as an impatient and unsuccessful driving instructor who has recently moved in with his partner and her teenage sons. Unfortunately, it wasn't renewed for a second series.

Westside – *New Zealand* – 2015 to 2017 - This prequel to Outrageous Fortune is set between 1974 and 1979, and it recounts stories of crime and passion in Auckland.

Whites – 2010 - Alan Davies (*Jonathan Creek*) stars alongside Katherine Parkinson

(The *IT Crowd, Doc Martin*) as a chef at a country house hotel.

White Van Men - 2011 - Will Mellor (*No Offence*) and Georgia Moffett (*The Bill*) are among the stars of this sitcom about a terribly incompetent handyman and his lazy assistant.

You, Me, & Them - 2013 to 2015 - Anthony Head and Eve Myles star in this sitcom about an age gap romance.

British History & Culture

100 Years of British Buses - 2016 - Enjoy this look back at one hundred years of British bus history and design.

Alexandria: The Greatest City - 2016 - Historian Bettany Hughes explores the one-grand city of Alexandria, founded by Alexander the Great and home to Cleopatra.

Ancient Egypt - Life and Death in the Valley of the Kings - 2013 - This documentary tells the story of the everyday lives of ancient Egyptians.

Art Deco Icons: Britain's Bling and Glamour – 2009 - David Heathcote visits four Art Deco icons around Britain – Claridge's, London Transport HQ, Casa Del Rio (an art deco home in Devon), and The Orient Express (as it leaves Victoria Station for Venice).

The Auction House – 2014 - Roger Allam appears in this docu-series about the eccentrics that populate the world of British auction houses.

A World Without Down's Syndrome - 2016 - British comedian Sally Phillips (*Miranda*) presents this series about the emotionally-charged debate surrounding Down's Syndrome and pregnancy termination.

Baroque - 2015 - Noted art critic Waldemar Januszczak traces the history of the Baroque movement from its start as a Vatican-approved religious art style to a bigger global movement.

Battle Castle - 2012 - Historian Dan Snow tells the stories of six famous castles with military significance.

Bomber Boys – 2005 - This PBS-aired documentary series intersperses modern upcoming "bomber boys" with World War II history and footage.

Bridges that Built London – 2012 - This hour-long special examines London's great bridges.

Britain AD: King Arthur's Britain - 2004 - Francis Pryor takes a look at British history including Roman times, the Dark Ages, and the invasion of the Anglo-Saxons.

Britain's Real Monarch - 2003 - Sir Tony Robinson takes a look at compelling new evidence that Kind Edward IV may have been illegitimate - and what that would mean for today's monarchy.

British Bouncers – 2013 - This isn't quite a travel show, but if you want to shatter all your posh illusions about Britain, this show about drunken Brits going up against bouncers might be just the thing.

British Passions on Film - 2012 - This BBC4 series takes a look at the hobbies, traditions, and transport methods of Brits throughout the last century.

Brushstrokes: Every Picture Tells a Story – 2013 - British art critic Waldemar Januszczak dives into the stories behind four works from Gauguin, Van Gogh, Cezanne, and Dobson.

Building Ireland – 2017 to 2018 - This new series explores the art, architecture, history, and culture of Ireland.

Castle Builders – 2015 - This series takes a look at what was involved in building the great castles of Europe.

Castles and Palaces of Europe - 2013 - Take a closer look at castles in Italy, France, Germany, Portugal, and Southern England.

Celtic Britain - 2000 - This docuseries takes a look at Celtic history in Scotland, Wales, and elsewhere in the British Isles.

The Celts – 2013 - This series takes a look at who the Celts were, where they came from, and how they influenced history and modern times.

The Celts: Blood, Iron, and Sacrifice with Alice Roberts and Neil Oliver – 2015 - Alice Roberts and Neil Oliver examine the origins of the Celts in this three-part documentary.

Chatsworth – 2008 - Explore this stately home in a one-hour video tour.

Churchill: Blood Sweat, & Oil Paint - 1970 - Hosted by Andrew Marr, this BBC special tells the fascinating story of Winston Churchill's lifelong love of painting. He meets Churchill's descendants and explores the connections between his private passion for painting and his public career as politician and statesman.

Civil War - 2002 - Dr. Tristram Hunt takes a look at the conflict that briefly toppled the English monarchy back in the 17th century.

Comfort Eating - 2017 - Comedian Nick Helm goes on the road seeking out Britain's best comfort foods in Islington, Camden, Leeds, Brighton, Berlin, St. Albans, Paris, Little Europe, Peckham, Essex, Soho, Wales, Notting Hill, Glasgow, and Borough Market.

Constable: A Country Rebel – 2018 - This program takes a closer look at John Constable, one of England's best-loved rural landscape painters.

The Cops - 2018 - Follow British cops equipped with body cams as they keep peace in Great Britain.

Cut from a Different Cloth – 2019 - This series takes a look behind the scenes at British fashion company Superdry as they attempt to launch a high-end men's collection with Idris Elba.

David Jason's Secret Service - 2017 - Sir David Jason hosts this fascinating docuseries about Britain's history of espionage.

Doctor Who: Tales Lost in Time - 2011 - Past cast and crew members take a look back at the Doctor Who series and some of its untold stories. The programme includes interviews with David Tennant, Peter Davison, Simon Pegg, Russell T. Davies, and many more.

Emergency Firefighters – 2005 - This series takes a look at the intense, demanding situations encountered by the Avon Fire and Rescue Service.

Empire: The Soul of Britannia - 2012 - Jeremy Paxman hosts this BBC series about the worldwide cultural impact of the British Empire.

The English Gentleman – 2016 - In this documentary, we get a look at where the "English Gentleman" stereotype came from, and whether it still exists today.

English Gypsies - 2017 - This series takes a look at a particularly interesting community, the "Gypsies" of England.

Exhibition on Screen: History's Greatest Artists – 2013 to 2016 - British documentarian Phil Grabsky produces artistic "immersions" around the world, many filmed in conjunction with galleries like London's National Gallery and the Royal Academy of Arts.

Fight Club: A History of Violence - 2017 - This series takes a look at fighting throughout British history.

The First Silent Night – 2014 - Actor Simon Callow uncovers the origins of the song Silent Night.

The Force: Manchester - 2015 - This reality series gives us a look inside the work being done by the Greater Manchester Police.

Gadget Man - 2012 to 2015 - Actors Stephen Fry (Series 1) and Richard Ayoade (Series 2-4) take a look at innovative products designed to make our lives easier. Note that Series 1 is listed entirely separate from Series 2-4, but at time of print, both are available on Prime Video.

Gauguin: The Full Story - 2003 - British art historian Waldemar Januszczak takes a look at the life and work of Paul Gauguin.

The Grand Tour – 2017 to 2019 - Jeremy

Clarkson, Richard Hammond, and James May roam around and drive unique, luxurious, and exotic automobiles.

Great Artists with Tim Marlow – 2001 to 2003 - British art historian Tim Marlow travels around the world, taking a closer look at some of its greatest artworks.

The Great British Benefits Handout – 2016 to 2017 - One of the problems with benefits systems is that they pay out tiny amounts over a long time, making it hard for recipients to get ahead or invest in themselves to get out of the mess. As a social experiment, this show offers benefits recipients the opportunity to quit benefits and receive a year's worth of payments in one lump sum. It follows as they invest in themselves and their new businesses.

Great Cars: British Elegance - 2018 - Each episode of this series focuses on a different British car - Aston Martin, Bentley, Jaguar, Land Rover, Lotus, MG, Mini, Morgan, and Rolls Royce.

Great Estates of Scotland – 2014 - This four-part series includes episodes on locations around Scotland, including Rosslyn Chapel (perhaps best known because of the *Da Vinci Code*).

The Green Park - 2015 - Learn the story behind the glamorous kosher hotel opened in 1943 on the British Riviera.

The Gypsy Matchmaker - 2014 - Follow two British Roma families as they continue in the tradition of early teenage marriage.

Hadrian's Wall: Antonine Wall - 2006 - Take a look at Rome's northernmost borders from their time in Britain.

Hairy Bikers: Pubs that Built Britain – 2016 - David and Si travel around Britain, visiting the island's best pubs.

The Harbour: Aberdeen – 2013 to 2015 - This documentary-style show explores the history and modern reality of Aberdeen Harbour, a busy industrial harbour along the Northeastern coast of Scotland.

Helicopter Search & Rescue – *Ireland* – 2016 - Watch real-life rescues by some of Ireland's most important rescue services – the Irish Coast Guard, the RNLI, Mountain Rescue Teams, Cork Fire Brigade, and the Irish Naval Services.

Holbein: Eye of the Tudors – 2015 - British art historian Waldemar Januszczak looks at how Hans Holbein recorded the most

notorious period in British history.

Horrible Histories – 2009 to present - While designed for children, this amusing educational program is every bit as entertaining for adults. The sketches cover different parts of history, but always with a dramatic or funny take on the event.

The Hotel Fixers – *Ireland* – 2017 - Hotel experts travel around Ireland and help struggling establishments.

The Impressionists – 2015 - British art critic Waldemar Januszczak travels around the world investigating the great Impressionists.

Inside the Ambulance – 2016 to 2018 - In this series, an ambulance is rigged with cameras to offer a new perspective on the lives of paramedics in the West Midlands region of the UK.

Inside the Merchant – 2016 - This series takes a behind-the-scenes look at the Merchant Hotel in Belfast, Northern Ireland.

The Irish Pub – 2013 - This documentary explores the history and culture of pubs in Ireland.

Iron Men - 2017 - Follow West Ham United as they bid farewell to Boleyn Ground after 112 years.

James May's Man Lab – 2010 to 2013 - James May sets out to teach modern men a few useful skills.

James May's Toy Stories – 2009 to 2014 - James May sets out on a mission to get kids away from screens and back to classic toys.

Julius Caesar with Mary Beard - 2018 - Historian Mary Beard reveals new insights on Julius Caesar and how he rose to power.

Keys to the Castle - 2014 - After four decades in their beloved Scottish castle, a couple prepares to downsize.

Know the British - 1973 - This hilarious short film was meant to educate American businessmen on the unusual habits and customs of the Brits.

The Last Days of Anne Boleyn - 2013 - This documentary takes a look at who Anne Boleyn really was, and why her life had to end in such a tragic, violent way.

Len and Ainsley's Big Food Adventure – 2015 - Two celebrities go on a culinary road trip of Britain.

Liam Dale's Ghostly Trails: Haunted Great Britain - 2009 - This short programmed visits haunted locations around Great Britain, including Cornwall's Jamaica Inn and Land's End. *See also: Ghostly Trails, Vol. 1 and Ghostly Trails, Vol. 2*

Living in the Shadow of World War II - 2017 - World War II affected more than just the people on the battlefield. Back home, the war cast a shadow over nearly every aspect of day-to-day life. This series takes a look at the ways the war affected people on the homefront.

Magic Numbers: Hannah Fry's Mysterious World of Maths - 2018 - Hannah Fry examines where math came from.

Meet the Romans - 2012 - British historian Mary Beard takes us along on a deep dive into what life was like during the Roman Empire.

Missing Persons Unit - *Australia* - 2006 to 2009 - This series uses footage captured over months of investigative work to show what happens when someone goes missing.

Most Haunted - 2002 to present - Yvette Fielding leads this paranormal investigation series that primarily focuses on the UK and Ireland.

Mysteries of Stonehenge - 2002 - Given recent discoveries, this will surely seem a bit dated - but it offers some lovely footage and history about Stonehenge.

The Nile: 5000 Years of History - 2018 - Historian Bettany Hughes takes us on a 900-mile adventure along the River Nile, sharing history and landmarks as she goes.

The Nurse – 2013 - This series takes a look at district nurses who travel around the UK, caring for patients at home.

One Born Every Minute - 2010 to 2018 - This popular documentary series highlights the drama of one of the most ordinary things people do – giving birth. Focusing on the human stories behind each situation, you'll see both the highs and lows of what happens in a maternity hospital.

The Only Way is Essex – 2010 to present - This reality series follows a group of young and "socially ambitious" individuals living in Essex, a region often stereotyped as being similar to New Jersey in the United States.

Pawnbrokers - 2010 - Take a look inside Uncles, a crazy British pawn shop that's been in business for three generations.

Rachel Allen's Cake Diaries - 2012 - Chef Rachel Allen offers tips for cakes of all types.

Renaissance Unchained – 2015 - British art critic Waldemar Januszczak explores the history of the Renaissance throughout Europe.

Return of the Black Death - 2014 - In this BBC documentary, scientists take a look at skeletons recently unearthed in a long-lost plague cemetery below London.

Rococo Before Bedtime – 2014 - British art historian Waldemar Januszczak examines the history and grandeur of the Rococo period.

Roman Britain: From the Air - 2014 - Christine Bleakley and Dr. Michael Scott check out remnants of Roman Britain that can be seen more clearly from the air than the ground.

Rome: Empire Without Limit - 2016 - Professor Mary Beard offers her take on the Roman Empire.

A Royal Hangover – 2015 - This series takes a look at British drinking culture and binge drinking.

Rubens: An Extra Large Story - 2015 - British host Waldemar Januszczak takes a look at the world of Sir Peter Paul Rubens.

Salt Beef and Rye – 2016 - This fun documentary looks at the characters who frequent London's Brick Lane.

Scarlet Woman: The True Story of Mary Magdalene - 2017 - British art historian Waldemar Januszczak takes a look at how faith and art come together in portrayals of Mary Magdalene.

Scotch! The Story of Whisky – 2015 - This short series takes a look at the history and science of the Scottish whisky industry.

Secrets of the Magna Carta - 2017 - Hugh Bonneville (*Downton Abbey*) narrates this look at the history of the Magna Carta.

Sharon Horgan's Women - 2012 - Sharon Horgan (*Catastrophe*) takes a look at what it takes to be a good mum, handle a midlife crisis, and maintain a solid marriage.

The Spy Who Went Into the Cold - 2013 - At the height of the Cold War in 1963, Kim Philby defected to Moscow after 30 years in senior positions in British intelligence offices. This documentary takes a look back at the scandal.

The Story of Europe - 2017 - Cambridge historian Sir Christopher Clark takes us on an engaging walk through the history of Europe.

The Story of the Mini - 2004 - Take a look at the history of the Mini, and how it came to be one of the most-loved cars ever made.

The Story of Women and Power - 2015 - Historian Amanda Vickery takes us on a tour of the 300-year battle for women's equality in Britain.

The Scottish Covenanters – 1998 - If you enjoy 17th-century Scottish history, you'll love this 54 minute program.

Scottish Myths and Legends - 2007 - From the Loch Ness monster to the shape-shifting kelpies, this programme takes a look at the legends of Scotland.

Shoreline Detectives - 2017 to 2019 - Dr. Tori Herridge and her team of historians and archaeologists explore seabeds and sand banks to find remnants of Britain's history.

Snowdonia 1890 - 2010 - Two families live as though they were 19th century farmers on Mount Snowdonia in Wales.

The Special Needs Hotel – 2015 - On the Somerset coast, a grand Victorian hotel trains special needs individuals for careers in hospitality.

A Stitch in Time – 2016 - Amber Butchart takes a look at historical figures through the clothing they wore.

Time Team - 1994 to 2014 - A group of archaeologists travel around Britain working on different excavation sites.

The Tower - 2004 - This eight-part series looks at the Tower of London throughout the ages.

Treasure Houses of Britain – 2011 - This series travels around Britain, exploring the history and architecture of some of the island's greatest estates.

The Tube: Going Underground – 2016 - This documentary gives you a behind-the-scenes look at what it takes to keep the Tube functioning.

Tudor Monastery Farm at Christmas – 2013 - Historians and archaeologists look at how the Tudors celebrated the 12 days of Christmas.

Walking Through History With Tony Robinson – 2013 to 2015 - Tony Robinson selects long walks around Britain for their combined scenery and historic merits.

Westminster: Behind the Closed Doors – 2008 - Learn what goes on behind closed doors of Westminster in this documentary filmed by Tony Benn over 12 months.

Home & Renovation

The Big House Reborn – 2015 - This series follows National Trust conservators as they work on restoring The Mount Stewart House.

Building Dream Homes - 2014 - This BBC series follows some of the country's top architects as they make housing dreams come true.

Design Doctors – *Ireland* – 2018 - This series helps Irish homeowners make their homes more attractive.

Double Your House for Half the Money - 2012 - British families see their homes transformed.

The Farm Fixer – Ireland – 2012 - This show visits struggling small farms around Ireland and attempts to help them improve their situations.

Half-Built House – 2012 - Property guru Sian Astley helps people who've started home renovations and gotten stuck.

Home of the Year: Ireland - *Ireland* - 2018 - This series travels around Ireland to look at the unique ways people have made their houses into homes.

The Home Show - 2008 - Architect George Clarke helps turn current homes into dream homes.

The House that 100k (GBP) Built – 2016 - Homes are expensive in the UK, but this series takes a look at people building homes from scratch – and on a budget.

The House that 100k Built: Tricks of the Trade – 2015 - This series takes a look at some of the low-cost building and renovation methods used to create really amazing spaces on a budget.

Make My Home Bigger – 2015 - Jonnie Irwin follows along as people seek to enlarge their homes.

Million Pound Properties - 2018 - This series takes a look at what you can get with a million pounds or more around the UK. From tiny London apartments to enormous Scottish castles, the value of a pound differs greatly from one market to another.

My Dream Derelict Home – 2014 - This series follows homeowners putting everything on the line to save and restore dilapidated properties around the UK.

Posh Neighbours at War – 2016 - This series looks at the multi-million pound disputes between London neighbours as they embark on messy and noisy building projects in cramped quarters.

Project Restoration – 2016 - Historical building surveyor Marianne Suhr travels the UK helping out on challenging restoration projects.

Restoration Home – 2010 - Actress Caroline Quentin (*Jonathan Creek, Blue Murder*) hosts this series about restoring neglected historic homes around Britain.

Room to Improve – 2013 to 2019 - Irish architect Dermot Bannan travels Ireland helping people create their dream homes.

Animals

Animal A&E – *Ireland* – 2010 - This series follows a team of emergency veterinary specialists who help animals in need of urgent care.

Animal Rescue Squad – 2007 - This series takes us along as professionals work tirelessly to rescue animals from dangerous situations.

Animal Squad – 2010 - This show follows RSPCA officers are they work to protect animals.

Anna's Wild Life – 2011 to 2012 - After buying a wildlife park with no actual experience in caring for wild animals, Anna and Colin are somehow surprised to find it's quite challenging to care for 100+ exotic creatures.

Man & Beast with Martin Clunes – 2012 - Animal lover and actor Martin Clunes sets out to explore the relationship between man and beast.

Martin Clunes & a Lion Called Mugie – 2014 - Martin Clunes travels to Kenya to meet an orphaned lion cub brought to the Kora National Reserve.

Martin Clunes: Heavy Horsepower – 2010 - *Doc Martin* star Martin Clunes investigates man's relationship with horses.

Martin Clunes: Last Lemur Standing – 2012 - Martin Clunes travels to the Indian Ocean to find out about the challenges facing lemurs.

Pet School – 2012 - In this series, children are taught what's really involved in providing proper care for the pets they'd love to have. If they're good students, they might just get the chance to bring a new animal companion into their homes.

Small Animal Hospital - 2014 - This series follows the action at the Small Animal Hospital at the University of Glasgow.

Walks With My Dog - 2017 - British celebrities like John Nettles and Robert Lindsay explore the countryside with their dogs.

Literary History

Brontë Country: The Life and Times of Three Famous Sisters - 2002 - This programme takes a look at the area of Yorkshire where the Brontë sisters lived. Though the quality of footage could be better, the scenery is still lovely.

The Brontë Sisters – 2006 - This series charts the lives of the Brontë sisters.

Charles Dickens' London Life - 2008 - This interesting series takes a look at the London locations that shaped the young man who would later grown into a much-loved novelist.

Charles Dickens: The Man That Asked for More - 2006 - This series offers an in-depth biography of author Charles Dickens.

Cracking the Shakespeare Code – 2017 - Codebreaker Petter Amundsen and historian Dr. Robert Crumpton investigate possible secrets buried in Shakespeare's first folio, also looking at a coded map.

Jane Austen Country: The Life and Times of Jane Austen - 2002 - This hour-long documentary offers background on Jane Austen's life and upbringing.

Jane Austen: Life – 2005 - This program wonders what author Jane Austen may have been like, visiting places she lived and examining her correspondence.

Legends of King Arthur – 2001 - This series takes a look at the enduring appeal of Arthurian legend.

Murder Rooms: Mysteries of the Real Sherlock Holmes – 2001 - This series takes a look at the influences on Sir Arthur Conan Doyle, particularly his mentor and medical instructor Dr. Bell.

The Mystery of Agatha Christie with David Suchet - 2014 - David Suchet (*Poirot*) embarks on a journey to learn more about Agatha Christie.

Narnia's Lost Poet: The Secret Lives and Loves of C.S. Lewis - 2013 - C.S. Lewis biographer A.N. Wilson embarks on a journey to find the man behind Narnia. He was incredibly secretive about his private life, and even his best friend (J.R.R. Tolkien) was unaware of his late-in-life marriage to a divorced American woman.

Rural Britain: A Novel Approach - 2008 - One part travel series, one part history lesson, this series walks you through Britain's most beautiful landscapes and talks about the authors who drew inspiration from them. The series looks at Jane Austen, Charles Dickens, the Brontë Sisters, George Eliot, Thomas Hardy, and D.H. Lawrence.

Shakespeare's Stratford - 2008 - This three-hour tour takes us all over Stratford to see the city that shaped Shakespeare.

Sherlock Holmes Against Conan Doyle – 2017 - This series takes a look at the enormous success of Sherlock Holmes – success that prompted some people of his time to contact Sir Arthur Conan Doyle in hopes that Holmes might help them.

To Walk Invisible: The Brontë Sisters – 2017 - This two-part series takes a look at the incredible Brontë sisters and their unexpected success in light of their male-dominated time period.

Royals & Upper Classes

British Royal Heritage: The Royal Kingdom - 2004 - This series looks at the historic relationships between the British royals and the ancient kingdoms of Sussex, East Anglia, Wessex, and Kent.

Charles I: Downfall of a King - 2019 - Historian Lisa Hilton takes a closer look at King Charles I's downfall and the political climate that led to it.

Crown and Country – 1998 to 2007 - HRH Prince Edward hosts this series that tours some of England's greatest landmarks.

Edward & Mary: The Unknown Tudors – 2002 - This two-part special tells the story of King Edward and Queen (Bloody) Mary, eldest daughter of Henry VIII and first English queen since Matilda.

Elizabeth I: Killer Queen - 2016 - Did Queen Elizabeth I really have a woman killed so she could continue sleeping with her husband? This documentary takes a look at the evidence.

Elizabeth I: War on Terror - 2014 - This documentary takes a look at Sir Francis Walsingham and how his work for Queen Elizabeth I protected her.

God Save the Queen – 2018 - This series explores the origins of British traditions.

Harrow: A Very British School – 2013 - A reality program set in a posh boarding school.

Henry VII: Winter King – 2013 - Author Thomas Penn dives into the world of the first Tudor King, Henry VII.

How to Get Ahead - 2013 - Presenter Stephen Smith takes a look at what it took to survive and do well in a variety of historic royal courts.

King Arthur's Lost Kingdom - 2019 - Professor Alice Roberts takes us inside a stone palace excavation in Cornwall, the supposed birthplace of King Arthur.

King of Scots – 2007 - This documentary looks a the life and times of Robert the Bruce.

Legends of Power with Tony Robinson – 2003 - Tony Robinson dives into the lives of some of the world's most powerful leaders.

Lord Montague – 2015 - *Upstairs, Downstairs* and *Downton Abbey* fans will enjoy this documentary on one of England's most controversial aristocrats.

Prince Charles: The Royal Restoration - 2013 - This factual programme takes a look at Princes Charles' efforts to preserve Dumfries House in Scotland.

Princess Elizabeth: The Early Years with Jane Dismore - 2018 - British author Jane Dismore talks about her book on the early life of Queen Elizabeth II.

The Private Lives of the Tudors - 2016 - This series takes a very personal look at one of Britain's most celebrated dynasties.

Queen Victoria's Letters: A Monarch Unveiled – 2014 - This series takes a look at Queen Victoria through her correspondence and writings.

Royal Britain: An Aerial History of the Monarchy - 2013 - Learn a bit of history while getting aerial views of the places the British royals have called home.

Royals & Animals: 'Til Death Do Us Part - 2013 - This documentary takes a look at Queen Elizabeth's passion for animals, particularly horses and dogs.

Serving the Royals: Inside the Firm - 2015 - This documentary looks at the roughly 1200 servants and employees working for the House of Windsor.

Wallis Simpson: The Secret Letters - 2016 - This series takes a look at the private correspondence of Wallis Simpson and what it says about the scandal.

Windsor Castle: After the Fire – 2006 - This one-hour program goes into the aftermath of the fire at Windsor Castle.

True Crime & Dark History

A is for Acid – 2002 - Though technically a movie, this one sees Martin Clunes playing John George Haigh, the "Acid Bath Murderer" who killed at least 6 people in 1940s England. Also stars Keeley Hawes.

Britain's Outlaws: Highwaymen, Pirates, and Rogues – 2015 - This series looks at some of the outlaws who ran wild in 17th and 18th century Britain.

Broadmoor: A History of the Criminally Insane – 2016 - This documentary sees criminology professor David Wilson using interviews and archives to look back at Britain's most dreadful criminals and the asylum that held them.

Crime & Violence in England – 2012 - This series takes you into the world of the people who work to combat gangs and street violence in England.

The Detectives –2015 to 2017 - More true crime than mystery, this documentary series follows a special sex crimes unit in the Greater Manchester Police.

Donal MacIntyre – *Ireland* – 2015 - In this series, Donal MacIntyre takes a look at youth crime and what causes it.

Fred Dinenage Murder Casebook – 2010 to 2013 - Fred Dinenage takes a modern forensic look at various murders that shocked the UK over the 20th century.

Halloween: Feast of the Dying Sun – 2010 - This documentary explores the Celtic origins of Halloween.

Inside the Tower of London: Crimes, Conspiracies, Confessions – 2017 - This four-part series goes into the gruesome history of the Tower of London.

Jack the Ripper – 2017 - UK murder squad detective Trevor Marriott builds a team in an effort to unveil the identity of the infamous killer.

Jack the Ripper: Conspiracies – 2002 - This documentary visits the sites of the Jack the Ripper murders, looking at available evidence and challenging the viewer to decide who really did it.

Jack the Ripper Revealed – 2017 - This series takes us back to 1888 and considers possible suspects for Jack the Ripper, alongside a bit of history for context.

Jack the Ripper: The Definitive Story – 2012 - This documentary attempts to dispel myths and misconceptions surrounding the Jack the Ripper case, offering what they believe to be the real truth.

The Life & Crimes of William Palmer – 1998 - Based on a true story, this miniseries tells the story of Victorian doctor and murderer William Palmer.

The Moors Murders – 2009 - Back in the mid-1960s, Ian Brady and Myra Hindley abducted, tortured, and murdered children and young teenagers, horrifying the British public. This documentary looks back at archival footage, creates dramatic reconstructions, and talks with some of those involved in the case.

Murdertown - 2018 to 2019 - This series tells the stories of shocking and true murders around the UK. The stories are grisly, but they show a fair bit of scenery around the cities and towns in question, so many will enjoy it on that alone.

Neighbourhood Blues – 2011 - This series takes a look at police operations in Avon and Somerset as they deal with typical, day-to-day crimes.

Scapegoat – 2017 - This story is the dramatisation of the real story of one of Ireland's most famous unsolved murders, which resulted in an innocent man being found guilty but insane. Not to be confused with *Scapegoat*, a 2012 film starring Matthew Rhys and Eileen Atkins.

The Secret Identity of Jack the Ripper – 1988 - Actor Peter Ustinov stars in this 1988 documentary which saw many of the world's best forensic scientists and criminologists reexamining the case.

This is Personal: The Hunt for the Yorkshire Ripper – 2000 - This short series is a dramatisation of the investigation into the Yorkshire Ripper murders of the 1970s, and the effect it had on the man who led the enquiry.

Tony Robinsons's Crime and Punishment – 2008 - *Blackadder* star Tony Robinson presents this four-part series about the history of Britain's legal system, along with commentary on the present and future.

Tony Robinson's Gods and Monsters – 2011 - Tony Robinson explores the dark corners of Britain's history, including witches, human sacrifice, demons, and sprites.

Gardening

Brilliant Gardens - 2012 - This programme features some of the loveliest gardens in Great Britain.

Gardens of the National Trust – 2007 - Four episodes take you to some of England's finest gardens.

Get Growing – New Zealand – 2014 to 2017 - Hosts Lynda Hallinan and Justin Newcombe encourage viewers to transform their outdoor living spaces.

Glorious Gardens from Above – 2014 - Horticulturist Christine Walkden explores some of Britain's loveliest gardens from a hot air balloon.

Greatest Gardens – 2015 - Our hosts set out to find the loveliest gardens in Northern Ireland.

The Great Gardens of England – 2007 - Alan Titchmarsh takes us on a tour of some of the finest gardens in England.

Ground Force - 2005 - Professional gardeners and landscapers help transform unattractive gardens.

Ground Force Revisited - 2004 - Each episode of this gardening series sees a worthy person getting a garden makeover.

My Dream Farm - 2010 - Monty Don follows first-time farmers as they learn to make a living from the land.

Nature: What Plants Talk About – *Canada* – 2013 - This series takes a look at plant behaviour.

Secret Gardens of England – 2007 - In this program, you'll visit 8 lesser-known but still very beautiful gardens in England.

Through the Garden Gate: A Diary of the English Countryside – 2010 - This series takes a look at everyday nature in the British countryside.

Treasure Gardens of England - 2006 - Alan Titchmarsh takes us on a tour of the gardens at ten stately homes around England.

Travel

Bath, England – Date Unknown - This extremely short 4-part series offers excellent views of Bath, and would be perfect for anyone who is considering including it on an upcoming trip.

Britain's Best Drives - 2009 - Richard Wilson (*One Foot in the Grave*) celebrates the 50th anniversary of Britain's first motorway with a trip around the country in six classic cars.

Daniel & Majella's B&B Road Trip – 2016 - This show offers a delightful journey through some of the loveliest B&Bs in Ireland.

Dan Snow's Norman Walks - 2010 - Presenter Dan Snow walks us through some of the areas of Britain with significant Norman history.

Derek Acorah's Ghost Towns – 2013 - This paranormal investigation show takes you around England with host Derek Acorah.

Discover England – 2004 - With 13 episodes on different regions of England, this series is a wonderful way to experience England when you can't actually be there.

Discover Ireland – 2000 - Once you've watched Discover England and Discover Scotland, why not check out Discover Ireland? Sadly, there is no Discover Wales or Discover Northern Ireland.

Discover Scotland – 2004 - Heavy on the history, this series offers four 1-hour episodes that take you around Scotland.

Edinburgh: More than Words - 2019 - This brief programme takes you on a quick tour through the streets of Edinburgh.

Galway, Ireland: Busy Streets and Irish Music in the Pubs – 2018 - This series looks around Galway, Ireland.

Grand Tours of Scotland's Lochs – 2017 - Historian Paul Murton takes us on an incredibly scenic journey around some of Scotland's most beautiful lochs.

Grand Tours of the Scottish Islands – 2013 to 2016 - Paul Murton guides us around some of Scotland's most beautiful islands.

Great Lighthouses of Ireland - 2019 - With gorgeous coastal footage, this series gives you a mix of history, science, and scenery - along with plenty of stories from lighthouse keepers of today and yesterday.

Guardians of the Night - 2007 - This series offers a look at the history of lighthouses, with on-location footage from lighthouses around the world.

Highlands and Islands: Where Scotland's Heart Beats Loudest - 2016 - Travel journalist Erik Peters visits the Scottish Highlands and islands.

Ireland with Ardal O'Hanlon – 2017 - This three-part series is a quick romp around Ireland with famed comedian Ardal O'Hanlon.

Ireland's Wild River - 2014 - Follow the River Shannon as it passes through the beautiful rural landscapes of Ireland.

Isle of Man: From the Air - 2014 - Between Great Britain and Ireland, you'll find the Isle of Man. This series take a look at the lovely island from above.

London: A City in Time - 2015 - This programme mixes live footage with historical documents and photos to tell the story of London. Though listed as 2015 on Amazon, it feels significantly older so that date may not be accurate.

London: A Tale of Two Cities – 2015 - This

hour-long documentary looks at the highs and lows London has faced over the years.

Love London - 2015 - A London taxi driver and a young Londoner travel the city to learn its secrets.

Memories of Scotland – Date Unknown - This 48-minute program focuses on the major tourist attractions in Scotland.

Mysterious Places of Scotland and Ireland: Swans of Loch Lomond – 2007 - No dialogue, just scenery. Enjoy the views.

On the Ballykissangel Trail – 2007 - This short documentary discusses the making of *Ballykissange*l, along with a tour of the area.

On the Whisky Trail: The History of Scotland's Famous Drink - 2003 - Learn more about the history of whisky and how it's made.

Over Ireland – 1998 - This video tour offers a look at some of Ireland's most famous landmarks and landscapes.

Oxford Street - 2017 - This series takes an in-depth look at one of Europe's largest shopping districts and its day-to-day activities.

Richard Wilson On the Road - 2014 - Richard Wilson (*One Foot in the Grave*) takes a trip around Britain with only his antique Shell travel guides to help him.

Rick Steves's Europe – 2000 to 2019 - Seasons 7 to 10 of this popular series are offered on Amazon. Of interest to Anglophiles will be: 7-8, London, 7-9 Northern England, 9-8 Western England, 9-9 Southeast England, 9-10 Cornwall, 10-1 Heart of England, 10-10 Scotland's Highlands, 10-11 Scotland's Islands, and 10-12 Glasgow.

Secrets of the Irish Landscape - *Ireland* - 2018 - Presenter Derek Mooney travels around Ireland and Europe to piece together the history of Ireland's landscape and how it came to be.

Secrets of the Stones - *Ireland* - 2016 - This series takes a look at some of Ireland's ancient monuments and what they tell us about the country's past.

The Shelbourne Hotel – *Ireland* - 2016 to 2017 - This reality show takes us behind the scenes at one of Dublin's poshest hotels.

Skye's the Limit - 2017 - Follow one woman as she circumnavigates the Isle of Skye on a stand-up paddleboard.

Smart Travels with Rudy Maxa – 2002 to 2006 - Although not exclusively about Great Britain, this series includes episodes in London, the London countryside, Dublin, Ireland's West Coast, Bath, South Wales, Edinburgh, and St. Andrews (not to mention a lot of other lovely cities around the world).

The Spirit of England: Part 1 - 2009 - This travel series takes you on a tour of some of the most popular tourist sites in England. Sites visited include Stonehenge, Rievaulx Abbey, and Dover Castle.

The Spirit of England: Part 2 - 2009 - This edition visits another set of tourist spots in England, including Framlingham Castle, Kenilworth Castle, and the Charles Darwin house.

Stephen Tompkinson's Australian Balloon Adventure – 2010 - Stephen Tompkinson (*Ballykissangel, DCI Banks*) stars in this three-part travel series checking out Australia by balloon.

The Story of London - 2014 - Six episodes walk us through different sites in London.

Terry Jones' Great Map Mystery – 2008 - *Monty Python* star Terry Jones travels around Britain to see if it's still possible to follow the earliest roadmaps of Wales.

Travel Scotland with James McCreadie – 2018 to 2019 - This half-hour special has James McCreadie taking you on a journey through the Trossachs.

Treyvaud Travels – 2015 - Paul Treyvaud travels around Ireland over the course of nine half-hour episodes.

Trolley Dollies – 2002 - This docu-soap features the lives of a charter flight crew that travels to some of the most popular vacation destinations in the world.

Visit Wales with Rachel Hicks – 2009 - This hour-long travel show explores a variety of locations around Wales.

Walks Around Britain – 2016 to 2019 - Britain is one of the greatest places in the world to go walking, and Amazon Prime lets you enjoy two series of short scenic walks around the countryside.

Walks Around Britain: The Great Glen Way – 2016 - This 48-minute programme shows rambler Andrew White walking The Great Glen Way from Fort William to Inverness. If you enjoy this one, also check out *Footloose in Scotland: The West Highland Way*. Together, the two journeys represent a walk all the way from Glasgow to Inverness.

My Welsh Sheepdog - 2016 - BBC presenter Kate Humble travels around Wales with her dog Teg to learn more about the rare Welsh sheepdog breed.

Whistlestop Edinburgh: Scotland's Beautiful Capital - 2014 - Tour guide Liam Dale leads us around some of Edinburgh's most interesting sites.

York, UK - 2016 - Tour guide Dennis Callan offers bite-sized videos taken around the city of York.

The Footloose Series

This series of travel videos features a British couple as they travel around Europe. We've only listed the episodes pertaining to the British Isles, but there are others set in mainland Europe if you search for them. They're great because instead of rushing through each bit and showing only the highlights, their videos are long and in-depth. Filming dates range from 1998 to present.

Footloose in the Cotswolds, Part 1 – UK filmmakers Debra and David Rixon visit Stow, Chipping Camden, Broadway, and the gardens of Kiftsgate and Hidcote.

Footloose in the Cotswolds, Part 2 – UK filmmakers Debra and David Rixon visit Cheltenham, Painswick, Tetbury, and the City of Bath.

Footloose in England: Along the Ridgeway - This two-hour walking film takes you along southern England's oldest green road. The 85-mile walk includes stone circles, hill forts, villages, and more.

Footloose in London: All the Best Sights of our Capital – UK filmmakers Debra and David Rixon offer budget-minded tips for visiting London and viewing its best sites.

Footloose in London: Undiscovered and Unusual – This episode takes a look at some of London's less conventional attractions and sites.

A Classic Tour of Scotland: Footloose Special – UK filmmakers Debra and David Rixon travel Scotland in an Airstream trailer, stopping off to visit locations like the Isle of Skye, Glasgow, Stirling Castle, Edinburgh, and Inverness.

Footloose in Scotland: The West Highland Way – This two hour programme follows David and Debra as they walk the 95-mile West Highland Way from Glasgow to Fort William.

Footloose in Ireland – This nearly two-hour programme sees David and Debra traveling to Dublin and walking the Dingle Way.

Narrowboats & Canals

100 Years of British Ships - 2007 - Though slightly broader than just narrowboats and canals, this series takes a look at all manner of British boats over the past 100 years.

Britain by Narrowboat - 2020 - Colin and his partner Shaun quit their jobs, sell their home, and start up life aboard a narrowboat.

Britain's Best Canals - 2015 to 2016 - BBC presenter John Sergeant takes us on a different canal journey with each episode.

British Inland Waterways – Date Unknown - If you've ever dreamed of lazily floating along the beautiful canals of England and Scotland, this series will be sure to delight.

Cruising the Cut - 2019 to present - This is another series about a different British man who quit his job to go live on the canals and travel.

Narrowboat Houseboating Through the English Countryside – 2001 - This instruction-oriented programme shows you what it takes to make the most of your houseboating adventure.

Travels by Narrowboat – 2018 to presents - Newer than many of the other narrowboating shows on Amazon, this one follows Kevin as he quits his job and embarks on a new life on the canals.

British Railway Journeys

100 Years of British Trains - 2016 - Follow along as this series traces the evolution of British trains throughout the 20th century.

100 Years of British Trams - 2007 - This documentary offers a history of trams and their use around Britain.

Best of British Heritage Railways - 2016 - Four episodes take us along some of Britain's rarest heritage railways. Look for episode 2 as a separate "Volume 2" listing.

Britain's Railways: Then and Now - 2010 - Using archival footage, this series takes a look at today's railways compared with those of the past.

Britain's Railways Then & Now: LNER - 2010 - This review begins at King's Cross Station and takes a look at the trains that travel her rails.

British Railway Journeys – 2012 - Each of these episodes is roughly an hour long, and they take you through interesting railway journeys around Britain. There is some commentary, and plenty of scenery around the rails (you're not just looking out a train window).

Journeys included: The Severn Valley and the Cotswolds, Southwest Scotland, East Anglia, The Lake District, The Peak District, The North East, North Wales, The South West, Northern England, and South Wales.

British Railways - 2016 - This series includes eight episodes about different trains around Great Britain. They are: Waterloo Sunset, Rails in the Isle of Wight, Vintage Southern, From Bewdley to Blaenau, British Narrow Gauge Miscellany, Steam in the Midlands, Channel Tunnel Trains, and English Branch Lines and Byways.

Byways of Steam: In Stephenson's Country - 2016 - This series takes a look at George Stephenson's impact on the British rail system and his enduring legacy.

Byways of Steam: In the Valleys and the Mountains – 2018 - The varied terrain within the British Isles presented many challenges for early trains, but it also makes for some gorgeous scenery in this 50 minute feature.

Classic British Steam Engines – 2015 - This series devotes nearly an hour each to several of Britain's most famous trains. Each edition is listed as a separate programme on Amazon, and you can look for the following episodes: Princess Margaret Rose , The Flying Scotsman , City of Truro, Duchess of Sutherland, Standards Class 4 Tanks, Best of British Heritage Railways

The Flying Scotsman: A Rail Romance - 2013 - Barbara Flynn narrates this hour-long story of the world's love affair with the Flying Scotsman.

The Flying Scotsman: Running the Legend - 2018 - At the National Railway Museum in York, they prepare the Flying Scotsman for a summer trip to Scarborough.

The Flying Scotsman Steam Train Comes Home - 2018 - After years away, the world's most famous locomotive train returns to its homeland.

The Magical World of Trains - 2007 - This hour-long feature celebrates all that is wonderful about trains - including train travel, the future of trains, and trainspotting.

Preserved Lines - 2009 - This series takes a look at a variety of heritage steam and diesel rail adventures to be had around Britain. Episodes include: Bluebell Railway, Avon Valley, Swanage, Gloucestershire Warwickshire Railway, and Didcot.

Railway Round-Up - 2016 - Take a look at some of the railway preservation work being done around the UK.

Smoke and Steam - 2007 - This series celebrates steam railways around Britain.

Vintage Steam Trains: Great British Steam – 2015 - This hour-long feature focuses exclusively on the British steam train and its history.

NETFLIX

Website: http://netflix.com

Description: One of the biggest and oldest streaming services, Netflix offers a wide variety of content from all over the world - along with quite a bit of their own original content.

Available On: Roku, Fire TV, Apple TV, Apple iPhone & iPad, Chromecast, Fire tablets, select Smart TVs, Android phones and tablets, and computer (via web browser).

Cost: $8.99/month (1 screen), $12.99 HD (2 screens same time), $15.99 UHD (4 screens same time)

Now Streaming
Mysteries & Crime Dramas

The A List - 2018 - This series blends romance, drama, suspense, and mystery when a group of young women go to a remote camp with a supernatural presence.

Broadchurch – 2013 to 2017 - When an 11-year-old boy is murdered in a quiet coastal community, town secrets are exposed. David Tennant (*Deadwater Fell*) and Olivia Colman (*Rev*) star.

Collateral – 2018 - When a pizza delivery man is gunned down in London, DI Kip Glaspie refuses to accept that it's just a random act of violence. Her investigation drags her into a dark underworld she never could have predicted. The series stars John Simm of *Life on Mars*, along with Nicola Walker (*River*), Billie Piper (*Doctor Who*), and Carey Mulligan (*Never Let Me Go*).

Criminal: United Kingdom – 2019 - This three-episode series takes a look at the intense interrogation of three different suspects in London. David Tennant makes an appearance in one episode.

Deadwind – *Finland* – 2018 to present - Detective Sofia Karppi investigates a murder with ties to a Helsinki construction firm.

The Five – 2016 - Years after a young boy disappears, his DNA turns up at a crime scene. Based on the novel by Harlen Coben.

The Frankenstein Chronicles – 2015 to 2017 - In 1827 London, a detective hunts a killer with an appetite for dismemberment.

Giri/Haji - 2019 - Japanese detective Kenzo Mori travels to London to figure out whether his brother Yuto, presumed dead, is actually dead. Yuto is believed to have killed the nephew of a Yakuza member, and the search draws Kenzo into the dark and dangerous criminal underworld of London.

Hinterland – 2013 to 2016 - This Welsh crime drama takes place in the coastal town of Aberystwyth, where DCI Tom Mathias is just getting started in a new job.

The Indian Detective – *Canada* – 2017 - A suspended Canadian police officer returns home to Mumbai and helps out with an investigation.

Intelligence – *Canada* – 2005 to 2007 - The female head of an organized crime unit faces off against the confident male leader of a drug-smuggling ring.

Kiss Me First – 2018 - Two girls become friends in the virtual world of an online game, and one is pulled into something much darker than she had imagined.

Lucifer - *United States* - 2016 to present - Though American, this Los Angeles-based procedural stars British actor Tom Ellis (*Miranda*). He plays Lucifer, the naughty son of God who's decided he's sick of Hell and wants to spend some time on Earth.

Marcella – 2016 to present - After her divorce, Marcella returns to work as a detective in London. A serial killer she once pursued may have done the same.

Paranoid – 2016 - What begins as a cozy British mystery quickly evolves into a massive European conspiracy.

Requiem – 2018 - After her mother commits suicide, a young woman finds evidence that might tie her to an abduction in Wales more than 20 years prior.

Retribution – 2016 - When a newlywed couple is killed, police question their feuding families and uncover more than they expected.

Ripper Street – 2012 to 2017 - This detective series is set in 1889 London in the aftermath of Jack the Ripper.

Safe – 2018 - Michael C. Hall (*Dexter*) tries on a British accent for his role in this series about a widowed surgeon whose teenage daughter goes missing.

Sherlock – 2010 to 2017 - Benedict Cumberbatch stars in this modern-day version of Sir Arthur Conan Doyle's *Sherlock Holmes* tales.

The Stranger - 2020 - Based on the Harlan Coben novel of the same title, this series sees a mysterious stranger tell a man a secret that destroys his otherwise peaceful life.

Tidelands – *Australia* – 2018 - When an ex-con returns to her hometown, it brings long-hidden truths to the surface.

Traitors – 2019 - Near the end of World War II, a young English woman assists a mysterious American agent as he tries to root out Russian infiltration in the British government.

Vexed – 2010 to 2012 - A young male and female detective team frustrate each other with their different attitudes and complicated personal lives.

Wanted – *Australia* – 2016 to 2018 - Two strangers become involuntary partners when they witness a murder and get framed for the crime.

Young Wallander – 2020 - Though the Kenneth Branagh adaptation of Wallander left Netflix this year, Netflix made this new series, an adaptation that imagines Kurt Wallander as a police officer in his early 20s in 2020 Sweden.

Dramas

Alias Grace – *Canada* – 2017 - In 19th-century Canada, a murderess might be deemed not guilty by reason of insanity. This limited series is based on Margaret Atwood's novel.

Anne With An "E" – *Canada* – 2017 to 2019 - Based on Anne of Green Gables, this series follows a spirited young orphan who goes to live with a spinster.

Between – *Canada* – 2016 - When a strange disease kills every town resident over the age of 21, the youthful inhabitants of the town are quarantined.

Black Earth Rising – 2018 - Investigator Kate Ashby is forced to investigate her own past when she takes on war crimes cases.

Black Mirror – 2007 to 2019 - This ominous modern thriller anthology gives

us glimpses into some very dark possibilities for the future.

Black Mirror: Bandersnatch – 2018 - In 1984, a programmer adapts a novel into a video game, growing less connected to reality as the project moves along. This is an interactive story with multiple endings.

Bodyguard – 2018 - Keeley Hawes and Richard Madden star in this hit drama about a veteran who helps thwart a terrorist attack and gets assigned to protect a prominent politician.

The Borgias – *Canada* – 2011 to 2013 - This period drama follows the notorious and frequently unethical Borgia family.

Call the Midwife – 2012 to present - This drama looks into the lives of dedicated midwives in impoverished East London of the 1950s and 60s.

Can't Cope, Won't Cope – *Ireland* – 2016 to 2018 - In Dublin, two young women realize their childish ways are wearing thin.

Cleverman – *Australia* – 2016 to 2017 - In a future world, powerful humanoid creatures try to survive in a world dominated by humans.

The Code - *Australia* - 2014 to 2016 - When two brothers, a hacker and a journalist, are facing the possibility of extradition to the US, the Australian National Security offers them a way out. They're taken to a government facility and told that if they help out, the slate will be wiped clean.

Creeped Out – 2017 to present - A masked figure known only as "The Curious" collects dark tales in this dramatic young adult anthology series.

The Crown – 2016 to present - This Netflix original follows some particularly dramatic times in Queen Elizabeth's reign during the last half of the 20th century. Claire Foy and Olivia Colman portray Queen Elizabeth II.

Dark Matter – *Canada* – Waking up on a spaceship with no memories, a crew must attempt to figure out who they are and how they got there.

Dead Set – 2008 - Housemates in a reality show are clueless as the undead attack the compound.

Degrassi : Next Class – *Canada* – 2016 to 2017 - This follow-up to the classic Canadian teen drama features a new generation of teenagers.

Doctor Foster – 2015 to 2017 - When a woman suspects her husband of having an affair, her investigations lead her down a dark path.

The End of the F***ing World – 2017 to present - A rebel and a psychopath embark on a teenage road trip.

The English Game – 2020 - This sports-themed period drama was developed by Julian Fellowes (*Downton Abbey*) for Netflix, and it follows the origins of modern football in England. Set in the 1870s, it brings us to a time when football was considered a sport for the wealthy – until two players from opposite ends of the social spectrum come together to change the game forever.

Free Rein – 2017 to present - A teenager from LA spends the summer in England

and bonds with a mysterious horse. See also: *Free Rein: The 12 Neighs of Christmas* and *Free Rein: Valentine's Day*

Freud - *Austria* - 2020 - In 1886 Vienna, a young Sigmund Freud hasn't yet risen to prominence. When a series of murders happens within Vienna high society, he teams up with a medium and a policeman to get to the bottom of things.

Frontier – *Canada* – 2016 to 2018 - In 18th-century North America, trappers and traders try to gain control in the fur trade.

Get Even - 2020 - At the elite Bannerman Independent School, a group of teenage girls band together to expose bullies and fight for justice. It's all going rather well until one of their targets is murdered and found holding a note pointing the finger at their group.

Glitch – *Australia* – 2015 to 2019 - In a small Australian town, seven local residents return from the dead in perfect condition.

H2O: Just Add Water – 2009 - A group of young girls deal with turning into mermaids.

Haven – *Canada* – 2010 to 2015 - In Haven, Maine, residents deal with a steady stream of supernatural difficulties. FBI agent Audrey Parker attempts to get to the bottom of it all.

Heartland – *Canada* – 2007 to present - A young woman deals with the stress of potentially losing the family ranch after the sudden death of her mother.

The Innocents – 2018 - Two teenage lovers find themselves in a world of trouble when one begins to show unexplainable abilities.

Land Girls - 2009 to 2011 - Land Girls follows four women in the Women's Land Army during WW2.

The Last Kingdom – 2020 - Set in the days of Alfred the Great, this Netflix Original takes us on one man's quest to reclaim his birthright.

Last Tango in Halifax – 2012 to present - Once upon a time, they were in love. Now, decades later, they meet again for a second chance. This time, there's a lot more baggage.

The Letter for the King - 2020 - Based on the 1962 Dutch novel *De brief voor de Koning* by Tonke Dragt, this series follows an aspiring knight as he attempts to deliver a secret letter to the king.

London Spy – 2015 - After his lover disappears, a fun-loving young man dives into the dangerous world of espionage.

Merlin - 2009 to 2013 - Colin Morgan (*The Fall*) stars as a young Merlin in his days as a mere servant to Prince Arthur of Camelot. In this version of Camelot, magic is banned and Merlin is forced to keep his talent hidden away.

Peaky Blinders – 2014 to present - Set in early 20th century Birmingham, this series focuses on gang boss Tommy Shelby and his family.

Pine Gap – *Australia* – 2018 - At a top-secret US and Australian defense facility, the alliance begins to show strain.

Rake - *Australia* - 2011 to 2018 - Defense lawyer Cleaver Greene makes a career out of hopeless cases, perhaps because his own personal life is troubled enough to help him relate.

The Rain - *Denmark* - 2018 to 2020 - After a virus wipes out most of the world's population, two siblings battle to survive their new reality.

Rebellion – 2016 - During WWI, three Irish women must choose sides in the revolt against English rule.

Republic of Doyle – *Canada* – 2010 to 2014 - Jake and Malachy Doyle are a father and son PI team in Newfoundland.

Secret City – *Australia* – 2016 - One student's protest leads to government scandal.

Skins – 2007 to 2013 - This racy classic offers a look into modern teenage life in England.

Top Boy – 2019 to present - This gritty drama focuses on drug dealers in London public housing. See also: Top Boy – Summerhouse.

Travelers – *Canada* – 2016 to 2018 - In the far future, special agents are tasked with traveling back in time to prevent the collapse of society.

Troy: Fall of a City – 2018 - This miniseries is a retelling of the siege of Troy, loosely based on the Iliad.

The Tudors – 2007 to 2010 - This series follows Henry VIII in 16th-century England.

Van Helsing – *Canada* – 2016 to present - After waking up from a coma, a young woman finds the world ravaged by vampires.

Wanderlust – 2018 - A middle-aged couple decides the answer to their marital doldrums is to see other people. Toni Collette and Steven Mackintosh star.

Watership Down – 2018 - This modern-day retelling of the British classic features a warren of rabbits on a daring journey to find a new place to call home.

Wentworth – *Australia* – 2013 to present - An innocent woman has to figure out how to survive in prison while awaiting trial for the murder of her husband.

The Witcher - 2019 - Henry Cavill stars in this upcoming series about a solitary monster hunter in a world full of wicked people. It's been billed as Netflix's attempt at a Game of Thrones-style series, and it's already been renewed for a second season. The series is based on the book series of the same name by Andrzej Sapkowski.

Wyonna Earp – *Canada* – 2016 to present - A descendant of Wyatt Earp teams up with an immortal Doc Holiday in this supernatural comic-inspired Wild West tale.

Comedies

After Life – 2019 to present - After losing his wife to cancer, a suicidal widower struggles to come to terms with his new life. Starring Ricky Gervais (in a series that will surprise many, especially those who aren't normally fans of Gervais).

Bad Education – 2012 to 2014 - In a fictional Hertfordshire school, teacher Alfie Wickers fails miserably at educating his students. *See also*: *The Bad Education Movie*

Borderline – 2016 to 2018 - This comedy follows an inept team of border patrol agents at a fictitious airport.

Bottersnikes and Gumbles - 2015 to present - Set in and near a junkyard, this animated programme sees the fun-loving Gumbles attempting to steer clear of the smelly Bottersnikes. Unfortunately, Netflix decided to re-dub the series with American accents.

Burnistoun – 2010 to 2019 - This Scottish sketch comedy is set in a fictional town near Glasgow.

Chewin' the Fat – 1999 - This irreverent Scottish sketch comedy was mostly filmed in Glasgow.

Crashing – 2016 - A group of young people live as property guardians in an unused hospital in London. Phoebe Waller-Bridge (*Fleabag*) stars.

Crazyhead – 2016 - 20-somethings work on becoming adults while also battling demons in this comedy.

Cuckoo – 2012 to 2019 - When a British woman brings an American hippie back home as her husband, it sets off turmoil in her polite and proper family.

Danger Mouse - 2015 to present - These modern episodes see Danger Mouse and hamster Penfold returning for more jet-setting spy adventures.

Danger Mouse: Classic Collection - 1981 to 1992 - This collection of classic episodes features the spy Danger Mouse and his sidekick Penfold as they foil evil plots around the world.

Dennis and Gnasher Unleashed - 2017 - This cartoon follows fearless Dennis, his dog Gnasher, and his friends as they seek out fun and adventure around their town.

Derek – 2012 to 2014 - Ricky Gervais stars in this comedy about a good-hearted but slow nursing home care assistant.

Derry Girls – 2018 to present - This Northern Irish sitcom takes place in 1990s Derry, where a group of young women grow up during the Troubles.

Extras – 2005 to 2007 - Ricky Gervais (*The Office*) stars as an actor reduced to working as an extra, forever making himself look bad as he attempts to get ahead.

Flowers – 2016 to 2018 - Olivia Colman and Julian Barratt star in this dark comedy about a very troubled English family.

Hoff the Record – 2015 to 2016 - This David Hasselhoff mockumentary sees him attempting to make a comeback in the UK.

The Inbetweeners – 2008 to 2010 - A comedy that follows four friends as they navigate their final years of school and entrance into adulthood.

The IT Crowd – 2006 to 2013 - Banished to the basement, two nerds and their clueless leader service the IT needs of a strange and generic corporation.

Jack Whitehall at Large – 2017 - This hour-long comedy special features the standup work of comedian Jack Whitehall.

Jack Whitehall: Christmas With My Father – 2019 - This Christmas special sees Jack Whitehall NOT travelling with his father – instead, taking the stage in London's West End with a host of celebrity guests.

Jack Whitehall: I'm Only Joking - 2020 - Comedian Jack Whitehall talks about life in hotels, human stupidity, and of course, his father.

Jack Whitehall: Travels with My Father – 2017 to present - A man and his father have little in common, but they come together as they travel around the world.

James Acaster: Repertoire – 2018 - This collection features four performances from quirky comedian James Acaster.

Kath & Kim – *Australia* – 2002 to 2007 - A quirky mother and daughter pair lead an interesting life in the suburbs of Melbourne.

Kim's Convenience – *Canada* – 2016 to present - This sitcom focuses on a Korean family that runs a small convenience store in Toronto

The Letdown – *Australia* – 2019 - A new mum meets strange friends in a new parents support group.

Limmy's Show – 2012 - This Scottish sketch comedy show sees Brian Limond playing roles like a TV psychic and costumed adventurer.

Loaded – 2017 - After four friends sell their startup for $300 million, life gets a bit more difficult. This series is based on the popular Israeli series Mesudarim (which is often described as an Israeli version of Silicon Valley meets Entourage).

Man Down – 2013 to 2017 - Dan is a child trapped in a man's body, and he's not loving adulthood.

Man Like Mobeen – 2017 to present - In Small Heath, Birmingham, Mobeen tries to be a good Muslim and make sure his sister grows up on the straight and narrow, despite his past as a drug dealer.

Meet the Adebanjos – 2012 to present - In South London, a Nigerian father tries to teach traditional African values to his modern British family – with entertaining results.

Monty Python's Almost the Truth – 2009 - Though this is technically a documentary, it made sense to include it here alongside the other Monty Python titles.

Monty Python and the Holy Grail – 1975 - King Arthur and his knights seek the Holy Grail, but they're not very well-suited to the task.

Monty Python Before the Flying Circus – 2000 - This documentary takes a look at how six talented men became the groundbreaking troupe, Monty Python.

Monty Python Best Bits – 2014 - This series compiles clips + opinions from prominent comedians, many of whom considered Monty Python to be influential on their careers.

Monty Python Conquers America – 2008 - This documentary takes a look at how Monty Python shaped a number of American comedians.

Monty Python's Fliegender Zircus – 1972 - This collection of sketches was created for German television. A must-watch for serious Monty Python fans.

Monty Python's Flying Circus – 1969 to 1974 - The classic British sketch comedy is now streaming on Netflix.

Monty Python's Life of Brian – 1979 - More Monty Python fun revolving around a man who deals with a particularly nasty case of mistaken identity.

Monty Python Live at Aspen – 1998 - The men of Monty Python reunite to discuss the making of their iconic show.

Monty Python Live at the Hollywood Bowl – 1982 - Clips and animations feature in this live-to-tape performance of Monty Python's greatest hits.

Monty Python Live (Mostly): One Down, Five to Go – 2014 - Live from London in a sold-out final show, the remaining members of Monty Python reunited to reprise their old roles.

Monty Python's Personal Best – 2005 - Members of the Monty Python troupe select their favorite sketches.

Monty Python: The Meaning of Live – 2014 - After a lengthy hiatus, the Monty Python crew reunited for this live performance.

Mr. Young – *Canada* – 2013 - After graduating at 14, a gifted young man returns to his high school as a teacher.

Pacific Heat – *Australia* – 2016 - This animated series features an unintelligent covert squad that handles crime on Australia's Gold Coast.

People Just Do Nothing – 2014 to 2018 - This mockumentary follows some very bad wannabe MCs from West London.

Rita - *Denmark* - 2017 to present - Danish schoolteacher Rita may be popular with her students, but she struggles with adults.

Schitt's Creek – *Canada* – 2015 to 2020 - After a wealthy family loses everything, they attempt to rebuild in the small town they once bought their son as a birthday gift gag.

Sex Education – 2019 to present - Though technically British, there's something VERY American-feeling about this series. It's a series about a socially awkward teen whose mother is a sex therapist.

Shaun the Sheep: Adventures from Mossy Bottom - 2020 - This classic animated programme features clever sheep Shaun, Bitzer the dog, and his friends at Mossy Bottom.

Sick Note – 2018 - When an aimless young man is misdiagnosed with cancer, his life starts to get exciting.

Simon Amstell: Set Free – 2019 - If you enjoyed *Grandma's House*, you might like this standup set from comedian Simon Amstell (star and co-writer of the British comedy). He's an introspective comic, and this set dives into love, ego, intimacy, and ayahuasca.

Some Assembly Required – *Canada* – 2015 - A teenager takes over control of a toy company.

Still Game – 2002 to 2019 - Scottish comedy about three old men in a Glasgow highrise.

Sunny Bunnies - 2015 to present - These furry, colourful bunnies seek fun and mischief wherever they go in this children's series.

Toast of London – 2013 to 2015 - A classically trained British actor struggles with both his personal and professional lives.

Trailer Park Boys – Canada – 2001 to present - This trailer park comedy follows a group of men in constant pursuit of a big score and an easier life. See also: *The Movie, The Animated Series, Countdown to Liquor Day, Out of the Park: USA, Out of the Park: Europe, Say Goodnight to the Bad Guys*, and *Live in F**kin Dublin*.

Turn Up Charlie - 2019 - Idris Elba (*Luther*) stars as Charlie, a struggling DJ and confirmed bachelor. When he sees a possible upside for his career, he reluctantly agrees to play nanny to a good friend's dreadful young daughter. Piper Perabo (*Coyote Ugly*) stars as his famous friend Sara.

Scrotal Recall (aka Lovesick) – 2014 to 2018 - After finding out he has an STD, a young man must attempt to contact former lovers.

Sisters – Australia – 2018 - A young woman suddenly finds out she has two sisters and more than 100 brothers.

W1A – 2014 to 2017 - This mockumentary-style show follows the new head of values at the BBC. Hugh Bonneville (*Downton Abbey*) stars, and the series features numerous cameos.

White Gold – 2017 to 2019 - This period comedy takes place in 1980s Essex, where obnoxious salesman Vincent Swan and his team do whatever it takes to sell double-glazed windows.

The Windsors – 2016 to present - This mockumentary parodies the current British royal family.

Workin' Moms – Canada – 2017 to present - When their (remarkably long Canadian) maternity leaves are over, a group of moms return to work.

The Worst Witch – 2017 to present - This young adult comedy follows a bumbling young witch who accidentally stumbles into witching school.

Documentary & Lifestyle

100% Hotter – 2017 - A team of professional stylists come together to help some of Britain's worst fashion disasters.

21 Again - 2019 - A group of young women disguise their mothers as 21-year-olds and send them out into the wild.

3 Wives, One Husband – 2018 - Originally created for British audiences, this series takes a look at modern polygamist families in Utah.

Amazing Interiors – 2018 - This British show travels the world to visit eccentric homeowners and their eccentric homes.

Baby Ballroom – 2018 - This series goes deep into the cutthroat world of children's ballroom dancing (which we didn't realise existed).

Battlefield Recovery – 2016 - In this series, a four-man team visits Latvia and Poland to unearth World War II artifacts and help uncover new truths about the conflict.

Behind Enemy Lines – 2001 - This series takes a look at some of the changes Winston Churchill instituted after WWII setbacks in 1940. He set out to create a force powered by intelligence, stealth, and cunning more than ruthless brute force, and it paid off.

The Big Family Cooking Showdown – 2017 to present - This unscripted reality show brings us some of Britain's most passionate amateur cooks.

The Big Flower Fight – 2020 - This one is best described as "the Great British Bake Off meets the RHS Chelsea Flower Show".

Cabins in the Wild with Dick Strawbridge – 2017 - An engineer and craftsman tour a set of unique cabins in Wales, then build their own.

Caught on Camera – 2015 - This series shows crimes caught on CCTV and cell phones, and how technology is used to solve otherwise unsolvable cases.

Churchill's Secret Agents: The New Recruits - 2018 - This reality series takes 14 modern contestants through the same selection process used for World War II spies.

Click for Murder – 2017 - This docuseries takes a look at the deadly dangers that lurk within the bowels of the internet.

Cocaine – 2005 - This series takes a look at

the cocaine industry and its impact on people of all walks of life.

The Code – 2011 - Not to be confused with the fictional TV series, this three-part documentary looks at the mathematics behind all of life.

Conspiracies – 2015 - This series dives into a number of potential coverups and secrets.

Crazy Delicious - 2020 - This food competition show rewards talented home chefs with a golden apple.

Edge of the Universe – 2008 - Astronomers reveal the latest discoveries about the world beyond Earth's atmosphere.

Everyday Miracles – 2014 - Scientist Mark Miodownik highlights the everyday miracles that make modern life so much better than the not-so-distant past.

Genius of the Ancient World – 2015 - Historian Bettany Hughes travels the world to study the lives of philosophers like Socrates, Confucius, and Buddha.

Genius of the Modern World – 2016 - Historian Bettany Hughes looks at the world that helped shape intellectual greats like Friedrich Nietzsche, Sigmung Freud, and Karl Marx.

Glow Up – 2020 - This series aims to see who can take the sexiest selfie – and the loser gets a makeover.

Grand Designs – 1999 to present- This British reality show that follows people as they attempt to build or massively overhaul homes.

The Great British Baking Show – 2010 to present - This popular British baking show sees amateurs facing off and trying to avoid the dreaded soggy bottom.

The Great British Baking Show: The Beginnings - 2012 - A dozen amateur bakers compete on this early edition of the Great British Baking Show.

Greatest Events of WWII in Colour – 2019 - This series also takes a look at WWII footage that's been restored with colour.

History 101 – 2020 - This educational series offers short history lessons for those challenged in the "attention span" department – everything from fast food to plastics to the space race and the rise of China.

Hitler's Circle of Evil – 2017 - This docuseries takes a look at the power struggles, plots, and betrayals that took place behind the scenes within Nazi leadership.

How to Live Mortgage Free with Sarah Beeny – 2018 - Sarah Beeny talks to people who've managed to free themselves of a mortgage or monthly rental payment.

I Am a Killer – 2020 - This show goes to America, where capital punishment is still legal, and listen to the stories of Death Row inmates.

Inside the Freemasons – 2017 - This brief series takes a look inside the free and often controversial Freemasons.

Inside the Real Narcos – 2018 - Ex-Special Forces commando Jason Fox takes us inside the world of drug traffickers and cartel members.

Inside the World's Toughest Prisons – 2016 to present - Journalists put themselves inside – behind bars – in some of the world's roughest prisons.

Interior Design Masters – 2019 - Aspiring interior designers transform a variety of spaces in a competition to win a contract with a fashionable London hotel.

The Investigator: A British Crime Story – 2018 - This British true crime series features criminologist Mark Williams-Thomas as he examines unsolved murders.

The Irish Mob – *Ireland* – 2016 - This series focuses on the rise of the Irish Mob in America.

Killer Women with Piers Morgan – 2017 - Women commit just a tiny fraction of all murders, making female murderers a particularly interesting group for study. Who are they? Why do they do it? Piers Morgan takes a closer look.

Million Pound Menu – 2019 - Young restaurateurs open pop-up restaurants in hopes of attracting and impressing investors.

Murder Maps – 2017 - Dramatic reenactments of famous British murders.

My Hotter Half – 2017 - Couples compete to see which member of the pair can take the better selfie.

Nadiya's Time to Eat – 2020 - Nadiya Hussain shows how modern families can make great food with limited time.

Nurses Who Kill – 2016 - While nurses are an overwhelmingly good and compassionate group of people, a handful use their positions to hurt, rather than heal. This series takes a look at what motivates them.

Operation Ouch - 2012 - This entertaining series takes a lighthearted approach to educating children about doctor visits and medical procedures.

The Repair Shop – 2017 to present - This delightfully calm series follows a group of craftspeople who help restore objects of importance, many of them antique.

The Royal House of Windsor – 2017 - This docuseries analyzes the British royal family's ability to hold onto power over the last century of struggles and changes.

Secrets of Great British Castles – 2016 - Documentary-style program highlighting some of the largest and most historically-important castles around Great Britain (including Stirling, York, and Edinburgh, among others).

Serial Killer with Piers Morgan – 2018 - Piers Morgan takes a closer look at three convicted serial killers and their crimes.

Stunt Science – 2018 - This series looks at the science behind daredevil stunts.

Sunderland 'Til I Die – 2020 - This docuseries follows the Sunderland Association Football Club through the 2017-2018 season as they try to make a big comeback.

They've Gotta Have Us – 2018 - This series interviews black entertainers to trace the history of black cinema.

Win the Wilderness – 2020 - This reality show pits six couples against each other to see who has the best survival skills. The winning couple gets the deed to a home in the wilds of Alaska.

Witches: A Century of Murder – 2015 - Historian Suzannah Lipscomb looks at the British witch hunts of the 17th century.

The World's Most Extraordinary Homes – 2017 to present - Caroline Quentin (*Jonathan Creek*) and architect Piers Taylor travel the world to view extraordinary and unusual homes.

World War II in Colour – 2009 - In this 13-episode series, WWII footage is restored and given new life – in colour.

HULU

Website: http://hulu.com

Description: Hulu is a hybrid service that can offer both streamed television and live TV with the addition of a more expensive plan.

Available On: Roku, Fire TV, Apple TV, Apple iPhone & iPad, Chromecast, Fire Tablets, Playstation 3 & 4, Nintendo Switch, Samsung TV (select models), LG TVs (Select models) Android phones and tablets, and computer (via web browser).

Cost: $5.99/month or $59.99/year, No Ads - $11.99/month, + live TV $54.99/month

Now Streaming
Dramas

The Accident - 2019 - Sarah Lancashire (*Happy Valley*) stars as a hairdresser named Polly in this series about a small Welsh community torn apart by a terrible accident. The series takes us through the aftermath - families waiting for news, lives changed forever, and the search for someone to blame.

Agatha Christie's Marple – 2004 to 2013 - Hulu offers six seasons of the classic Agatha Christie sleuth.

Apple Tree Yard - 2017 – This miniseries is based on Louise Doughty's novel by the same name, and it's a suspenseful combination of sex and murder. When a woman gets an intriguing proposition, it excites her – until she realizes it may not be quite what it seemed. Emily Watson and Ben Chaplin star.

Atlantis – 2013 - A young man washes up on the shores of ancient Atlantis.

Banished – 2015 - British convicts are sent to Australian to pay for their crimes, and both they and the soldiers have a great deal of adapting to do.

Bedlam – 2011 to 2012 - When a haunted former asylum is turned into a high-end apartment building, it has unexpected consequences for the building's new tenants.

Being Erica – *Canada* – 2009 to 2011 - A young woman participates in a strange form of therapy that involves time travel.

Bleak House – 2005 - This classic BBC Dickens adaptation is based on the legal drama of the same name. The central story surrounds a person who left several versions of his will when he died.

Butterfly – 2018 - When a young boy named Max decides he would prefer to live as a girl named Maxine, his parents have to decide how to handle it.

City Homicide – *Australia* – 2007 to 2011 - In Melbourne, Australia, a group of homicide detectives work to find justice for victims of murder.

Clique - 2017 to 2019 - When two best friends go off to university in Edinburgh, it seems like everything will be amazing. When one of them is pulled into a clique of popular, powerful women, however, their university lives take a dark turn.

Coronation Street - 1960 to present - Running since 1960, and there are more than 9400 episodes of this daytime drama classic. The show is set in the fictional area of Wetherfield, where residents walk cobbled streets among terraced houses and the ever-present Rovers Return pub.

Criminal Justice – 2008 to 2009 - Each of the two seasons of this crime drama follow an accused criminal through the criminal justice system.

Daniel Deronda – 2002 - This adaptation of George Eliot's final novel focuses on a Victorian man torn between the love of two women.

David Copperfield – 1999 - Daniel Radcliffe (*Harry Potter*) stars as young David in this adaptation of the Dickens novel.

DCI Banks – 2010 to 2016 - Stephen Tomkinson (Ballykissangel, Wild at Heart) stars as DCI Alan Banks, a skilled but stubborn Yorkshire-based investigator.

The Fades – 2011 - A young man is haunted by dreams he can't explain, and he begins to see spirits around him – some of them malicious.

Hard Sun – 2018 - Two detectives work together to fight crime in a world that may be doomed anyway.

Harlots – 2007 to 2019 - In 18th century London, a brothel owner struggles to raise her daughters. The series was inspired by historian Hallie Rubenhold's book, *The Covent Garden Ladies*.

Harrow - *Australia* - 2018 to present - Welshman Ioan Gruffudd stars as Dr. Daniel Harrow, a forensic pathologist with authority issues. Still, his empathy for the dead makes him brilliant at what he does.

Hollyoaks - 1995 to present - This young adult soap opera is set in the fictional village of Hollyoaks, a suburb of Chester. As a youth-oriented programme, it frequently covers topics considered taboo.

In the Flesh – 2013 - After the government gets a handle on the recent zombie epidemic, they begin to rehabilitate zombies for re-entry into society. They aren't always warmly received.

Intruders – 2014 - John Simm (*Life on Mars*) stars as an ex-cop whose wife goes missing. The ensuing investigation leads him to Seattle, and a secret society dedicated to chasing immortality by hiding in the bodies of others. Based on Michael Marshall Smith's novel.

Jane Eyre – 2006 - This two-part adaptation of the classic Charlotte Bronte novel tells the story of a young woman who falls in love with the dark and brooding Mr. Rochester.

Killing Eve – 2018 to present - A bored but highly competent MI5 officer trades her life behind a desk to pursue an elusive and particularly aggressive female serial killer.

Lark Rise to Candleford - 2008 to 2011 - Set in the late 19th century in the small Oxfordshire hamlet of Lark Rise and the nearby market town of Candleford, this period drama follows a young woman who moves towns to work in a post office. The series is based on Flora Thompson's semi-autobiographical novels about living in the English countryside.

Legends - *United States* - 2014 to 2015 - Brit Sean Bean stars as deep cover operative Martin Odum, a man with an abnormally strong ability to change his identity as needed for the job at hand.

Line of Duty – 2012 to present - This suspenseful British police series is set in the fictional "anti-corruption unit" AC-12, where the police police the police. Yes, we know that sounds a bit odd. Lennie James, Vicky McClure, Martin Compston, and Adrian Dunbar all feature.

Lip Service – 2010 - This dramedy focuses on the romantic lives of lesbian women in the Scottish city of Glasgow.

Murdoch Mysteries - *Canada* - 2008 to present - Set in the 1890s, Murdoch uses early forensics to solve murders. Yannick Bisson stars as Detective William Murdoch, Helene Joy plays Dr. Julia Ogden, and Thomas Craig and Jonny Harris fill the roles of Inspector Thomas Brackenreid and Constable George Crabtree, respectively. Hulu has the first 10 seasons.

The Musketeers – 2014 to 2016 - This modern retelling of the classic Dumas novel includes appearances by Peter Capaldi, Tom Burke, and Rupert Everett.

My Mad Fat Diary – 2013 to 2015 - In 1990s Lincolnshire, a young woman grapples with depression and body image.

New Tricks – 2003 to 2015 - This long-running series focuses on a group of police who come out of retirement to work unsolved cases.

Normal People – *Ireland* – 2020 – This series follows a couple navigating their relationship after secondary school. Though from the same small Irish town, their different social classes cause friction.

Oliver Twist – 2007 - In this adaptation of the Dickens classic, we see appearances from Morven Christie, Tom Hardy, and Sarah Lancashire, among others. The story focuses on the difficult life of a young orphan after he's sold into an apprenticeship with an undertaker.

Paradox – 2009 - This sci-fi police drama focuses on a group of investigators who seek out evidence for crimes that haven't yet occurred.

Prey – 2014 to 2015 - Manchester detective Marcus Farrow (played by John Simm) is on the run, accused of a crime and desperate to prove his innocence. All the while, his former friends and colleagues do their best to hunt him down. This series reunites Philip Glenister and John Simm, who also appeared together in *Life on Mars*.

Pride & Prejudice – 1995 - Colin Firth and Jennifer Ehle star in this adaptation of the classic tale of Elizabeth Bennet and the snobbish but enticing Mr. Darcy.

Prime Suspect - 1991 to 2006 - Helen Mirren stars as Detective Jane Tennison, battling crime as well as sexism on the job.

Primeval – 2008 to 2011 - When strange things start happening around England, a professor and his team are forced to capture a variety of unusual creatures from other time periods. Includes Ben Miller (of *Death in Paradise*).

Run - 2013 - Olivia Colman and Lennie James star in this miniseries about four unconnected people whose lives intersect after a random act of violence.

Scott & Bailey - 2011 to 2016 - Two very different female police detectives enjoy a close friendship and good partnership.

The Secret of Crickley Hall – 2012 - Suranne Jones and Tom Ellis star in this supernatural miniseries about a family that relocates to a grand old estate up north after the disappearance of their young son.

Sense & Sensibility – 2008 - When a woman finds herself newly widowed and destitute with three unmarried daughters, she downsizes and attempts to find good husbands for them.

Silk – 2011 to 2014 - This series focuses on the challenges modern-day barristers face in their careers.

The Split - 2018 to 2020 - After a 30 year absence, a family of female lawyers has enough trouble dealing with their personal lives...and then their long-absent father returns.

Upstairs Downstairs - 2010 to 2012 - This series picks up the *Upstairs Downstairs* saga shortly after the period covered by the original series. Covering 1936 to 1939, it tells the story of the new owners of 165 Eaton Place, ending with the outbreak of World War II. Ed Stoppard (*Home Fires*) and Keeley Hawes (*Bodyguard*) play new owners Sir Hallam Holland and Lady Agnes Holland.

Whitechapel - 2009 to 2013 - An inspector, a detective sergeant, and a historical homicide expert look at crimes that may have connections to the Whitechapel district.

Comedies

Absolutely Fabulous - 1992 to 2012 - In this groundbreaking classic, two wild women do everything but act their age. The series was based on a sketch comedy called "Modern Mother and Daughter" by Dawn French (*Vicar of Dibley*) and Jennifer Saunders (Edina Monsoon in *Absolutely Fabulous*). Joanna Lumley stars alongside Saunders as Patsy Stone, and Julia Sawalha plays Edina's daughter Saffron.

The Aliens – 2016 - After aliens crash-land in the Irish Sea, they're allowed onto British soil but forced to live in a ghetto called Troy. Border guard Lewis helps to maintain the separation, but it becomes a tough position to hold when he learns he's half-alien.

Blackadder - 1983 to 1989 - Rowan Atkinson stars as antihero Edmund Blackadder, accompanied by Sir Tony Robinson as his sidekick Baldrick. Each series of this quirky comedy is set in a different period within British history, and Edmund carries different titles throughout. The "essence" of each character remains largely the same in each series, though.

Black Books – 2000 to 2004 - Bernard Black runs a bookshop, but he's not particularly good with customers.

Brassic - 2019 to present - This working-class comedy follows a young man named Vinnie (Joe Gilgun) and his occasionally criminal friends as they go about their lives in the northern English town of Hawley. It's a lively, rough-around-the-edges comedy about desperate small-town life and the ever-present question of whether there might be something better elsewhere. *Brassic* gets its name from Cockney rhyming slang. It's a shortening of "boracic lint", slang for "skint".

Coupling – 2000 to 2004 - Six young adults in London navigate the work, love, and the transition into responsible adulthood. Many have called this "the British Friends".

Dead Boss – 2012 - Helen Stephens has been wrongly convicted of killing her boss, and while she hopes she'll be cleared soon, everyone she knows wants her in prison.

Dirk Gently's Holistic Detective Agency – 2016 to 2017 - While this reinterpretation of the famous Douglas Adams detective is technically American, it's based on the work of a British author, so we'll include it. In this one, a holistic detective investigates cases involving the supernatural.

Doc Martin - 2004 to present - Martin Clunes (*Men Behaving Badly*) stars in this comedy about a brilliant but grumpy London surgeon who suddenly develops a fear of blood. He leaves his high-flying career and takes a post in a Cornish fishing village where he spent holidays as a child with his Aunt Joan. His bad attitude and lack of social skills makes it a challenge to adapt to his new life.

Dream Corp LLC – 2016 to present - Though this animated series is not strictly British, Brit Stephen Merchant plays a lead role as T.E.R.R.Y., and the series includes guest appearances from Liam Neeson, Toby Kebbell, and Rupert Friend. It's a workplace comedy that takes place in a dilapidated dream therapy centre in a strip mall. Patients come to have their dreams recorded, studied, and occasionally, adjusted. Darren Boyd (*The Salisbury Poisonings*) stars.

Gameface – 2014 to 2019 - A young woman navigates her 30s with the help of her friends, a questionable life coach, and her eternally patient driving instructor.

Getting On – 2009 to 2012 - This dark comedy follows the staff and residents in a geriatric ward.

Hang-Ups - 2018 - Stephen Mangan (*Dirk Gently*) stars as a therapist whose practice has collapsed, leaving him to conduct therapy sessions via webcam. Katherine Parkinson (*The IT Crowd*) also stars.

The Hitchhiker's Guide to the Galaxy - 1981 - Arthur Dent is one of the last surviving members of the human race. Still in his dressing gown, he's dragged through an intergalactic portal and sent on an adventure through the universe. The series is based on Douglas Adams' novel of the same name, and he adapted it.

Horrible Histories – 2009 to present - While designed for children, this amusing educational program is every bit as entertaining for adults. The sketches cover different parts of history, but always with a dramatic or funny take on the event.

Hunderby – 2012 to 2015 - Julia Davis stars in this dark period comedy about a woman who washes ashore after a shipwreck off the English coast.

Inside No. 9 - 2014 to 2020 - Dark humor, crime, drama, and horror are showcased in this anthology series. Every episode incorporates the number nine in some way, so keep an eye out as you watch.

The Kennedys – 2015 - Katherine Parkinson (*The IT Crowd*) stars in this comedy about a family moving from a housing estate to a home, eager to move up the social ladder.

Kingdom - 2007 to 2009 - Stephen Fry (*QI*) stars as a country solicitor in the small town of Market Shipborough. Working with his trusty secretary Gloria and reasonably capable assistant Lyle, it should be a peaceful life. The only problem? He has a crazy sister and he recently lost his half-brother in mysterious circumstances. Hermione Norris (*Cold Feet*) and Celia Imrie (*Bergerac*) also star.

Ladhood - 2019 to present - This coming-of-age sitcom takes a look at mischief and modern masculinity.

Maxxx – 2020 – Maxx is a has-been boy band star working on a comeback, but between the distractions in his life and his massive ego, he'll have some challenges.

The Mighty Boosh – 2003 to 2007 - Two young men work for a madman at a zoo.

Miranda – 2009 to 2013 - Miranda Hart stars as a lovably awkward woman who runs a joke shop with her best friend and specialises in getting herself into pickles.

Misfits – 2009 to 2013 - A group of young offenders develops superpowers when they're struck by lightning.

Moone Boy – 2012 to 2014 - A young boy copes with life in a small Irish town, thanks to his imaginary friend.

Mr. Bean - 1992 to 1995 - Bumbling Mr. Bean rarely speaks and has some very peculiar ways of doing things, but it usually works out for him. Rowan Atkinson (*Maigret*) stars as the iconic character.

The Office - 2001 to 2003 - Before there was Michael Scott in the US, there was David Brent in Slough, England. Written by Ricky Gervais (*After Life*) and Stephen Merchant (*Hello Ladies*), this mockumentary-style programme takes place in the office of the fictional Wernham Hogg paper company. Mackenzie Crook (*Detectorists*) and Martin Freeman (*Sherlock*) are also among the stars.

Outnumbered - 2007 to 2014 - Hugh Dennis and Claire Skinner star in this sitcom about a couple who are outnumbered by their three children.

Peep Show – 2003 to 2015 - Two dysfunctional and very different friends share a flat in London and attempt (rather poorly) to grow up.

Shameless - 2004 to 2013 - Before he created *No Offence*, Paul Abbott created Shameless - the story of a rough-around-the-edges family living in a Manchester housing estate. It was later adapted into an American series starring William H. Macy. This one contains some strong language and sexual content, so it's not for everyone.

Spaced – 1999 to 2001 - To get an affordable flat in North London, two young people pretend to be a couple. Simon Pegg (*Shaun of the Dead*) and Jessica Hynes (*There She Goes*) star.

Spy – 2011 to 2012 - When a man loses his self-esteem and the respect of his son, he has to take drastic action to get it back. He applies for a job as a civil servant, but accidentally ends up becoming a spy.

The Thick of It – 2005 to 2012 - This political satire takes place among the team at the Department of Social Affairs and Citizenship, where everything seems to be one giant farce.

This Way Up - 2019 - Aisling Bea (*Trollied, Finding Joy*) stars as Aine, a single Irish Catholic woman who has a nervous breakdown while living in London and teaching English as a second language. Sharon Horgan (*Catastophe*) co-produces and co-stars as Shona, her older sister.

Uncle - 2014 to 2017 - Nick Helm stars as Andy, a 30-something slacker who's left to care for his nephew in spite of the fact that he's utterly unsuited to the task.

Wasted – 2016 - In the fictional West Country village of Neston Berry, young slackers spend their days getting drunk and smoking marijuana at "Stoned Henge", a souvenir shop and tattoo parlour.

Whose Line Is It Anyway? – 1988 to 1999 - While the US has since made its own version, this is the original *Whose Line*, the show where four performers create characters, songs, and scenes on the spot based on prompts they receive from the host or audience.

The Wrong Mans – 2013 to 2014 - After a council worker answers a ringing phone at the site of a crash, he and an acquaintance in the same building become entangled in a web of crime and corruption. James Corden (*Gavin & Stacey*) and Mathew Baynton (*Horrible Histories*) star.

Documentary & Lifestyle

Gordon Ramsey's 24 Hours to Hell & Back – 2018 to present - In this series, Gordon Ramsay attempts to help failing restaurants in just 24 hours.

Gordon Ramsay's The F Word – 2005 to 2010 - Each episode of this cooking series features Gordon Ramsay preparing a meal for 50 guests at The F Word restaurant. In between, there are segments about cooking, farming, and various challenges with guests.

Gordon Ramsey's Ultimate Home Cooking – 2013 - This series helps people learn to cook simple, healthy, practical meals in their own home kitchens.

Hell's Kitchen – 2004 to 2009 - This series

pits prospective chefs against one another, with the winner getting a head chef position.

Jamie: Keep Cooking and Carry On – 2020 – Jamie Oliver shows recipes, tips, and tricks aimed at the unique times we live in. The recipes are prepared with limited ingredients and substitutions.

Jamie's Quick and Easy Food – 2017 to present - Chef Jamie Oliver shows off quick and easy recipes using just five ingredients.

Kitchen Nightmares - 2007 to 2014 - Acclaimed British chef Gordon Ramsay hosts this series in which he visits struggling American restaurants and spends a week trying to help them be more successful.

Love Island – 2015 to present - This reality series places singles on an island and eliminates contestants based on audience voting.

The Only Way is Essex – 2010 to present - This reality series follows a group of young and "socially ambitious" individuals living in Essex, a region often stereotyped as being similar to New Jersey in the United States.

Tea with the Dames - 2018 - Dames Maggie Smith, Judi Dench, Eileen Atkins, and Joan Plowright come together to share stories of their lives and careers.

Travel Man – 2015 to present - Richard Ayoade (*The IT Crowd*) takes 48 hour trips to various destinations, always bringing along a celebrity guest.

The Wine Show – 2016 to 2018 - In this reality series, actor Michael Goode travels around learning about wine, drinking wine, and generally celebrating the existence of wine.

SUNDANCE NOW

Website: http://sundancenow.com

Description: Sundance Now is a cousin to Acorn TV, and it has a broader focus. Their offerings include a good mix of international titles and indie productions. A number of the titles on Sundance Now are also on Acorn TV.

Available On: Roku, Amazon Fire TV, Apple TV, Apple iPhone & iPad, Android TV, Android phones and tablets, Google Chromecast, computer (via web browser). You can also subscribe via Amazon Prime Video.

Cost: $6.99/month, $59.99 billed yearly

Now Streaming

A Discovery of Witches – 2018 to present – When an Oxford historian and reluctant witch is able to access a book no one else can, it sets off a chain of events involving an eternal feud between witches and vampires.

Being Human - *Canada* - 2011 to 2014 - This is the North American adaptation of the British series about a set of supernatural roommates trying to keep their secrets and live normal lives.

Black Work – 2015 – Sheridan Smith (Gavin & Stacey) is crushed when her detective husband is killed in an abandoned warehouse, but when she learns he was working undercover at the time of his death, she starts to question everything she knew about him.

Born to Kill – 2017 – This miniseries follows Sam, a charismatic but sociopathic teenage boy on the verge of acting out his worst impulses.

Brief Encounters – 2016 – In the early 1980s, a group of British women shake things up in their community by becoming saleswomen for a company that specialises in "marital aids" and lingerie.

Britain's Bloodiest Dynasty - 2014 - Historian Dan Jones tells the story of the Plantagenets, one of Britain's darkest and most brutal dynasties.

Britain's Bloody Crown - 2016 - Dan Jones presents this four-part documentary about the War of the Roses.

Cheat - 2019 - When university lecturer Dr. Leah Dale confronts a student about suspected cheating, the student takes it as a personal attack. A simple academic issue soon spirals out of control, putting both women at risk. Katherine Kelly (*Happy Valley*) and Molly Windsor (*Three Girls*) star in this chilling psychological drama.

Close to the Enemy - 2016 - After WW2, a German engineer is taken to Britain in hopes of gaining his cooperation. Jim Sturgess (*Across the Universe*) and Charlotte Riley (*Press*) star.

The Crimson Petal and the White – 2011 – In late 1800s London, a prostitute finds her position greatly improved after becoming the mistress to a powerful man.

The Cry - *Australia* – 2018 – Jenna Coleman stars in this miniseries about a young couple dealing with the abduction of their baby.

Dead Lucky - *Australian* - 2018 – When a dangerous armed robber resurfaces in Sydney, two very different detectives are forced to work together to catch him.

The Fall - 2013 to 2016 - Gillian Anderson (*The X-Files*) and Jamie Dornan (*50 Shades of*

Grey) star in this series about a senior investigator who goes head-to-head with a serial killer who's attacking young professional women in Belfast.

Fingersmith – 2005 – In Victorian England, a young female thief hatches a plan to get close to an heiress and scam her. It doesn't go as planned.

Innocent – 2018 – Innocent is set around the beautiful southern coast of England, and it tells the story of a man rebuilding his life after his conviction for the murder of his wife is overturned.

Law & Order: UK – 2009 to 2014 – This popular procedural is adapted from the American series *Law & Order*. Though set within a different legal system, the basic formula is the same. In the first half of an episode, police investigate a crime. In the second half, prosecutors take the case to court.

Leverage - *United States* - 2008 to 2012 - This series follows a group of high-tech criminals who attempt to steal from wealthy people who don't deserve their money. Though it's American, it stars British actress Gina Bellman (*Coupling*). For a British series that's somewhat similar in tone, check out *Hustle*.

Liar – 2017 to 2020 – After a seemingly pleasant date, a schoolteacher accuses a prominent local surgeon of rape. The situation continues to spiral out of control as more information comes to light. The second series takes a different angle, but there's little we can say without it being a spoiler.

The Little Drummer Girl – 2018 – An English actress is recruited by the Israelis to help infiltrate a Palestinian assassin's terrorist cell.

Loch Ness - 2017 - Highlands Detective Annie Redford faces her first murder case when a human heart is found.

McMafia – 2018 to present - James Norton (*Grantchester*) stars as the English-raised son of a Russian mafia figure who was exiled from his country. Though his familiy tried to correct course, a murder draws them back in. A second series is on the way, though we've yet to see a date for it.

Midwinter of the Spirit – 2015 – This creepy drama follows a country vicar as she trains to be an exorcist for the Church of England. Before she's able to get much

experience, she finds herself faced with powerful supernatural threats.

Motherland – 2016 to present – Mums take on the challenges of middle-class motherhood, and it's not always pretty. This 30-minute comedy aims to show real motherhood, not the pretty and acceptable public idea of what motherhood should be.

Murder Trial: The Disappearance of Margaret Fleming - 2020 - Two carers were accused of murdering a 35-year-old woman and claiming benefits in her name for 16 years. This series takes a look at their trial.

The Name of the Rose - 2019 - In 1327, a friar and his apprentice investigate deaths at a nearby abbey. They soon find themselves mixed up in something much bigger than they might have imagined. Rupert Everett (*My Best Friend's Wedding*) and John Turturro (*Barton Fink*) star.

Next of Kin – 2018 – A GP is devastated after hearing her brother was kidnapped on his way home to the UK.

Penance - 2020 - After her son's death in Thailand, a woman begins having lusty thoughts about a young man she met in grief counseling (who just happens to look a lot like her dead son). Julie Graham (*Queens of Mystery*), Neil Morrissey (*Men Behaving Badly*), and Nico Mirallegro (*Hollyoaks*).

Raised by Wolves – 2015 – Six home-schooled siblings live with their survivalist mother, mostly isolated from the real world. This comedy follows the family as the children begin to come of age.

The Red Shadows - *France* – 2019 – In 1993, a five-year-old girl was kidnapped. 25 years later, her sister uncovers clues that suggest she may still be alive.

The Restaurant - *Sweden* – 2017 to 2018 – At the end of WWII, two strangers cross social classes with a kiss that has lasting repercussions. This series has been called a Swedish *Downton Abbey*.

Restless – 2012 – This two-part TV movie is based on a bestselling spy novel by William Boyd. It focuses on a young woman who finds out her mother was a spy for British intelligence during WWII, and that she's been on the run ever since.

Rillington Place – 2016 – This three-part miniseries is a dramatization of the murders at 10 Rillington Place in the 1940s and 50s.

Riviera – 2017 to present – Riviera is a UK production set in France. When a newlywed's wealthy husband is killed in an explosion, she's stunned to learn what lurked behind the facade of their upper class lifestyle.

Rosehaven - *Australia* – 2016 to present – In this half-hour comedy, a young man returns home to Tasmania to help his mother with her business.

Safe House – 2015 to 2017 – Christopher Eccleston (*Doctor Who*) stars in this series about a married couple asked to turn their guest house into a safe house.

Secret State – 2012 – In a miniseries that will reassure you that the US isn't the only place where government and big business are way too close, Secret State shows a Deputy Prime Minister entangled in an international conspiracy.

The Split – 2018 to 2020 - After a 30 year absence, a family of female lawyers has enough trouble dealing with their personal lives...and then their long-absent father returns.

State of the Union - 2019 - Chris O'Dowd (*The IT Crowd*) and Rosamund Pike (*Pride & Prejudice*) star in this short-form comedy about a couple that visits a pub each week before their marriage counseling session.

Stella Blomkvist - *Icelandic* – 2017 – A young and morally dubious lawyer takes on dangerous murder cases.

Straight Forward - *Denmark / New Zealand* - 2019 - After attempting to get revenge for her father's death, a Danish conwoman is forced to flee to New Zealand.

Striking Out - *Ireland* - 2017 - Amy Huberman (*Finding Joy*) stars as Tara Rafferty, a successful Dublin lawyer who abandons her safe life after discovering that her fiancé is cheating on her. She cancels the wedding, quits her job, and begins a new and unconventional private practice. Neil Morrissey (*Men Behaving Badly*) and Rory Keenan (*War & Peace*) also star.

Upright - *Australia* - 2020 - Comedian Tim Minchin stars in this series about two people trying to get an upright piano from one side of Australia to the other.

Wisting - *Norway* - 2019 – Norwegian detective William Wisting discovers a corpse at a Christmas tree farm that may be connected to an American serial killer. He may be living among them.

TUBI TV

Now Streaming
Mysteries & Crime Dramas

Blue Murder - 2003 to 2009 - Caroline Quentin (*Jonathan Creek*) stars in this series about a single mom struggling to raise four kids while also heading up a team of homicide detectives.

Cadfael - 1994 to 1998 - In 12th century Shrewsbury, a monk solves mysteries. Derek Jacobi (*Last Tango in Halifax*) stars.

Case Histories - 2011 to 2013 - Based on the Jackson Brodie novels by Kate Atkinson, this Edinburgh-based series features a tough guy PI with a heart of gold.

City Homicide – *Australia* – 2007 to 2011 - In Melbourne, Australia, a group of homicide detectives work to find justice for victims of murder.

Cracker – *United States* - 1997 to 1998 - While this is the US version, we're including it here because it's inspired by the original British show, *Cracker*. It's the story of an unlikeable, anti-social criminal psychologist who proves brilliant in assisting on tough cases.

Eternal Law – 2012 - In the lovely, historic city of York, a group of angels find themselves assisting in court cases. Though the premise is a bit silly,

remarkably few British television shows are set in the city of York, making it a

Exile – 2011 - John Simm (*Life on Mars*) stars in this mystery-thriller about a man who returns home after his life falls apart – only to find a different kind of trouble there.

The Fall - 2013 to 2016 - Gillian Anderson (*The X-Files*) and Jamie Dornan (*50 Shades of Grey*) star in this series about a senior investigator who goes head-to-head with a serial killer who's attacking young professional women in Belfast.

Gracepoint - *United States* - 2014 - This American *Broadchurch* adaptation sees David Tennant put on an American accent and return to the central role, this time as Detective Emmett Carver. It tells the story of a coastal California town turned upside-down when a young boy is found dead on the beach.

Hidden – 2011 - David Suchet (*Poirot*) and Philip Glenister (*Life on Mars*) star in this series about a London solicitor who's unwittingly drawn into the investigation of his own brother's murder and a political conspiracy. Not to be confused with the Welsh *Hidden* (aka *Craith*) on Acorn TV.

Hustle - 2004 to 2012 - Adrian Lester (*Bonekickers*), Robert Vaughn (*The Man from U.N.C.L.E.*), and Robert Glenister (*Paranoid*) star in this series about grifters who live by the motto, "you can't cheat an honest man". The specialise in long cons on the undeserving wealthy.

Kavanagh QC - 1995 to 2001 - John Thaw (*Inspector Morse*) stars as James Kavanagh QC, a barrister with a working-class background and a strong sense of right and wrong. It was one of Thaw's final roles before he died of cancer at the age of 60. Pay close attention to the guest stars in this one, as it's loaded with actors who went on to well-known roles, including Lesley Manville (*Mum*), Larry Lamb (*Gavin & Stacey*), Barry Jackson (*Midsomer Murders*), Phyllis Logan (*Downton Abbey*), Bill Night (*Love Actually*), and Julian Fellowes (*Downton Abbey*).

Leverage - *United States* - 2008 to 2012 - This series follows a group of high-tech criminals who attempt to steal from wealthy people who don't deserve their money. Though it's American, it stars British actress Gina Bellman (*Coupling*). For a British series that's somewhat similar in tone, check out *Hustle*.

Midsomer Murders - 1998 to present - In Midsomer County, the landscapes are beautiful, the villagers all have secrets, and murder is rampant. This British mystery classic features John Nettles as DCI Tom Barnaby through the first 13 seasons, with Neil Dudgeon as DCI John Barnaby for the later seasons.

The Saint - 1962 to 1969 - Roger Moore stars as Simon Templar, a wealthy adventurer who travels the world solving crimes and engaging in all manner of secret agent hijinks. Though the settings are occasionally exotic, nearly every episode was filmed at a studio in Hertfordshire using "blue-screen" technology. The series was based on the Simon Templar novels by Leslie Charteris.

Sherlock Holmes: The Classic Collection - 1942 to 1946 - This "series" is actually a collection of four performances by Basil Rathbone. Though the movies are old, many consider him to be the definitive Sherlock Holmes. Frequently typecast as a villain, Rathbone was excited to play Holmes, stating, "For once, I got to beat the bad guy instead of play him."

Ultimate Force - 2002 to 2007 - Ross Kemp (*EastEnders*) stars in this action series about a Special Air Service team that stops things like anthrax poisonings, assassinations, and bank sieges.

Vincent – 2005 to 2006 - Suranne Jones and Ray Winstone star in this series about an ex-cop turned PI who brings incredible skill and determination to his cases.

Trinity – 2009 - Convinced her father's death is somehow linked to prestigious Trinity College, Charlotte enrolls there to get to the bottom of the mystery. Charles Dance stars as Dr. Edmund Maltravers, and Antonia Bernath plays Charlotte.

Dramas

A Family At War - 1970 - In this classic family saga, we follow the daily life of the Ashtons, a working-class family in Liverpool during the time of WWII.

Being Human - 2008 to 2013 - Aidan Turner (*Poldark*) stars in this series about a werewolf, vampire, and ghost attempting to live together. This is not to be confused with the American version of the series that was made a few years later.

Brideshead Revisited - 1981 - Jeremy Irons and Anthony Andrews star in this adaptation of Evelyn Waugh's novel by the same name. *The Telegraph* awarded it the top position in its list of greatest television adaptations of all time.

Camelot - 2011 - This short-lived adventure series was created by Michael Hirst (*The Tudors*) and Chris Chibnall (*Broadchurch*), and it focuses on the period of time after King Uther's death when Merlin puts forth Arthur as the new king.

Camomile Lawn – 1991 - Felicity Kendal (*The Good Life*) and Jennifer Ehle (*Pride & Prejudice* '95) star in this series about a family spending the summer of 1939 together, just as World War II begins.

The Crimson Petal & the White – 2011 - A deeply indebted writer finds an escape from his everyday life in the arms of a prostitute named Sugar.

The Darling Buds of May - 1991 to 1993 -

Based on the 1958 H.E. Bates novel of the same name, this series is set in rural 1950s Kent and follows the Larkin family as they go about their daily lives. This early 90s dramedy was a breakout role for Welsh actress Catherine Zeta-Jones.

The Devil's Mistress – 2008 - This two-part series takes place against the backdrop of the English Civil War, following a young woman as she moves between poverty and power.

Heartbeat - 1992 to 2010 - This Yorkshire-based period crime drama ran for 18 seasons and 372 episodes, focusing on the lives of characters in a small village. Initially, it focused on a central couple, PC Nick Rowan and Dr. Kate Rowan, but as time went on, it branched out to include storylines all over the village. The series is based on the "*Constable*" novels written by Peter N. Walker under the pseudonym Nicholas Rhea.

Jason and the Argonauts - *United States* - 2000 - Though this was a Turkish-American co-production, you'll likely spot a number of familiar British faces in this adaptation of the classic mythological story of Jason and the Argonauts. Derek Jacobi (*Cadfael, Last Tango in Halifax*) stars alongside Angus Macfadyen (*Braveheart*), Ciarán Hinds (*Above Suspicion*), Adrian Lester (*Hustle*), and Olivia Williams (*Emma*).

Lip Service - 2010 to 2012 - This serial drama takes a look at the lives of a group of lesbian women living in Glasgow, Scotland.

Lost in Austen – 2008 - A bored young Pride and Prejudice fan is changed forever when Elizabeth Bennet stumbles into her modern bathroom. This miniseries includes Hugh Bonneville (*Downton Abbey*) as Mr. Bennet, Morven Christie (*Grantchester*) as Jane Bennet, and Jemima Rooper (*Gold Digger*) as lead Amanda Price.

McLeod's Daughters - 2002 to 2009 - Two sisters separated as children are reunited when they jointly inherit a ranch in the Australian bush: the ndependent Claire McLeod (Lisa Chappell, *Gloss*) and her estranged half-sister, Tess (Bridie Carter, *800 Words*), a stubborn city girl with a drive to change the world. Together, they build an all-female workforce and commit to life at Drovers Run. Nearby, the men of the Ryan family help keep things interesting.

Merlin - 2009 to 2013 - Colin Morgan (*The Fall*) stars as a young Merlin in his days as a mere servant to Prince Arthur of Camelot. In this version of Camelot, magic is banned and Merlin is forced to keep his talent hidden away.

Merlin's Apprentice - *United States/Canada* - 2005 - This miniseries is a follow-up to the 1998 NBC miniseries called *Merlin*, not the longer-running British TV show *Merlin*. The series features British actress Miranda Richardson (*Blackadder*) as The Lady of the Lake, and much of the rest of the cast is from the Commonwealth.

The Mill - 2013 to 2014 - This period drama is based on the real stories of textile mill workers in 1830s England. Set in Cheshire, it depicts the harsh realities of the Industrial Revolution.

Moll Flanders – 1996 - Daniel Craig stars in this miniseries adaptation of the classic Daniel Defoe novel.

Nero: The Obscure Face of Power - 2004 - John Simm (*Life on Mars*), Liz Smith (*Lark Rise to Candleford*), and Ian Richardson (*House of Cards*) are among the British actors that appear in this epic British-Italian miniseries about the Roman empire.

The Other Wife - 2012 - This two-part drama tells the story of a woman who finds out about her husband's secret life after he dies in a plane crash. Rupert Everett (*Parade's End*), John Hannah (*McCallum*), Natalia Wörner (*Berlin Station*), and Phyllida Law (*Kingdom*) star.

Our Girl - 2014 to present - This series follows a young woman from East London as she embarks on her career as an army medic. Lacey Turner (*EastEnders*) stars as Molly Dawes, with Michelle Keegan (*Brassic*) entering later as Georgie Lane.

Peak Practice - 1993 to 2002 - This drama takes place in and around a GP surgery in the fictional town of Cardale in Derbyshire's Peak District (mostly filmed in the real-life village of Crich, also in Derbyshire). The series was popular during its run, lasting for 12 series and 147 episodes. Fair warning, though: it ends on a cliffhanger. Cast members over the years included Kevin Whately (*Lewis*), Amanda Burton (*Silent Witness*), Clive Swift (*Keeping Up Appearances*), and Sarah Parish (*Bancroft*).

Prisoners' Wives - 2012 to 2013 - In South Yorkshire, four different women struggle to deal with life after men in their lives go to prison. Iain Glen (*Jack Taylor*) fans will be delighted to see him opposite Polly Walker (*Age Before Beauty*).

The Royal – 2003 to 2011 - This *Heartbeat* spinoff is set in the 1960s and focuses on an NHS hospital serving the seaside Yorkshire town of Elsinby.

Shameless - 2004 to 2013 - Before he created *No Offence*, Paul Abbott created Shameless - the story of a rough-around-the-edges family living in a Manchester housing estate. It was later adapted into an American series starring William H. Macy. This one contains some strong language and sexual content, so it's not for everyone.

Space: 1999 - 1975 to 1977 - This British-Italian sci-fi series begins when nuclear waste on the far side of the moon explodes, sending both it and its inhabitants out of orbit and into space. At the time it was produced, *Space: 1999* was the most expensive British television series ever produced. Married American actors Martin Landau and Barbara Bain starred.

Truckers - 2013 - Stephen Tompkinson (*DCI Banks*) stars in this drama about a group of truck drivers in Nottinghamshire.

Wild at Heart - 2006 to 2013 - Stephen Tompkinson (*DCI Banks*, *Ballykissangel*) stars in this series about a British veterinarian who takes his family along to South Africa to release an animal back into the wild. When he sees the area and meets pretty game reserve owner Caroline (Hayley Mills), he ultimately decides to stay.

Wolfblood - 2012 to 2017 - This British-German young adult series revolves around the lives of "wolfbloods", creatures that look like humans but have the ability to transform into wolves at will - and with the full moon. The series focuses on the challenges of growing up and the added difficulties of occasionally transforming.

Comedies

At Home With the Braithwaites - Amanda Redman (*Good Karma Hospital*) and Peter Davison (*Doctor Who*) star in this dramedy about a woman who wins the lottery and starts a charity with the winnings instead of telling her family.

At Last the 1948 Show – 1967 - This sketch series preceded *Monty Python's Flying Circus*, and included several cast members.

Black Books – 2000 to 2004 - Bernard Black runs a bookshop, but he's not really cut out for customer service. He spends most of his time having adventures with his employee and a nearby shopkeeper.

Blandings – 2013 to 2014 - This fun period comedy follows an eccentric aristocratic family and their crumbling ancestral home. It's based on the writings of PG Wodehouse, and stars Timothy Spall and Jennifer Saunders.

Bounty Hunters - 2017 - Rosie Perez and Jack Whitehall star in this comedy about an oddball partnership between a British man and a New York City bounty hunter.

Boy Meets Girl - 2009 - After a freak accident, a man and woman find themselves trapped in each other's bodies. Martin Freeman (*Sherlock*) and Rachael Stirling (*Detectorists*) star in this dramedy.

Bridget & Eamon – 2016 to 2019 - Bridget and Eamon are an Irish couple living with an unknown number of children in the Midlands in the 1980s.

Budgie - 1971 to 1972 - Pop star Adam Faith (*Love Hurts*) starred in this series about a recently released prisoner who alwyas manages to find trouble. The first four episodes were filmed in black and white due to the ITV Colour Strike of late 1970 to early 1971.

Carters Get Rich - 2017 - This British sitcom follows a family after their child develops an app and sells it for £10 million. James van der Beek (*Dawson's Creek*) appears as the wealthy CEO who buys the app and later tries to mentor the young programmer.

Clone – This 2008 British comedy includes Mark Gatiss (*Sherlock*) and focuses on the disastrous unveiling of the world's first human clone.

Count Arthur Strong – 2013 to 2017 - An aging, unemployed actor struggles to reconcile his real life with the inflated way he views himself. The series is based on the BBC Radio 4 programme Count Arthur Strong's Radio Show, but it picks up at a different phase of his life with a different cast of supporting characters.

Crims - 2015 - This sitcom follows two young men sent to a young offenders' institution after one got the other involved in a bank robbery without his knowledge.

Doc Martin - 2004 to present - Martin Clunes (*Men Behaving Badly*) stars in this comedy about a brilliant but grumpy London surgeon who suddenly develops a fear of blood. He leaves his high-flying career and takes a post in a Cornish fishing village where he spent holidays as a child with his Aunt Joan. His bad attitude and lack of social skills makes it a challenge to adapt to his new life.

Doctor at Large - 1971 - Bill Oddie, John Cleese, Graham Clapham, and a number of other British comedy greats were involved in the script for this short-lived series about a group of newly-qualified doctors heading to work. The first six episodes were filmed in black and white due to the ITV Colour Strike of late 1970 to early 1971.

Grafters - 1998 to 1999 - Robson Green (*Grantchester*) and Stephen Tompkinson (*Ballykissangel*) starred in this dramedy about two brothers who run a building company together and move to London to renovate a house.

Green Wing – 2004 to 2007 - This zany medical comedy features a largely incompetent staff that does very little actual medical work. Among the stars are Tamsin Greig (*Friday Night Dinner*), Mark Heap (*Friday Night Dinner*), Olivia Colman (*Broadchurch*), and Stephen Mangan (*Hang-Ups, Episodes*).

The Inbetweeners – 2008 to 2010 - This raunchy teen comedy focuses on a group of young men who aren't quite as cool as they'd like to be.

The Inbetweeners Movie - 2012 - Though not a TV series, this Is the natural sequel to the series, and it sees the gang together again on holiday.

London Irish – 2013 - This occasionally off-colour comedy focuses on a group of Northern Irish ex-pats in the city of London. The series was written by Lisa McGee, best known as the writer and creator of *Derry Girls*.

Lunch Monkeys – 2008 to 2011 - This workplace comedy focuses on the administrative support staff at a busy law firm.

Man Stroke Woman – 2005 to 2007 - This British sketch comedy includes appearances by Nick Frost, Daisy Haggard, Nick Burns, and Amanda Abbington.

Men Behaving Badly – 1992 to 2014 - Two young male flatmates act like...a couple of young male flatmates. The two explore adult life and love, frequently acting like cads. Stars Martin Clunes (*Doc Martin*), Neil Morrissey (*Unforgotten*), and Caroline Quentin (*Jonathan Creek*).

Monday Monday – 2009 - When a supermarket chain moves their head office to Leeds, it's a bit of adjustment for the staff.

Outnumbered - 2007 to 2014 - Hugh Dennis and Claire Skinner star in this sitcom about a couple who are outnumbered by their three children.

Parents - 2012 - Sally Phillips (*Miranda*) starred in this sitcom about a middle-class fortysomething woman who moves her family out of London to live with her parents in Kettering. Though well-reviewed, a second series was never made.

Peep Show – 2003 to 2015 - Two oddly-matched roommates get into all manner of trouble together as they try to navigate the basics of day-to-day adult life. Stars a young Olivia Colman alongside David Mitchell and Robert Webb.

Plus One – 2009 - A man attempts to find a date to an ex's wedding.

Sam's Game - 2001 - This short-lived comedy starred TV presenter Davina McCall as Sam, a single woman living in a London flat over a High Street shop. To help pay the rent, she illegally sublets to Alex (comedian Ed Byrne), an Irishman who seems to find no end of troubles.

Smack the Pony – 2003 - This British sketch comedy features an all-female cast, including Fiona Allen, Doon Mackichan, and Sally Phillips.

Spaced – 1999 to 2001 - When a young man and woman struggle to find affordable housing, they're tempted to lie.

Spy – 2011 to 2012 - When a man loses his self-esteem and the respect of his loved son, he has to take drastic action to get it back. He applies for a job as a civil servant, but accidentally applies to become a spy.

Teachers - 2001 to 2004 - This dramedy follows the teachers and students in one British school. Andrew Lincoln (*The Walking Dead*) stars, but it's also one of James Corden's earliest appearances. You'll also spot a young Shaun Evans (*Endeavour*) and Mathew Horne (*Gavin & Stacey*) in this series.

Vicious - 2013 to 2016 - Sir Ian McKellen and Sir Derek Jacobi star as an aging gay couple with a hilariously snarky love/hate relationship. The two live together in a Covent Garden flat, entertaining frequent guests, hoping for Freddie's big acting break, and checking to make sure their elderly dog is still alive.

White Van Men - 2011 - Will Mellor (*No Offence*) and Georgia Moffett (*The Bill*) are among the stars of this sitcom about a terribly incompetent handyman and his assistant.

The Young Person's Guide to Becoming a Rock Star - 1998 - A young Gerard Butler (*P.S. I Love You*) stars in this series about a young Glasgow band trying to get their big break.

Thriller & Horror

Chiller – 1995 - Martin Clunes and Nigel Havers star in this horror series about a group of friends who receive prophecies during a seance in the basement of a London cafe.

Hammer House of Horror – 1980 - This classic anthology series tells tales of mystery, suspense, and horror.

Thriller – 1973 to 1976 - This long-running 1970s anthology series includes a few supernatural tales, but mostly a lot of suspense and mystery. It also includes a surprising number of American guest stars.

Tales of the Unexpected – 1979 to 1988 - This anthology series features terrifying tales and a variety of well-known Brits, including Roald Dahl and Timothy West (*Great Canal Journeys*).

The House that Dripped Blood – 1971 - This anthology series tells stories about a haunted home in the UK. Christopher Lee and Peter Cushing are featured.

The Prisoner – 1967 to 1968 - After his resignation, a secret agent wakes up to find himself stuck in a strange coastal prison known as The Village. They want information he's not prepared to share, and he makes numerous attempts to escape. The series is set in the Welsh village of Portmeirion, the lovely but unusual creation of Sir Clough Williams-Ellis.

Secret Agent – 1960 to 1968 - Patrick McGoohan stars as John Drake, an M9 agent who specialises in handling subversive elements that threaten world peace. Though he travels the world on his adventures, the first episode takes him to the Welsh seaside resort village of Portmeirion (where he would later set *The Prisoner*).

Documentary & Lifestyle

Aerial Britain - 2019 - Enjoy aerial scenery from England, Scotland, and Wales. Each episode has a theme - stately homes, work and industry, and spiritual locations.

Animal 24/7 - 2006 - This fly-on-the-wall docuseries shows us what it's like to do animal rescue work in Britain.

Animal Madhouse - 2010 - In the Warwickshire countryside, there's a clinic that helps animals of all types and sizes. This series is similar to Yorkshire Vet, but a bit wilder.

Animal Rescue School - 2018 - Follow Royal Society for the Prevention of Cruelty to Animals candidates as they progress through the grueling 10 month training process.

At Your Service – 2016 - This documentary series takes a look at people who specialise in the lost art of service and hospitality. Though it's set in Ireland, it's part of the British Isles – so we're including it.

Auction - 2015 - This series travels the world, looking at some of the most impressive items up for auction. Episodes feature everything from pop art in New York to the letters of Winston Churchill and a clear-out at Chatsworth.

The Auction House - 2014 - This series goes behind the scenes at Lots Road Auctions in London, where the hardworking staff does their best to find unusual items for wealthy clients. *Endeavour* fans will recognise Roger Allam's voice doing the narration.

A Very British Sex Shop - 2019 - Get a look behind the scenes of a family-run sex shop empire in Brighton, England.

Baby Beauty Queens - 2009 - This series follows three young girls, aged seven through nine, as they enter Britain's very first pre-teen beauty pageant.

Booze Britain – 2004 - In this series, the cameras follow hard-drinking Brits in a variety of locations, including Newcastle and Isle of Man.

Boozed Up Brits Abroad – In mainland Europe, British tourists have something of a reputation for being drunk and disorderly. This series follows a number of British tourists as they set out on vacations and stag parties.

The Bridal Coach – A former model and current bridal coach helps British brides-to-be as they prepare for the big day.

Designer Darlings – This series follows the Bassi family as they run a business selling expensive clothing to parents who don't mind spending a fortune to keep their kids looking fashionable.

Discovering the World - 2019 - London-based Belgian journalist Pierre Brouwers travels the world, going beyond the typical tourist attractions. Though the British Isles don't factor in too heavily, one episode does visit Scotland.

The Dog Rescuers – 2017 - Alan Davies (*Jonathan Creek, QI*) appears in this series about dog rescues around the UK.

Edwardian Farm - 2010 - In this series, the creators of *Victorian Farm* turn their attention to the Edwardian period, looking at the way farming life looked a little more than 100 years ago.

Emergency Firefighters – 2005 - This series takes a look at the intense, demanding situations encountered by the Avon Fire and Rescue Service.

Fat Men Can't Hunt - 2008 - Four overweight British men and women are taken to the African desert to try out the hunter-gatherer diet.

The Farmer's Country Showdown - 2016 - This celebration of rural Britain shows off farming families and the events that show off their hard work.

The French Collection - 2016 - British bargain hunters cross the channel to scour French antique markets for bargains.

Get a Life – This series aims to help people with basic life skills like confidence, flirting, style, and courage.

Girlfri3nds - 2012 - Three single British women live together while searching for Mr. Right.

Give a Pet a Home – Amanda Holden (Wild at Heart) stars in this series about celebrities and animal adoption in the UK.

Grime Fighters – 2009 - This series looks at the people who clean up some of the UK's most disgusting messes.

Hidden Europe - 2002 - British zoologist Bobbie Fletcher travels Europe in search of overlooked places and rare animals.

The Hotel - 2011 - This hilarious docu-series follows overconfident hotelier Mark Jenkins as he attempts to work in a variety of hotel settings. Hugh Bonneville (*Downtown Abbey*) narrates series two through four.

Husbands from Hell - 2019 - Marrying a British man isn't all charming accents and afternoon teas. This series takes a look at some of the worst husbands in the nation.

The Irish Pub – 2013 - This documentary explores the history of pubs in Ireland.

The Kangaroo Gang – 2014 - This two-part documentary tells the story of brazen Australian thieves who moved to London and pulled off a number of high-profile, daring heists.

Ladette to Lady – 2008 - This series follows a group of young women as they attend a finishing school to teach them proper etiquette, deportment, and elocution.

Laura McKenzie's Traveler - *United States* - 2002 - Though not a British series, this one features three episodes set in the British Isles - London, Dublin, and Edinburgh.

Lily Allen: From Riches to Rags - 2011 - This documentary series follows early-2000s pop singer Lily Allen as she and her sister launch a fashion line.

Killer Roads - 2011 - The UK has a number of dangerous roads that host more than their fair share of devastating accidents.

Made Over By - 2016 - This series sees experts transforming some of the UK's most fashion-challenged residents.

Make Me Perfect - 2006 - This series uses

major cosmetic intervention (including surgery) to help people feel better about their looks and get over past trauma.

Married to a Celebrity – 2017 - This series takes a look at the worst things about being married to a celebrity.

Masterpiece - 2018 - Alan Titchmarsh stars in this series about antiques enthusiasts separating trash from treasure.

My Pet Shame - 2010 - Joanna Page of Gavin & Stacey presents this series about Britain's most embarrassing pet problems.

No Ordinary Party – 2011 - This series takes a look at incredible and extreme parties in the UK – including a puppy party, a naturist party, and a festish party in Edinburgh.

Older Than Ireland – 2015 - This series interviews 30 Irish centenarians to build a living history of modern-day Ireland.

The Only Way is Essex - 2010 to present - Proof that British TV isn't all thoughtful dramas and intelligent mysteries, this reality series follows a group of wild young people living in Essex.

Oxford Street Revealed - 2017 - This series takes a closer look at one of the UK's most famous streets.

Park Life: London – 2016 - This program takes a look at London's Hyde Park through the seasons.

Personal Services Required – 2007 - Two well-off families seek someone to manage their households.

Quizeum - 2018 - Griff Rhys Jones stars in this quiz show set at some of the most remarkable museums in Britain.

Retail Therapy – 2011 - This series follows Brits who need serious help as they embark on a shopping excursion.

Salt Beef and Rye – 2016 - This fun documentary looks at the characters who frequent London's Brick Lane.

Secrets of the Stones – 2018 - This two-part series dives into the history and archaeology of Ireland.

The Shelbourne Hotel – 2017 - This reality series takes a look at what goes on behind the scenes of an upscale hotel.

Small Animal Hospital - 2014 - This series follows the action at the Small Animal Hospital at the University of Glasgow.

Snowdonia 1890 - 2010 - Two families live as though they were 19th century farmers on Mount Snowdonia in Wales.

Spendaholics - 2005 - This show follows a variety of Brits with major spending problems and the debt to match.

Thelma's Big Irish Communions – 2015 - A dressmaker explores the world of Irish Catholic Holy Communion celebrations – and the dresses that go along with it.

Time Team – 1994 to 2014 - A group of archaeologists visits different excavation sites. Amazon currently offers Set 20 of this long-running British series. If you like that one, you can go here for more.

Tower Block Kids – 2017 - In an attempt to house their poor, the UK built more than 4000 bleak tower blocks. This is the two-part story of kids growing up in those buildings.

Trouble in Poundland – 2017 - The modern economy challenges businesses of all types, and this series looks at what Poundland is doing to survive.

Tudor Monastery Farm at Christmas - 2013 - This fascinating series takes a look at Christmas celebrations as they would have been practiced on rural farms in Tudor England during the 15th century.

Very British Problems – 2016 - This hilarious series takes a look at what it means to be British.

Victorian Farm - 2009 - On the Acton Scott Estate in rural Shropshire, things continue as they might have been more than 100 years ago.

Victorian Farm: Christmas Special - 2009 - This series shows us how the Victorians changed the way we celebrate Christmas.

Walks With My Dog - 2017 - British celebrities like John Nettles and Robert Lindsay explore the countryside with their dogs.

Wedding SOS - 2008 - A top British wedding planner helps couples whose weddings seem doomed.

Wild Animal Rescue - 2016 - This series follows animal rescue missions to some of the wildest places on the planet.

The Yorkshire Vet - 2015 to present - This engaging series follows the staff of Skeldale Veterinary Centre as they work with the animals.

Medical, Police, & Rescue

24 Hours in Police Custody - 2014 - This long-running docuseries goes behind the scenes at the Luton Police Station.

999 What's Your Emergency? - 2012 - Take a look at what goes on behind the scenes when you dial 999 (the "British 911").

Air Ambulance ER - 2014 - When terrain and road access make it hard for regular ambulances to reach an area quickly, air ambulance teams step in.

Ambulance – 2016 - This series follows the London Ambulance Service as they struggle to prioritize resources for those who need them most.

An Hour to Save Your Life - 2015 - Talented British doctors make life-or-death choices in the first hour of emergency care.

Baby Baby – 1997 - This documentary series follows couples as they bring multiples into the world.

Baby Hospital – 2005 - This British reality series takes a look at growing families in a variety of different situations.

Cars, Cops, & Criminals - 2008 - The Association of Vehicle Crime Intelligence Service fights vehicle-related crimes.

Children's Hospital - 1993 - The Royal Manchester Children's Hospital opens its doors to let viewers see the challenging work they do.

Extreme A&E – 2012 - This graphic series follows top paramedics as they deal with major emergencies around the world - including an episode in London.

Helicopter ER - 2017 - This series follows the doctors and paramedics of the Yorkshire Air Ambulance.

Helicopter Search & Rescue - *Ireland* - 2018 - If you've ever wondered what goes on behind the scenes of Ireland's key rescue agencies, you'll want to check out this series that takes a peek at the work being done by the Irish Coast Guard, Cork Fire Brigade, the RNLI, the Irish Naval Services, and mountain rescue teams.

Inside the Ambulance - 2016 - This series goes behind the scenes with a West Midlands ambulance crew.

Kids on the Edge – 2015 - This three-part series takes a look at families involved with the Tavistock Gender Identity Development Service, the NHS's gender identity clinic for children with gender dysphoria.

Nursing the Nation – 2013 - This series follows district nurses around the UK, taking a look at their day-to-day lives.

One Born Every Minute UK – 2010 to present - This series follows families as their children are born.

One Born Every Minute UK: What Happened Next? – 2011 - This series follows up with families from *One Born Every Minute*, seeing how life is going for them after the birth of their children.

Secret Eaters - 2012 - Anna Richardson visits households around the UK to help people learn why they're gaining weight.

Street Hospital – 2013 - This series follows paramedics as they deal with some of the wildest emergencies the UK has to offer – stag parties gone wrong, births in nightclub basements, and so, so many drunks.

Supersized Hospitals – 2010 - This two-part series takes a look at the opening of the New South Glasgow Hospital, the largest medical campus in Western Europe.

Trauma Rescue Squad - 2017 - Britain's toughest medics are ready to go when the worst disasters strike.

Food & Cookery

Catherine's Family Kitchen - 2018 - Chef Catherine Fulvio celebrates Irish cooking.

Celebrity Restaurant in Our Living Room - 2010 - Two celebrity couples turn their homes into restaurants to see who can create the best dining experience.

Chef's Protégé - 2014 - This BBC2 series follows three Michelin star chefs as they return to their old schools and choose protégés to train.

Cook Yourself Thin UK - 2007 - This series focuses on helping Brits lose weight by transforming unhealthy dishes.

Choccywoccydoodah - 2011 - This now-defunct Brighton bakery was once famous for its quirky cakes and celebrity clients.

Comfort Eating - 2017 - Comedian Nick Helm goes on the road seeking out Britain's best comfort foods in Islington, Camden, Leeds, Brighton, Berlin, St. Albans, Paris, Little Europe, Peckham, Essex, Soho, Wales, Notting Hill, Glasgow, and Borough Market.

Hairy Bikers: Pubs that Built Britain – 2016 - David and Si travel around Britain, visiting the island's best pubs.

Hell's Kitchen – 2004 to 2009 - This series pits prospective chefs against one another, with the winner getting a head chef position.

Home of the Fabulous Cakes - 2009 - British pastry chef Fiona Cairns invites viewers to learn her best baking secrets.

How to Cook Well With Rory O'Connell - 2018 - The famed Irish chef and instructor teaches classic cooking techniques.

James & Thom's Pizza Pilgrimage – 2017 - James and Thom travel around Italy to learn about pizza, and even sell a bit of it on the street in London.

James Martin's United Cakes of America – 2012 - British chef James Martin travels the United States in search of cake.

James Martin's Mediterranean – 2011 - James Martin shows off what might be the best job in the world as he sails around the Mediterranean and eats...a lot.

James Martin Home Comforts – 2015 - James Martin tackles cool weather comfort foods – including jacket potatoes and Toad in the Hole.

Kitchen Nightmares - 2007 to 2014 - Acclaimed British chef Gordon Ramsay hosts this series in which he visits struggling American restaurants and spends a week trying to help them be more successful.

Mary Berry's Absolute Favourites - 2014 to 2015 - Britain's favourite home cook shares some of her favourite recipes from a lifetime of cooking.

Mary Berry's Foolproof Cooking – 2015 - Mary Berry offers tips and demonstrations for simple, foodproof recipes.

Modern Irish Food - *Ireland* - 2013 - Award-winning chef Kevin Dundon demonstrates traditional Irish dishes with modern twists.

My Life on a Plate – 2014 - A variety of notable Brits like Mary Berry and Nigel Havers take a look back at their lives and the foods that accompanied them.

Nigel Slater Eating Together – 2014 - Nigel Slater explores modern British home cooking with basics like noodles, soup, custard, and hotpots.

Rachel Allen Home Cooking - *Ireland* - Irish chef Rachel Allen goes into the home kitchens of well-known chefs to see how they operate when they're at home.

Rachel Allen's Dinner Parties - *Ireland* - 2010 - Chef Rachel Allen shows viewers how to throw the perfect dinner party.

Remarkable Places to Eat - 2018 - Top chefs in England walk us through some of the best dining experiences in the world, visiting Venice, Edinburgh, Paris, and San Sebastian.

Restaurant in Our Living Room – 2010 - In each episode, two couples turn their homes into restaurants and compete for the best takings.

Scotch! The Story of Whisky – 2015 - This short series takes a look at the history and science of the Scottish whisky industry.

The Story of Tea: The History of Tea & How to Make the Perfect Cup – 2007 - This documentary offers a look at the history and enduring appeal of tea.

Home & Garden

Art Deco Icons: Britain's Bling and Glamour – 2009 - Designer and lecturer David Heathcote visits four Art Deco icons around Great Britain – Claridge's, the London Transport HQ, Casa Del Rio (an art deco home in Devon), and The Orient Express (as it leaves Victoria Station for Venice).

Best Laid Plans – 2017 - Charlie helps couples tackle major home renovations around the UK.

Brand New House on a Budget - 2014 - This show features home makeovers on a budget.

Brick by Brick: Rebuilding Our Past – 2011 - Dan Cruickshank and Charlie Luxton follow along with the reconstruction of historic British buildings.

Build a New Life in the Country – 2005 to 2010 - This series follows families as they relocate to the countryside and build new lives.

Build a New Life in the Country Revisits – 2007 - This programme is a follow-up to the last entry on this list, revisiting families who have relocated to the British countryside.

Dermot Bannon's Incredible Homes - *Ireland* - 2018 - Renowned Irish architect Dermot Bannon explores some of the most incredible homes in the world, visiting Sydney, Melbourne, Sweden, London, New York, and Los Angeles.

Design Doctors – 2018 - British couples get design help in this reality series.

Double Your House for Half the Money - 2012 - British families see their homes transformed.

First Homes – This series focuses on first-time homebuyers around the UK, with locations including Glasgow, Chester, and Northampton.

Getting the Builders In – 2017 - In this series, teams of builders pitch to win a variety of construction and renovation jobs.

Grand Designs – 1999 to present - Kevin McCloud follows people as they attempt to build or restore their dream homes. Projects featured on *Grand Designs* are notoriously ambitious.

Greatest Gardens - 2017 - Diarmuid Gavin and Helen Dillonare look for the best private gardens in Northern Ireland.

Home of the Year: Ireland - *Ireland* - 2018 - This series travels around Ireland to look at the unique ways people have made their houses into homes.

Homes By Design - *Canada* - 2007 - This show takes a look at extraordinary homes around North America and Europe, including some properties in England and Scotland.

Honey, I Bought the House – 2014 - Couples hunting for a home allow one members of the couple to make the final property decision.

The House that 100k (GBP) Built – 2016 - Homes are expensive in the UK, but this series takes a look at people building homes from scratch – and on a budget.

The House that 100k Built: Tricks of the Trade – 2015 - This series takes a look at some of the low-cost building and renovation methods used to create really amazing spaces on a budget.

Location, Location, Location - 2000 to present - This popular, long-running British house-hunting show has hosts Kirstie Allsopp and Phil Spencer helping guests find the right house in the right location.

Make My Home Bigger – 2015 - Jonnie Irwin follows along as people seek to enlarge their homes.

Millionaire Basement Wars – 2015 - In the increasingly crowded and expensive City of London, many homeowners are building down rather than up. The construction of large and eloborate basements is both noisy and time consuming, making life miserable for neighbours.

Million Pound Properties - 2018 - This series takes a look at what you can get with a million pounds or more around the UK. From tiny London apartments to enormous Scottish castles, the value of a pound differs greatly from one market to another.

My Flat Pack Home - 2010 to 2012 - This British series takes a look at unusual prefab homes and the people who buy them.

Nick Knowles: Original Home Restoration – 2014 - This series follows families as they renovate their historic homes.

Restoration Home – 2010 - Actress Caroline Quentin (*Jonathan Creek, Blue Murder*) hosts this series about restoring neglected historic homes around Britain.

Project Restoration – 2016 - Historical building surveyor Marianne Suhr travels the UK helping out on challenging restoration projects.

Restoration Man – 2014 - Architect George Clarke helps people all over the UK as they take on ambitious renovations and transformations of unique and historic spaces.

Restoration Man Best Builds – 2014 - George Clarke looks at a number of his favourite dramatic building transformations, including old churches, industrial conversions, and towers – including one in the Outer Hebrides islands of Scotland.

Room to Improve – *Ireland* - 2007 to present - This Ireland-based series follows a variety of housing situations, including people seeking to downsize, upsize, and renovate.

To Build or Not to Build - 2013 - This series follows people who've decided to build their own homes, watching as they learn the necessary skills and battle with their local councils to get the proper permissions.

Unreal Estate - *Australia* - 2015 - This series takes a look at some of the most incredible and over-the-top homes in Australia, along with the extravagant folks who live in them.

What the Neighbours Did – This show follows Brits as they renovate spaces in their homes.

Young, Rich, and Househunting – 2010 - This house hunting show focuses exclusively on young buyers at the upper end of the British home market. These lucky buyers are largely financed by relatives.

PLUTO

Website: http://pluto.tv

Description: Pluto is another ad-supported streaming service, but they also offer the option to watch some shows through their "live" streaming. The major downside to Pluto is that they don't have a search function.

Available On: Roku, Fire TV, Apple TV, Apple iPhone & iPad, Chromecast, Android phones and tablets, and computer (via web browser).

Cost: Free with ads

Now Streaming

999 What's Your Emergency? - 2012 - Take a look at what goes on behind the scenes when you dial 999 (the British equivalent of 911).

Ambassadors - 2013 - David Mitchell and Robert Webb (both of *Peep Show*) star in this series about employees at the British embassy in the fictional Asian country of Tazbekistan.

Ancient Egypt - Life and Death in the Valley of the Kings - 2013 - This documentary tells the story of the everyday lives of ancient Egyptians.

Anna Karenina - 1978 - Nicola Pagett (*Upstairs Downstairs*) stars as Anna Karenina in this retelling of Tolstoy's classic tale of family passions in 1870s Russia.

Antiques Roadshow - 1979 to present - Filmed at a variety of stately homes around the country, this series allows members of the public to bring in cherished items for expert appraisal.

Arabian Nights - 2000 - This British-American co-production covers several of the stories from *One Thousand and One Nights*. The cast includes Jim Carter (*Downton Abbey*) and Rufus Sewell (*The Pale Horse*), among others.

Archangel - 2006 - Daniel Craig stars as a middle-aged former Oxford historian whose studies in a Moscow Library lead him into the middle of a dark and dramatic plot. This series was produced by the BBC and also includes Gabriel Macht of *Suits*.

Bedlam – 2011 to 2012 - When a haunted former asylum is turned into a high-end apartment building, it has unexpected consequences for the building's new tenants.

Being Human - 2008 to 2013 - Aidan Turner (*Poldark*) stars in this series about a werewolf, vampire, and ghost attempting to live together. This is not to be confused with the American version of the series that was made a few years later.

Big School - 2013 to 2014 - A new French teacher arrives at Greybridge School and gives the long-time Deputy Head of Science second thoughts about resigning.

Black Harbour - *Canada* - 1997 to 1998- When her mother gets ill, Katherine and her husband Nick give up their prestigious careers in Los Angeles to move back home to Nova Scotia.

Blood Ties - *Canada* - 2007 - When a Toronto detective begins losing her eyesight, she becomes a PI and teams up with a 470-year-old vampire (also the illegitimate son of Henry VIII). The series is based on Tanya Huff's *Blood* novels.

Bluestone 42 - 2013 to 2015 - This dark comedy follows the lives of British soldiers working in a bomb disposal detachment in Afghanistan.

Bomb Girls - *Canada* - 2012 to 2013 - Set during World War II, BOMB GIRLS tells the stories of women who risked their lives in factories to make bombs for the Allied Forces. The series stars Meg Tilly (*The Big Chill*), Jodi Balfour (*Quarry*), Charlotte Hegele (*When Calls The Heart*) and Ali Liebert (*Ten Days in the Valley*).

Brick by Brick: Rebuilding Our Past – 2011 - Dan Cruickshank and Charlie Luxton follow along with the reconstruction of historic British buildings.

Britain's Best Bakery - 2012 to 2014 - Experts travel Great Britain in search of the best independent bakeries.

Bromwell High - 2005 - This animated comedy follows a group of naughty schoolgirls at an under-funded South London secondary school.

The Cars That Made Britain Great - 2016 - Celebrity car lovers walk us through some of their favourite British vehicles.

The Case - 2011 - This legal drama tells the story of a man put on trial for the murder of his terminally ill partner after he helped her commit suicide.

Case Histories - 2011 to 2013 - Based on the Jackson Brodie novels by Kate Atkinson, this Edinburgh-based series features a tough guy PI with a heart of gold.

Celtic Britain - 2000 - This docuseries takes a look at Celtic history in Scotland, Wales, and elsewhere in the British Isles.

Code 9 - 2008 - This *Spooks* (*MI-5*) spin-off takes place after a 2012 terrorist attack on London, and it sees young MI-5 officers trying to make Britain feel safe again. Georgia Tennant and Joanne Froggatt star.

Conviction: Murder at the Station - 2016 - This two-part series takes a look at the work of a British charity which investigates miscarriages of justice.

Conviction: Murder in Suburbia - 2018 - This true-crime documentary takes another look at the evidence that brought about the murder conviction of Glyn Razzell in 2003.

Cop Car Workshop - 2018 - This unusual documentary takes a look at the work being done at one of Britain's police car workshops.

Critical - 2015 - This medical drama is set in a fictional major trauma center.

Dead Man's Shoes - 2004 - Paddy Considine (*Peaky Blinders*) stars in this miniseries about a soldier looking for revenge on thugs who targeted his mentally-challenged brother.

The Deep - 2010 - James Nesbitt (*Cold Feet*) and Minnie Driver (*Good Will Hunting*) star in this series about oceanographers who become stranded in the Arctic while looking for new forms of life.

Desperate Romantics – 2009 - In 1851 London, a group of artists lead colorful lives amidst the chaos of the Industrial Revolution.

The Devil's Mistress, aka The Devil's Whore – 2008 - This two-part series takes place against the backdrop of the English Civil War, following a young woman as she moves between poverty and power.

The Diplomat - 2009 - This two-part television miniseries follows a British diplomat who's been arrested on charges of working with the Russian mafia. Richard Roxburgh (*Rake*) and Claire Forlani (*Meet Joe Black*) are among the stars.

Doc Martin - 2004 to present - Martin Clunes (*Men Behaving Badly*) stars in this comedy about a brilliant but grumpy London surgeon who suddenly develops a fear of blood. He leaves his high-flying career and takes a post in a Cornish fishing village where he spent holidays as a child with his Aunt Joan. His bad attitude and lack of social skills makes it challenging.

The Dog Rescuers – 2017 - Alan Davies (*Jonathan Creek, QI*) appears in this series about dog rescues around the UK.

Drifters – 2013 to 2016 - Meg, Bunny, and Laura share a flat in Leeds and face the ups and downs of post-university life.

Extreme Ghost Stories - 2006 - This British reality series investigates hauntings.

The Fades – 2011 - A young man is haunted by dreams he can't explain, and he begins to see spirits around him – some of them malicious.

Father Ted - 1995 to 1998 - Father Ted lives with two other very strange priests on the not-so-quiet Craggy Island in Ireland.

The Field of Blood - 2011 to 2013 - Set in early 1980s Glasgow, a young woman solves murders on a squad full of men.

Unfortunately, her dedication to the truth also puts her in danger. The series stars Jayd Johnson (*River City*) as Paddy Meehan, working alongside Peter Capaldi (*Doctor Who*) and David Morrissey (*The Missing*).

Fifth Gear - 2002 to present - This series talks cars, offering reviews, close-up looks, and industry information.

Fight Club: A History of Violence - 2017 - This series takes a look at fighting throughout British history.

Forensic Investigators - *Australia* - 2004 to 2006 - This reality series focuses on real Australian crimes and the hard work that goes into solving them.

Frankie - 2013 - Eve Myles (*Keeping Faith*) stars as the head nurse on a traveling nursing team.

Fred Dinenage Murder Casebook – 2010 to 2013 - Fred Dinenage takes a modern forensic look at various murders that shocked the UK over the 20th century.

Gangsters: Faces of the Underworld - 2009 - This true-crime series takes a look at some of the world's most notorious gangsters.

Getting On - 2009 to 2012 - This dark comedy follows the residents and staff in a geriatric ward.

Ghost Chasers - 2016 - Paranormal investigators visit some of Europe's most haunted locations.

The Ghost Squad - 2005 - Similar to *Line of Duty*, this series follows an Internal Affairs division designed to help find and fix corruption within the police. Elaine Cassidy (*No Offence*) stars.

Gordon Behind Bars, aka Ramsay Behind Bars - 2012 - Gordon Ramsay goes behind bars to help a group of prisoners start a bakery.

Great Interior Design Challenge - 2014 to 2017 - Amateur designers attempt to transform inside spaces.

Him & Her - 2010 to 2013 - This sitcom follows a twenty-something working-class couple. The series portrays the couple with a brutal honesty that can make it a bit uncomfortable to watch, particularly if you don't like swearing or adult situations.

Hyperdrive - 2006 to 2007 - This sci-fi comedy follows a group of astronauts tasked with getting businesses to relocate to Britain.

The Incredible Journey of Mary Bryant - 2007 - After stealing a woman's picnic, starving Mary Broad is convicted to death. Before realizing that fate, however, she's granted mercy and allowed to live in a penal colony in New South Wales, Australia.

Inside Men - 2012 - This miniseries tells the story of three employees who plan and execute a major heist.

The Irish Mob – *Ireland* – 2016 - This series focuses on the rise of the Irish Mob in America.

Jamie and Jimmy's Food Fight Club - 2012 - Jamie Oliver and Jimmy Doherty open a pop-up restaurant.

Jonathan Creek - 1997 to 2016 - After meeting a pushy investigative journalist, an eccentric magic trick developer finds himself investigating murders.

K-9 - 2009 - This *Doctor Who* spin-off follows the robot dog companion K-9.

Lip Service – 2010 - This dramedy focuses on the romantic lives of lesbian women in the Scottish city of Glasgow.

Little Dorrit – 2008 - Claire Foy and Matthew Macfayden star in this adaptation of Dickens' story of struggle in 1820s London.

Love London - 2015 - Guided by a London taxi driver, you'll follow a young Londoner trying to learn more about her city.

Man Stroke Woman - 2005 to 2007 - This sketch comedy series features a variety of well-known British actors including Amanda Abbington, Daisy Haggard, and Nick Frost.

McLeod's Daughters - 2002 to 2009 - Two sisters separated as children are reunited when they jointly inherit a ranch in the Australian bush: the independent Claire McLeod (Lisa Chappell, *Gloss*) and her estranged half-sister, Tess (Bridie Carter, *800 Words*), a stubborn city girl with a drive to change the world. Together, they build an all-female workforce and commit to life at Drovers Run. Nearby, the men of the Ryan family help keep things interesting.

Meet the Romans - 2012 - British historian Mary Beard takes us along on a deep dive into what life was like during the Roman Empire.

Merlin - 2009 to 2013 - Colin Morgan (*The

Fall) stars as a young Merlin in his days as a mere servant to Prince Arthur of Camelot. In this version of Camelot, magic is banned and Merlin is forced to keep his talent hidden away.

Midsomer Murders - 1998 to present - In Midsomer County, the landscapes are beautiful, the villagers all have secrets, and murder is rampant. This British mystery classic features John Nettles as DCI Tom Barnaby through the first 13 seasons, with Neil Dudgeon as DCI John Barnaby for the later seasons.

Moby Dick - 1998 - Sir Patrick Stewart stars as Captain Ahab in this adaptation of Herman Melville's novel.

Most Haunted - 2002 to present - Yvette Fielding leads this paranormal investigation series that primarily focuses on the UK and Ireland.

Mr. Bean - 1992 to 1995 - Bumbling Mr. Bean rarely speaks and has some very peculiar ways of doing things, but it usually works out for him. Rowan Atkinson (*Maigret*) stars as the iconic British character.

My Kitchen Rules, aka MKR + UK - 2017 - This British cookery show looks for the UK's top home cooks.

The New Tomorrow - *New Zealand* - 2005 - After a virus kills all the adults, kids are left to take care of themselves.

One Born Every Minute UK – 2010 to present - This series follows families as their children are born.

The Only Way is Essex - 2010 to present - Proof that British TV isn't all thoughtful dramas and intelligent mysteries, this reality series follows a group of wild young people living in Essex.

The Palace – 2008 - A fictional British royal family deals with all manner of upper class problems.

Paradox – 2009 - This sci-fi police drama focuses on a group of investigators who seek out evidence for crimes that haven't yet occurred.

Peak Practice - 1993 to 2002 - This drama takes place in and around a GP surgery in the fictional town of Cardale in Derbyshire's Peak District (mostly filmed in the real-life village of Crich, also in Derbyshire). The series was popular during its run, lasting for 12 series and 147 episodes. Fair

warning, though: it ends on a cliffhanger. Cast members over the years included Kevin Whately (*Lewis*), Amanda Burton (*Silent Witness*), Clive Swift (*Keeping Up Appearances*), and Sarah Parish (*Bancroft*).

Pete vs. Life - 2010 to 2011 - Journalist Pete is a pretty normal guy, except that he's constantly observed and analysed by a couple of sports commentators.

Plus One - 2009 - When a man is invited to his ex-girlfriend's wedding to a pop star, he needs a plus one. Miranda Raison (*Silks*) and Daniel Mays (*Good Omens*) star.

Primeval – 2008 to 2011 - When strange things start happening around England, a professor and his team are forced to capture a variety of unusual creatures from other time periods. Includes Ben Miller (of *Death in Paradise*).

The Prisoner –1967 - Patrick McGoohan stars in this surprisingly well-aged series about a secret agent who's abducted and taken to a mysterious prison dressed up as an idyllic seaside village.

Prison: First and Last 24 Hours - This docuseries follows convicted criminals on their first and last days in Scottish prisons.

Rachel Allen: Easy Meals - 2011 - Irish chef Rachel Allen focuses on meals anyone can replicate in their homes.

Rachel Allen's Cake Diaries - 2012 - Chef Rachel Allen offers tips for cakes of all types.

Ramsay's Best Restaurant - 2010 - Gordon Ramsey sorts through 12,000 public nominations for the best restaurant in England and then takes a closer look at the final 16 to see which are best.

Restoration Home – 2010 - Actress Caroline Quentin (*Jonathan Creek, Blue Murder*) hosts this series about restoring neglected historic homes around Britain.

Richard Hammond's Engineering Connections - 2011 - *Top Gear* presenter Richard Hammond looks at the engineering behind the world's most advanced structures. From the tallest hotel to a Formula 1 car to space shuttles and earthquake-proof bridges, he makes engineering feel accessible and exciting.

Richard Wilson On the Road - 2014 - Richard Wilson (*One Foot in the Grave*) takes a trip around Britain with only his antique Shell travel guides to help him.

Robin Hood – 2006 - After fighting in the Crusades, Robin Hood returns home to find a corrupt, changed Nottingham.

Rome: Empire Without Limit - 2016 - Professor Mary Beard offers her take on the Roman Empire.

Rovers – 2016 - This working class comedy centers around the people who spend time at the Redbridge Rovers Football Club.

The Shadow Line - 2011 - DI Jonah Gabriel returns to work after a near fatal return, quickly finding himself going deep into the dangerous world of drug dealing.

Shameless - 2004 to 2013 - Before he created *No Offence*, Paul Abbott created *Shameless* - the story of a rough-around-the-edges family living in a Manchester housing estate. Contains some strong language and sexual content.

The Silence – 2010 - While struggling to integrate into the hearing world, a young girl with a new cochlear implant witnesses the murder of a police officer. Douglas Henshall (*Shetland*) stars.

Simply Nigella - 2015 - Nigella Lawson teaches viewers how to prepare quick, simple comfort food dishes.

Speed with Guy Martin - 2013 to 2016 - Motorcycle racer Guy Martin performs a variety of speed challenges.

The Suspicions of Mr. Whicher: Beyond the Pale - 2014 - Whicher is hired to investigate threats made to the son of an important government employee, leading him to some of the most dangerous parts of Victorian London. Paddy Considine (*Informer*) stars.

The Suspicions of Mr. Whicher: The Murder at Road Hill House - 2011 - Based on Kate Summerscale's best-selling novel, this series sees DI Whicher pursuing the murderer of a three-year-old boy. Paddy Considine (*Informer*) stars.

The Suspicions of Mr. Whicher: The Murder in Angel Lane - 2013 - Whicher investigates the death of a young girl, pitting him against some of London's wealthiest and most powerful individuals. Paddy Considine (*Informer*) stars.

The Suspicions of Mr. Whicher: The Ties That Bind - 2014 - This entry sees Whicher taking on what appears to be a simple infidelity case, but it soon turns much darker. Paddy Considine (*Informer*) stars.

Terrahawks - 1983 to 1986 - This series follows the missions of a space defense group tasked with protecting Earth from Martians.

Terry Jones' Great Map Mystery – 2008 - *Monty Python* star Terry Jones travels around Britain to see if it's still possible to follow the earliest roadmaps of Wales.

Terry Pratchett's Hogfather – 2006 - The Hogfather has gone missing on Hogswatch, and Death must take his place.

To the Ends of the Earth – 2005 - This BBC series is based on William Golding's novels of a sea journey to Australia from England in 1812-13. Benedict Cumberbatch (*Sherlock*) stars.

Travel Man – 2015 to present - Richard Ayoade (*The IT Crowd*) takes 48 hour trips to various destinations, always bringing along a celebrity guest.

Treasure Island - 2012 - Eddie Izzard stars as Long John Silver in this retelling of the classic Robert Louis Stevenson story.

Truckers - 2013 - Stephen Tompkinson (*DCI Banks*) stars in this drama about a group of truck drivers in Nottinghamshire.

Ultimate Force - 2002 to 2007 - Ross Kemp (*EastEnders*) stars in this action series about a Special Air Service team that stops things like anthrax poisonings, assassinations, and bank sieges.

Wild at Heart - 2006 to 2013 - Stephen Tompkinson (*DCI Banks*, *Ballykissangel*) stars in this series about a British veterinarian who takes his family to South Africa to release an animal. When he sees the area and meets pretty game reserve owner Caroline (Hayley Mills), he decides to stay.

Wired – 2008 - Jodie Whittaker stars in this suspenseful London-based thriller about a young woman whose high-profile promotion carries unexpected costs. She's quickly pushed into a criminal underworld she had no desire to be a part of.

Wolfblood - 2013 - Wolfblood teenagers have a number of heightened abilities, but their powers also bring danger and a need for secrecy.

Young Dracula - 2006 to 2014 - Count Dracula is a single father, and he's moved his kids Vlad and Ingrid to modern-day Britain. Now, little Vlad wants nothing more than to be a normal British kid and fit in with his friends.

IMDB TV

Website: https://www.imdb.com/tv/

Description: IMDb TV is a free, ad-supported streaming service that offers a variety of programming from the US and abroad. Though most of their shows are older, they will be premiering the new *Alex Rider* series later this year.

Available On: Roku, Amazon Fire TV, Apple TV, Apple iPhone & iPad, Android TV, Android phones and tablets, Google Chromecast, computer (via web browser). You can also watch via Amazon Prime Video.

Cost: Free with ads

Now Streaming

Air Ambulance ER - 2014 - When terrain and road access make it hard for regular ambulances to reach an area quickly, air ambulance teams step in.

Animal Park - 2000 to 2018 - Presenters Ben Fogle and Kate Humble go behind the scenes at Longleat Estate and Safari Park in Wiltshire, telling the stories of the people and animals who make the park and home so unique.

Archangel - 2006 - Daniel Craig stars as a middle-aged former Oxford historian whose studies in a Moscow Library lead him into the middle of a dark and dramatic plot. This series was produced by the BBC and also includes Gabriel Macht of *Suits* fame.

The Ballymurphy Precedent - 2018 - In August 1971, 10 apparently innocent Catholics were killed in Northern Ireland by an elite British Parachute Regiment. Officially, the British army claimed (and continues to claim) they were armed terrorists.

Banged Up - 2008 - This docuseries follows a unique experiment fronted by British Home Secretary the Rt. Hon David Blunkett. For 10 days, the empty Scarborough Prison is re-opened to take in a group of out of control teenagers.

Battle of Kings: Bannockburn - 2014 - King Robert the Bruce's campaign against King Edward II of England culminated in the Battle of Bannockburn in 1314. This docudrama tells the story.

Black Harbour - *Canada* - 1997 to 1998- When her mother gets ill, Katherine and her husband Nick give up their prestigious careers in Los Angeles to move back home to Nova Scotia.

Blue Murder - 2003 to 2009 - DCI Janine Lewis struggles with the challenge of being a single mom to four kids while leading a team of detectives through homicide investigations. Caroline Quentin (*Jonathan Creek*) stars.

Britain's Best Bakery - 2012 to 2014 - Experts travel Great Britain in search of the best independent bakeries.

Case Histories - 2011 to 2013 - Based on the *Jackson Brodie* novels by Kate Atkinson, this Edinburgh-based series features a tough guy PI with a heart of gold.

City Homicide – *Australia* – 2007 to 2011 - In Melbourne, Australia, a group of homicide detectives work to find justice for victims of murder.

Classic Mary Berry - 2018 - In this series, famed British chef Mary Berry travels around England, cooking dishes inspired by the various locales she visits. This includes ethnically-diverse South London, the classic British countryside, and even Port Isaac on the Cornish coast (aka Portwenn from *Doc Martin*).

The Colour of Magic - 2009 - This series is based on the *Discworld* series of novels by Terry Pratchett, and features Sean Astin as tourist Twoflower alongside Sir David Jason as wizard Rincewind. When a fire breaks out during Twoflower's holiday, the two flee the city together, beginning an interesting magical journey.

The Crest - 2019 - Two cousins meet for the first time in Ireland to celebrate their shared heritage and love of surfing.

Diana: The New Evidence - 2017 - This documentary takes a look at new evidence in the case of Lady Diana's death.

Edward and Mrs. Simpson - 1978 - This seven-part series is a dramatisation of the events surrounding the abdication of King Edward VIII.

England's Forgotten Queen: The Life and Death of Lady Jane Grey - 2018 - Historian Helen Castor guides us through this documentary series about Lady Jane Grey, the young woman who served as first reigning queen of England. Though she had a reputation as one of the most learned young women of her time, her reign would last just nine days and end in tragedy.

Escape to the Country – 2002 to present - Each episode follows a different set of homebuyers looking to leave crowded areas and find new homes in the British countryside.

Enid Blyton Adventure Series – *UK/New Zealand* – 1996 - This series sees a group of kids on adventures in New Zealand, and it's based on Enid Blyton's novels.

Enid Blyton Secret Series – *UK/New Zealand* – 1997 - This fanciful young adult series is based on author Enid Blyton's much-loved *Secret* novels, and it's a follow-up to the Adventure Series.

Eternal Law - 2012 - In *Eternal Law*, angels live among us and help humans when they're at their most desperate – in this case, the angels are lawyers in the lovely and historic city of York.

The Fenn Street Gang – 1971 to 1973 - This spin-off of *Please Sir!* follows the students after they leave school.

George III: The Genius of the Mad King - 2017 - This documentary takes a look at the newly-unlocked personal papers and documents of King George III.

The Grand - 1997 to 1998 - This period drama was written by Russell T Davies (*Doctor Who*) and takes place in 1920s Manchester. It follows the Bannerman family as they re-open The Grand after WWI.

Grand Designs – 1999 to present - Kevin McCloud follows people as they attempt to build their dream homes.

The Great Hip Hop Hoax - 2013 - This documentary tells the story of two Scottish students who faked American accents and identities in pursuit of rap careers in California.

Heartbeat - 1992 to 2010 - This Yorkshire-based period crime drama ran for 18 seasons and 372 episodes, focusing on the lives of characters in a small village. Initially, it focused on a central couple, PC Nick Rowan and Dr. Kate Rowan, but as time went on, it branched out to include storylines all over the village. The series is based on the "*Constable*" novels written by Peter N. Walker under the pseudonym Nicholas Rhea.

Home of Fabulous Cakes - 2013 - In this brief series, Leicestershire baker Fiona Cairns shares some of her top cake baking secrets. Royal fans will likely remember Ms. Cairns as the creator of the lovely eight-tiered cake for the wedding of the Duke and Duchess of Cambridge back in 2011. She doesn't attempt anything quite so massive in this series, opting instead for practical tips any baker can put to use in their own confections.

Idris Elba: King of Speed - 2013 - Idris Elba explores the world's greatest raceways, contemplating the question of why we're so obsessed with speed. In his quest, he travels from London to America to Finland.

Imagine a School: Summerhill - 2008 - Summerhill is a "free school" in England where students do as they please so long as they aren't hurting anyone else. Not surprisingly, the school has had some issues with the government. This documentary takes a look at their battle.

The Incredible Journey of Mary Bryant - 2007 - After stealing a woman's picnic, starving Mary Broad is convicted to death. Before realizing that fate, however, she's granted mercy and allowed to live out her life on a penal colony in New South Wales, Australia.

Inside the Crown: Secrets of the Royals - 2020 - This documentary pairs archived film, historical documents, and eyewitness interviews to offer new insights into Queen Elizabeth II's life.

It Came From Connemara - 2017 - In the mid 1990s, legendary Hollywood producer Roger Corman decided to open a production studio in Ireland. In the following years, he would make numerous feature films using an Irish crew (and a fair bit of funding from the Irish government). This documentary looks at Corman's work in Ireland.

The Joy of Techs - 2017 - A technophobe and a technophile join forces to test some of the world's top gadgets. Rather than simply grabbing an iPhone and reviewing it, they put the products into taxing real world situations. They attempt to destroy indestructible gadgets, navigate the French Alps, survive off the grid, and romance women, among other things.

Kitchen Nightmares - 2007 to 2014 - Acclaimed British chef Gordon Ramsay hosts this series in which he visits struggling American restaurants and spends a week trying to help them be more successful.

Legends - *United States* - 2014 to 2015 - Brit Sean Bean stars as deep cover operative Martin Odum, a man with an abnormally strong ability to change his identity as needed for the job at hand.

Lily Allen: From Riches to Rags - 2011 - This documentary series follows early-2000s pop singer Lily Allen as she and her sister launch a fashion line in London.

Living the Tradition: An Enchanting Journey into Old Irish Airs - 2017 - This documentary takes the viewer on a journey into the world of traditional Irish music.

London's Burning - 1988 to 2002 - This series about a London fire brigade began as a TV movie and evolved into a long-running drama series.

The Man Who Cracked the Nazi Code - 2018 - This documentary celebrates the awkward but brilliant man, Alan Turing, whose work helped to make the D-Day landings possible.

The Man Who Killed Richard III – 2015 -

This documentary attempts to prove that King Richard III was killed by Welshman Sir Rhys ap Thomas of Carew Castle in Pembrokeshire. Richard III's death paved the way for the Tudor monarchy, thus giving Britain its current queen. Many believe we owe ap Thomas a debt of gratitude for that reason, and though a strong case can be made, it's impossible to be 100% certain he was the one who committed the act of regicide.

Martin Clunes: A Man and His Dogs - 2010 - Martin Clunes takes a closer look at how and why we've decided to share our lives and homes with dogs.

McLeod's Daughters - 2002 to 2009 - Two sisters separated as children are reunited when they jointly inherit a ranch in the Australian bush: the ndependent Claire McLeod (Lisa Chappell, *Gloss*) and her estranged half-sister, Tess (Bridie Carter, *800 Words*), a stubborn city girl with a drive to change the world. Together, they build an all-female workforce and commit to life at Drovers Run. Nearby, the men of the Ryan family help keep things interesting.

Men Behaving Badly – 1992 to 2014 - Two young male flatmates act like...a couple of young male flatmates. The two explore adult life and love, frequently acting like cads. Stars Martin Clunes (*Doc Martin*), Neil Morrisey (*Line of Duty*), and Caroline Quentin (*Jonathan Creek*).

Midsomer Murders - 1998 to present - In Midsomer County, the landscapes are beautiful, the villagers all have secrets, and murder is rampant. This British mystery classic features John Nettles as DCI Tom Barnaby through the first 13 seasons, with Neil Dudgeon as DCI John Barnaby for the later seasons.

Miranda – 2009 to 2013 - Miranda Hart stars as a lovably awkward woman who runs a joke shop and seems to specialize in getting herself into pickles.

Missing Persons Unit - *Australia* - 2006 to 2009 - This series uses footage captured over months of investigative work to show what happens when someone goes missing.

Monroe - 2011 to 2012 - James Nesbitt stars in this medical drama about a brilliant but quirky neurosurgeon and the talented doctors who work with him.

Mummy's Little Murderer - 2013 - This true crime documentary tells the story of

Elliot Turner, a boy whose mother helped him cover it up when he murdered his girlfriend.

Murder, She Wrote - *United States* - 1984 to 1996 - British-born Angela Lansbury stars in this classic series about a novelist who seems to encounter murder everywhere she goes.

The New Tomorrow - *New Zealand* - 2005 - After a virus kills all the adults, kids are left to take care of themselves.

Nothing Trivial – *New Zealand* – 2011 to 2014 - For one group of thirtysomething friends, a weekly trivia night is the only thing that's constant in their lives.

Older Than Ireland – 2015 - This series interviews 30 Irish centenarians to build a living history of modern-day Ireland.

One Night Stand with Anne Sibonney - *Canada* - 2014 - This Canadian food and travel series includes an episode in Glasgow.

On the Yorkshire Buses - 2014 - Buses make up roughly two-thirds of all public transport usage in the UK today, but what's it like to be one of the legion of bus drivers who keep Britain moving? This series follows a number of bus drivers over the course of the summer holiday season in Yorkshire. This is not to be confused with *All Aboard!*, the series that takes you through scenic journeys, including one bus ride through the Yorkshire Dales (on BritBox).

Outrageous Fortune – *New Zealand* – 2005 to 2010 - A trashy family of criminals tries to clean up their act.

The Queen at 90 - 2016 - Featuring interviews with family members and those close to Queen Elizabeth II, this documentary takes a look back at her first 90 years.

The Real Middle Earth - 2007 - Sir Ian Holm narrates this look at the buildings and places that helped shape J.R.R. Tolkien's Middle Earth.

Restoration Home – 2010 - Actress Caroline Quentin (*Jonathan Creek, Blue Murder*) hosts this series about restoring neglected historic homes around Britain.

Richard Hammond's Engineering Connections - 2011 - *Top Gear* presenter Richard Hammond goes on a quest to discover engineering connections behind

some of the most advanced structures in the world. From the world's tallest hotel to a Formula 1 car to space shuttles and earthquake-proof bridges, he makes engineering feel accessible and exciting.

Ross Kemp: Back on the Frontline - 2011 - Actor Ross Kemp returns to Afghanistan in 2011 to find out how things have changed since 2001 and 9/11

Ross Kemp: Return to Afghanistan - 2009 - Ross Kemp and his team visit Britain's frontline in Helman province, Afghanistan, offering a view of what it's really like to fight the Taliban.

The Royal – 2003 to 2011 - This *Heartbeat* spinoff is set in the 1960s and focuses on an NHS hospital serving the seaside Yorkshire town of Elsinby.

Sara Dane - *Australia* - 1982 - This miniseries follows a young woman banished from England to Australia for a crime she didn't commit.

Secret Nature - 2004 - This series opens up Oxford Scientific Films' archives to take a look at some of the most difficult animals to capture on film.

Single-Handed - 2007 to 2010 - *Ireland* - Jack Driscoll is transferred back to his hometown to take over the Garda Sergeant role his father left.

Spaced – 1999 to 2001 - To get an affordable flat in North London, two young people pretend to be a couple. Simon Pegg (*Shaun of the Dead*) and Jessica Hynes (*There She Goes*) star.

Step Dave – *New Zealand* – 2014 to 2015 - A young slacker in New Zealand meets the woman of his dreams, only to realize she's 15 years older than him and comes with major baggage.

Surgery School - 2010 - Follow the lives of 10 junior doctors setting out as surgical trainees.

Then There Were Giants - 1994 - John Lithgow, Michael Caine, and Bob Hoskins star in this miniseries about how Roosevelt, Churchill, and Stalin navigated the events of World War II.

The Take - 2009 - Shaun Evans (*Endeavour*) and Tom Hardy (*Peaky Blinders*) star in this four-part 2009 miniseries about a man newly released from prison (Hardy) who learns his cousin (Evans) is trying to build a criminal reputation on the back of his reputation. Fun fact: Tom Hardy met Charlotte Riley (*Press*) while filming this series, and the two later married.

The Toilet: An Unspoken History - 2012 - This quirky programme takes a look at toilets throughout the ages.

The Tribe – *New Zealand* – 1999 - In a world where all the adults were killed off by a virus, a group of young people try to stay alive.

Vincent - 2005 to 2006 - Vincent is an ex-cop who becomes a private investigator and takes on the tough cases. Ray Winstone (*The Trials of Jimmy Rose*) and Suranne Jones (*Doctor Foster*) star.

Whisky: The Islay Edition - 2010 - This special takes a look at what goes on at Islay, the Scottish capital of whisky.

Wild at Heart - 2006 to 2013 - Stephen Tompkinson (*DCI Banks*, *Ballykissangel*) stars in this series about a British veterinarian who takes his family along to South Africa to release an animal back into the wild. When he sees the area and meets pretty game reserve owner Caroline (Hayley Mills), he ultimately decides to stay.

The Witness - 2016 - This suspenseful documentary takes a look at the Kitty Genovese murder - the shocking case where 38 witnesses watched a woman get stabbed to death during an hour-long attack.

Wycliffe - 1993 to 1998 - Based on W.J. Burley's novels, this Cornwall-based series features DS Charles Wycliffe, a man who investigates murders with a unique level of determination and accuracy.

IMDB TV

TOPIC

Website: http://topic.com

Description: This new service focuses on international programming, and it includes a number of countries often overlooked (including the Middle East and African countries). Their British library is relatively small but there are some good titles.

Available On: Roku, Fire TV, Apple TV, Apple iPhone & iPad, Android phones and tablets, and computer (via web browser). You can also subscribe via Amazon Prime Video.

Cost: $5.99/month, $59.99/year

Now Streaming

Against the Law - 2017 - When Peter Wildeblood and Edward McNally fell in love in 1952, it was still a crime in Britain. This film takes a look at the devastating consequences for each of the two men.

B.B. King: The Life of Riley - 2012 - This documentary takes a look at the life and career trajectory of famed musician B.B. King.

Babs - 2018 - This short film sees a young man make a shocking discovery about how his father lived and loved.

Biggie & Tupac - 2002 - English documentarian Nick Broomfield conducts an intense investigation into the unsolved murders of two rap musicians called Biggie Smalls and Tupac Shakur, and his evidence points to involvement of the LAPD and an imprisoned recording executive, Marion Knight.

Bringing Babs Home - 2018 - In this short film, a young man brings his dead father's lover home.

Capital - 2015 - When property values soar on a once middle-class London street, residents receive mysterious postcards saying, "We want what you have."

Chimerica - 2019 - Based on real events, this series follows a photojournalist attempting to uncover the identity of the protester who stood in front of the tanks in Tiananmen Square.

Cla'am - 2019 - In this short comedy, a man becomes convinced that a large-scale conspiracy is driving the rapid gentrification of his London neighbourhood.

Come Home - 2018 - After nineteen years of marriage, a woman suddenly walks out on her family.

Death Over Dinner - 2019 - This series invites strangers to dine together and talk about death.

Down from London - 2019 - This British comedy follows a couple that attempts to ignore their relationship troubles by taking trips away from London.

Enterprice - 2019 - In this BBC Three sitcom, a couple of young entrepreneurs in South London attempt to launch their new delivery service, Speedi-Kazz.

Exile – 2011 - John Simm (*Life on Mars*) stars in this mystery-thriller about a man who returns home after his life falls apart – only to find a different kind of trouble there.

Getting High for God? - 2016 - This hour-long documentary follows Mawaan Rizwan as he explores whether drugs can bring you closer to your maker.

How Gay is Pakistan? - 2015 - Though it's illegal to be homosexual in Pakistan, the country has a growing gay community. Mawaan Rizwan takes a look at what life is like for gay Pakistanis.

Hugh the Hunter - 2019 - This short film sees a man wandering the Scottish moors in search of prey.

Intruders – 2014 - John Simm (*Life on Mars*) stars as an ex-cop whose wife goes missing. The ensuing investigation leads him to Seattle, where a secret society chases immortality by hiding in the bodies of others.

Jamie's American Road Trip - 2009 - In this series, Jamie Oliver travels around the US to discover its food - including stops in Wyoming, New York, Louisiana, LA, Georgia, Florida, and Arizona.

Jamie's Food Escapes - 2010 - Jamie Oliver visits Marrakesh, Andalucia, Stockholm, Venice, the French Pyrenees, and Athens to experience their unique foods and cultures.

Jamie's Super Food - 2015 - Jamie Oliver travels the world in search of super foods in their native homelands.

Louis Theroux's Altered States: Choosing Death - 2018 - In this hour-long documentary, Louis spends time with individuals facing the decision to end their own lives.

Louis Theroux's Altered States: Take My Baby - 2018 - In this hour-long documentary, Louis heads to the open adoption state of California, where he talks with women handing over their babies to families paying tens of thousands of dollars.

Miriam's Big American Adventure - 2018 - Miriam Margolyes (*Call the Midwife, Bucket*) sets off on a fun and entertaining road trip around the United States. She begins in Chicago before moving on to an Indiana summer camp and a prison in Ohio. In the final entry, she ponders whether the United States is actually "the Divided States".

Monkman & Seagull's Genius Guide to Britain - 2018 - This fun travel series originally aired on BBC Two in the UK, and it follows a couple of quiz show champions as they visit some of the country's greatest triumphs of science and engineering. If you

enjoy great scenery and more insight into the way things work, you'll love this one. One episode is dedicated to each of the four countries of the UK.

Moses Jones - 2009 - After a body is discovered in the Thames, DI Moses Jones investigates possibilities of witchcraft in London's Ugandan exile community. Shaun Parkes (*Line of Duty, Hooten & the Lady*) stars as DI Moses Jones, with Matt Smith (*Doctor Who*) and Dennis Waterman (*New Tricks*) in supporting roles.

Not Safe for Work - 2015 - When budget cuts move Katherine's civil servant job to Northampton, she reluctantly goes along with the relocation.

The Office - 2001 to 2003 - Before there was Michael Scott in the US, there was David Brent in Slough, England. Written by Ricky Gervais (*After Life*) and Stephen Merchant (*Hello Ladies*), this mockumentary-style programme takes place in the office of the fictional Wernham Hogg paper company. Mackenzie Crook (*Detectorists*) and Martin Freeman (*Sherlock*) are also among the stars.

Pulp: A Film About Life, Death and Supermarkets - 2014 - This rock documentary follows the Britpop band Pulp as they head back to Sheffield for one last concert.

Run - 2013 - Olivia Colman and Lennie James star in this four-part miniseries about four seemingly unconnected people whose lives intersect after a random act of violence.

Shut Up & Play the Hits - 2012 - This music documentary takes a look at the last days of LCD Soundsystem.

Song of Granite - 2017 - This documentary takes a closer look at Joe Heaney, a shy boy born in a remote Irish village who would later grow up to become one of the country's most loved traditional vocalists.

The Sunshine Makers - 2017 - This documentary shares the untold story of Nicholas Sand and Tim Scully, a duo at the heart of the 1960s LSD/counterculture movement in America.

Transsiberian - 2008 - Woody Harrelson, Kate Mara, Emily Mortimer, and Ben Kingsley star in this dramatic film about an American couple who encounter a pair of mysterious travelers on a train journey from China to Moscow.

The Virtues - 2019 - When his personal life falls apart, Joseph travels to Ireland in hopes of making amends with his estranged sister Anna. In doing so, he unearths the horrors of his past while also finding a path to move forward. Stephen Graham (*Snatch*) stars.

Weapons of Mass Production - 2019 - This docuseries takes a look at the price people in Britain are paying for the country's arms business.

The Witness - 2016 - This suspenseful documentary takes a look at the Kitty Genovese murder - the shocking case where 38 witnesses watched a woman get stabbed to death during an hour-long attack.

Wuthering Heights - 2012 - This artsy adaptation of Brontë's classic stars James Howson and Kaya Scodelario as an older Heathcliff and Cathy, with Solomon Glave and Shannon Beer as younger version of themselves. Reviews of this nontraditional retelling were mixed, but it's a must-watch for anyone who enjoys Brontë.

Year of the Rabbit - 2019 - Matt Berry (*The IT Crowd*) stars in this period comedy about an eclectic group of Victorian detectives who fight crime whilst mingling with street gangs, spiritualists, politicians, Bulgarian princes, and even the Elephant Man.

STARZ

Website: http://starz.com

Description: Starz is a premium cable network owned by Lions Gate Entertainment. They focus on first-run television shows and major motion pictures. They don't offer a lot of British programming, but what's there is usually quite good.

Available On: Roku, Amazon Fire TV, Apple TV, Apple iPhone & iPad, Android TV, Android phones and tablets, computer (via web browser). You can also subscribe via Amazon Prime Video or your cable company.

Cost: $8.99/month

Now Streaming

American Gods - *United States* - 2017 to present - Though it's an American production, American Gods is based on the novel of the same name by British-born author Neil Gaiman, and the series stars Ian McShane (*Lovejoy*). It tells the story of a prisoner who's just days away from release when he gets the news that his wife has been killed in an accident. After his early release, he encounters a strange men, Mr. Wednesday (McShane), who offers him a job that ultimately brings him into a world of magic and old gods.

Dancing on the Edge – 2013 - In early 1930s London, a black jazz group is coming up in the world. Unfortunately, tragedy strikes before they can fully appreciate their success. This six-episode series features a mixture of British high society and the much uglier underbelly of racism and poverty in London at the time.

Da Vinci's Demons - 2013 to 2015 - This historical fantasy offers a fictional retelling of Leonardo da Vinci's early life.

Dublin Murders - 2019 - Based on the Dublin Murder Squad book series by Tana French, the first season of this British-American-Irish co-production features eight episodes adapted from In the Woods and The Likeness. Killian Scott (*C.B. Strike*) stars as Rob Reilly, and English detective dispatched to investigate the murder of a young girl just outside Dublin. The case forces Reilly to confront his own dark past, and it puts his relationship with partner Cassie Maddox (Sarah Greene, *Penny Dreadful*) to the test.

Howards End – 2017 - This miniseries is based on the E.M. Forster novel, and it examines class differences in 1900s England through the lens of three families.

Little Dorrit - 1987 - Sir Derek Jacobi stars in this classic Dickens tale of a young girl, her indebted father, and the benefactor who helps her.

Luther – 2010 to 2019 - Idris Elba stars as a brilliant London detective who frequently gets into trouble because of his passion for the job.

The Missing – 2014 to 2017 - James Nesbitt (*Cold Feet*) stars in this drama about the disappearance of a 5-year-old and the manhunt that follows.

MotherFatherSon - 2019 - Richard Gere stars in his first major television role as Max Finch, American newspaper owner. The 8-part series is a psycho thriller about power, politics, and the media. Helen McCrory (*Peaky Blinders*), Sarah Lancashire (*Happy Valley*), Sinéad Cusack (*Marcella*), and Ciarán Hinds (*Above Suspicion*) are among the other cast members.

Outlander - 2014 to present - In 1945, an English nurse is mysteriously transported back in time to Scotland in 1743. The massively-popular series is based on the novels of Diana Gabaldon.

The Pillars of the Earth - 2010 - This miniseries is based on the 1989 Ken Follett novel of the same name, and it follows the construction of a cathedral during the 12th century.

The Rook - 2019 - Emma Greenwell stars as Myfanwy Thomas, a young woman who finds herself at the Millennium Bridge in London surrounded by corpses and no memory of how she ended up there. While the series is American, it features a largely British cast, and it takes place in London. It was based on the novel of the same name by Daniel O'Malley, originally adapted by Stephenie Meyer of *Twilight* fame.

Save Me - 2018 - Lennie James and Suranne Jones star in this series about a man who will do anything to find his missing daughter.

The Spanish Princess - 2019 - This period drama is based on the novels *The Constant Princess* and *The King's Curse* by Philippa Gregory, and it's a sequel to the previous miniseries *The White Queen* and *The White Princess*. The series follows teenage princess Catherine of Aragon as she travels to England to meet her husband by proxy.

The White Princess - 2017 - Based on the Philippa Gregory book of the same name, this miniseries tells the story of Elizabeth of York and her marriage to Henry VII. It's the sequel to *The White Queen*.

The White Queen - 2013 - This miniseries is based on Philippa Gregory's historical series, *The Cousins' War*, and it tells the story of the women involved in the conflict for England's throne during the War of Roses.

World Without End - 2012 - This miniseries is a sequel to *The Pillars of the Earth*, and it's set 150 years later in the same English town of Knightsbridge. This time, they're facing the outbreak of the Black Death and the Hundred Years' War. It's based on the Ken Follett novel of the same name.

STARZ

CINEMAX

Website: http://cinemax.com

Description: Cinemax is an older premium cable service, and they're owned by HBO. Programming mostly consists of older movies, original action series, and documentaries, but they do have a handful of British shows.

Available On: Roku, Amazon Fire TV, Apple TV, Apple iPhone & iPad, Android TV, Android phones and tablets, computer (via web browser). You can also subscribe via Amazon Prime Video or Hulu.

Cost: $9.99/month

Now Streaming

C.B. Strike (aka Strike) - 2017 to present - Based on the *Cormoran Strike* novels written by JK Rowling under the Robert Galbraith pseudonym, this series sees war veteran Cormoran Strike team up with a highly-competent assistant who helps him solve cases and transform his ailing business.

Hunted - 2012 - After an attempt on her life, a spy goes back undercover as a nanny, unsure of who she can trust.

Rellik - 2017 - DCI Markham and his team hunt down a killer in this mystery told in reverse. The serial killer is a man who attacks his victims with acid, and the investigating officer becomes a surviving victim of the killer.

Strike Back- 2010 to 2020 - This British/American spy series is based on the 2007 novel of the same name by former SAS soldier Chris Ryan. It follows the goings on of Section 20, a secret branch of the British Defence Intelligence service who conduct high-risk, high-priority missions around the world. Jed Mercurio (*Line of Duty*) was among the writers, and stars have included Richard Armitage (*North & South*), Andrew Lincoln (*The Walking Dead*), and Robson Green (*Grantchester*).

HBO

Website: http://hbo.com

Description: Both HBO and HBO Max are owned by WarnerMedia, and they focus on a mix of original series, and other premium content. Below, shows only on HBO Max are underlined.

Available On: Roku, Fire TV, Apple TV, Apple iPhone & iPad, Chromecast, Android phones and tablets, and computer (via web browser). You can also subscribe via Amazon Prime Video or Hulu. **HBO Max** is NOT available on Amazon or Roku.

Cost: $14.99/month

Now Streaming

The Alienist - *United States* - 2018 - Though American, this series stars Welshman Luke Evans. It's a period crime drama set in late 1800s New York City, with the first season focusing on finding someone who's killing boy prostitutes. The second season sees some of the characters working as private detectives to find a kidnapped infant.

Avenue 5 - *United States* - 2020 - Hugh Laurie and Josh Gad star in this science fiction comedy about a space cruise ship. They've been thrown off course, and it's estimated that it will take them three years to get back to Earth - but they only have enough supplies for eight weeks. Along with Hugh Laurie, you'll spot a number of popular British actors including Daisy May Cooper (*This Country*) and Matthew Beard (*Vienna Blood*).

The Casual Vacancy - 2015 - This miniseries is based on JK Rowling's novel of the same name, and it tells the story of a town resident's sudden death and how it impacts the local community.

Catherine the Great - 2019 - Helen Mirren stars as Catherine the Great in this four-part miniseries. The series covers the later portion of her life, from 1764 until her death in 1796. Jason Clarke (*Zero Dark Thirty*), Rory Kinnear (*Penny Dreadful*), Richard Roxburgh (*Rake*), and Paul Ritter

(*No Offence*) also appear.

Chernobyl - 2019 - Screenwriter Craig Mazin created this moving five-part historical adaptation of the Chernobyl nuclear disaster. The series includes a number of actors likely to be familiar to British TV fans, including Jared Harris (*The Crown*), Stellan Skarsgård (*Pirates of the Caribbean*), Paul Ritter (*No Offence, Friday Night Dinner*), and Emily Watson (*Miss Potter*).

Doctor Who - 1963 to present - A mysterious Time Lord travels through time and space, exploring and saving the world in equal measure. HBO Max has all the modern Doctor Who episodes.

Elizabeth I - 2006 - Helen Mirren, Jeremy Irons, and Hugh Dancy star in this two-part miniseries about the later half of Queen Elizabeth I's reign.

Family Tree – 2013 - This hilarious series follows one man's efforts to track down long-lost members of his family tree.

Five Days - 2007 to 2010 - Each series covers five non-consecutive days in a major police investigation.

Game of Thrones - 2011 to 2019 - In a mythical world, families fight for control of the Iron Throne. The series is based on the novels of George R.R. Martin, and the show is estimated to have had the largest cast on television.

Gentleman Jack - 2019 to present - The incomparable Sally Wainwright (*Happy Valley, Last Tango in Halifax*) ventures into historical drama, bringing us the story of 19th century English industrialist, landowner, and lesbian Anne Lister. Suranne Jones (*Doctor Foster*) stars as Lister, a Yorkshire woman who was very much ahead of her time. Other cast members include Sophie Rundle as Ann Walker, Timothy West as Jeremy Lister, and Stephanie Cole as Aunt Ann Walker.

Ghosts - 2019 to present - When a young married couple inherits a crumbling old estate, they decide to move in and make a go of it. Unfortunately, it's also home to more than a few ghosts. Since neither can leave, they have to learn to get along.

Gunpowder - 2017 - Kit Harington (*Game of Thrones*) stars in this three-part period drama about the Gunpowder Plot of 1605.

His Dark Materials - 2019 - Based on the trilogy by Oxford novelist Philip Pullman, this eight-episode fantasy series takes place in an alternate world where each human has an animal companion called a daemon. A young orphan girl living at Jordan College, Oxford, is drawn into a dangerous puzzle when her friend, a fellow orphan, is kidnapped. Among the stars are Lin-Manuel Miranda (*Hamilton*), Ruth Wilson (*Luther*), James McAvoy (*Shameless*), David Suchet (*Poirot*), and Andrew Scott (*Fleabag*). Dafne Keen (*The Refugees*) plays Lyra.

I May Destroy You - 2020 - Michaela Coal stars in this series about a woman trying to rebuild her life after she's raped.

Life's Too Short - 2011 to 2012 - Warwick Davis stars as a scheming actor aiming to be nothing less than Britain's number one little person.

Hello Ladies – *United States* - 2013 - While not technically British, this series comes from Stephen Merchant, a British actor and writer who has partnered with Ricky Gervais. See also - *Hello Ladies: The Movie*

Little Britain USA – 2008 - British tourists Lou and Andy travel around the United States.

Miss Sherlock - *Japan* - 2018 - This Japanese adaptation of the Sherlock Holmes story sees a young "Miss Sherlock" working alongside the Tokyo police.

The No. 1 Ladies' Detective Agency - 2009 - Based on the novels of Scottish author Alexander McCall Smith, this series follows a young woman in Botswana as she opens her country's first female-owned detective agency.

Parade's End - 2013 - Benedict Cumberbatch (*Sherlock*) stars in this series adapted from Ford Madox Ford's tetralogy of novels. It focuses on the lives and relations of three Brits just before and at the outset of World War I.

Perry Mason - *United States* - 2020 - Welshman Matthew Rhys stars in this prequel to the original *Perry Mason*. It's set in 1932 Los Angeles, when Mason is struggling to get back on track after a divorce and his war trauma.

Run - *United States* - 2020 - This comedy-thriller begins with two people who once made a promise that if either ever texted the word "RUN" to the other, they'd drop everything and meet in Grand Central Terminal and travel the country together. While this is an American series, Brit Phoebe Waller-Bridge is both executive producer and a recurring character. One of the leads, Domhnall Gleeson, is Irish.

Sally4Ever - 2018 - A woman decides to leave a boring man to have an affair with a woman instead.

Sarah Jane Adventures - 2007 to 2011 - This children's show is a *Doctor Who* spin-off that follows former companion Sarah Jane Smith, now an investigative journalist.

Torchwood - 2006 to 2011 - A secret agency called Torchwood fights off threats from aliens and the supernatural. The series is a spin-off of *Doctor Who*.

Years and Years - 2019 - This series follows the Manchester-based Lyons family as they their lives progress through 15 years of politics, technology, and human events. Emma Thompson, Rory Kinnear, and Anne Reid are among the cast.

HBO

SHOTIME

Now Streaming

The Affair - *United States* - 2014 to 2019 - A man (Dominic West) and woman (Ruth Wilson) have an affair that leads to a complex series of events.

Back to Life - 2019 to Present - Following an 18-year prison sentence, Miri Matteson (*Daisy Haggard*) returns home to Hythe, Kent, and attempts to rebuild her life.

Brotherhood - 2006-2008 - Irish-American brother's lives intertwine as they go their own way.

Episodes - 2011 to 2017 - Two married British TV producers are offered a deal in the US, and then everything goes wrong. Stephen Mangan (*Hang-Ups*) and Tamsin Greig (*Friday Night Dinner*) star.

Flack - 2019 to Present - A PR executive specializes in cleaning up after her selfish clients in London. Anna Paquin stars.

Guerrilla - 2017 - Set in early 1970s London, Guerrilla tells the story of a politically active couple whose relationship and values are tested when they liberate a political prisoner and form a radical underground cell.

Happyish - *United States* - 2015 - Brit Steve Coogan (*The Trip*) stars as a depressed middle-aged man who contents himself with feeling merely "happy-ish".

Just Another Immigrant - 2018 - Comedian Romesh Ranganathan uproots his entire family and moves to the United States.

Patrick Melrose - 2018 - Based on the semi-autobiographical Patrick Melrose novels by Edward St. Aubyn, this miniseries tells the story of an upper class man's addictions and family troubles.

Penny Dreadful - 2014 to 2016 - A group of explorers and adventurers team up to fight supernatural threats in Victorian England.

Secret Diary of a Call Girl - 2007 to 2011 - Billie Piper (*Doctor Who*) stars as a high-end London call girl.

Shameless - *United States* - 2011 to present - This American series is an adaptation of Paul Abbott's British series of the same name and features an ensemble cast led by William H. Macy and Emmy Rossum.

The Tudors - 2007 to 2010 - The Tudors is a drama about Henry VIII and his extensive love life.

We Hunt Together - 2020 - This drama sees two conflicted detectives tracking down a pair of deadly killers. Starring Eve Myles (*Torchwood*).

PEACOCK

Website: http://peacocktv.com

Description: This NBC-owned subscription service is the major online home of NBCUniversal content. British programming is limited.

Available On: Roku, Amazon Fire TV, Apple TV, Apple iPhone & iPad, Android TV, Android phones and tablets, most recent game consoles, Google Chromecast, computer (via web browser).

Cost: Limited Free Membership, Peacock Premium - $4.99/month or $49.99/year, Peacock Premium Plus for an additional $5/month to watch without ads.

Now Streaming

The Affair - *United States* - 2014 to 2019 - A man (Dominic West) and woman (Ruth Wilson, *Luther*) have an affair that leads to a complex series of events.

Alfred Hitchcock Presents - 1955 to 1962 - The English master of suspense hosts this anthology series full of mystery and murder.

Brave New World - 2020 - Jessica Brown Findlay (*Downton Abbey*) is among the stars of this adaptation of Aldous Huxley's classic dystopian novel.

The Capture - 2019 - Holiday Grainger (*C.B. Strike*) stars in this series about a detective who uncovers a massive conspiracy while investigating the charges against a British soldier.

Downton Abbey - 2010 to 2015 - This popular period drama follows the lives of the Crawley family and their servants during the early 1900s.

Escape to the Chateau - 2016 to 2019 - This British reality series follows Dick Strawbridge and Angela Adoree as they buy and renovate the 19th-century Château de la Motte-Husson in Martigné-sur-Mayenne, France.

Hell's Kitchen – 2004 to 2009 - This series pits prospective chefs against one another, with the winner getting a head chef position.

Hitmen - 2020 - This comedy follows two best friends who have fallen into a career in contract killing. Mel Giedroyc (*Spies of Warsaw*) and Sue Perkins (*The Great British Baking Show*) star.

Intelligence - 2020 - An NSA agent joins forces with a computer analyst to establish a new cyber crimes department in the UK. American David Schwimmer (*Friends*) stars.

Murder, She Wrote - *United States* - 1984 to 1996 - British-born Angela Lansbury stars in this classic series about a novelist who seems to encounter murder everywhere she goes.

RENEWALS & CANCELLATIONS

This list is based on the best information available at print time (early August 2020). Last-minute changes can always occur, and that's doubly true in pandemic times.

For returning shows, we've not added dates because very few are able to make accurate predictions given the constant changes in pandemic restrictions.

Shows Not Expected to Return

No Offence
Scarborough
Detectorists
Wild Bill
Warren

Age Before Beauty
Sanditon*
Turn Up Charlie
Harlots
Hard Sun

Cold Feet
Mum
Still Game
Black Mirror

Returning for Another Season

Shakespeare & Hathaway
Shetland
Vienna Blood
Agatha Raisin
Finding Joy
Ms. Fisher's Modern Murder
Mysteries
Father Brown
Manhunt
Death in Paradise

Call the Midwife
Vera
Life on Mars
Endeavour
The Bletchley Circle: San
Francisco
Miss Scarlet and the Duke
Year of the Rabbit
Grantchester
Sex Education

Top Boy
After Life
My Life is Murder
Harrow
Killing Eve
Avenue 5
American Gods
Flack
Doc Martin**

Not Yet Announced

Good Karma Hospital
Friday Night Dinner

Dead Still
The Split

*Amazon has hinted at possibly bringing this one back

**Though not officially confirmed by ITV, director Nigel Cole said they're coming back.

COMING SOON

As with the list on the previous page, this list is both incomplete and subject to change. Some services don't provide many updates about what's coming, and others have press embargoes that prevent information from being released before a certain date - so what you see here is what's able to be shared based on the expected shipping date of this guide.

For PBS, keep in mind that many shows stream the day after they air on television.

Acorn TV

The Advocates - 1991 to 1992 - September 28

This Scottish legal drama is set in the high-powered world of lawyers and advocates

The Badness of King George IV - 2004 - September 14

Oliver Ford Davies (*Star Wars: Episodes 1 and 2*) plays the highly unpopular monarch in this film that explores his failings as a monarch.

Bang, Series 2 - 2020 - September 21

The new season will see officer Gina Jenkins and her partner Luke Lloyd investigating a series of murders possibly connected to a historic rape allegation.

The Black Velvet Gown - 1991 - September 28

Set in 1830s Northumberland, this two-part film explores what happens when a mother and daughter are set apart by their shared ability to read and write.

Bloodlands - 2020 - November TBD

Produced by Jed Mercurio (*Line of Duty*), this series begins when an expensive car is pulled out of the water with a suicide note but no body. James Nesbitt (*Cold Feet*) stars as Northern Ireland police detective Tom Brannick, who instantly sees a connection to a cold case.

The Mystery of a Hansom Cab - 2012 - September 21

Set in 1880s Melbourne, this period drama is based on the bestselling novel by Fergus Hume. It follows the murder of a man connected to a wealthy benefactor, along with an accused man unable to provide an alibi.

Mystery Road, Series 2 - 2020 - October 12

Aaron Pedersen stars in this Australian Outback-based mystery series.

Public Enemies - 2012 - September 7

This series tells the story of a young man recently released from prison after serving 10 years, and the parole officer working with him after returning from a professional suspension.

The Sounds - 2020 - September 3

A happily married Canadian couple moves to New Zealand to escape the husband's domineering family, but when he disappears soon after relocating, long-buried secrets come to light.

Two episodes will premiere on the 3rd, with remaining episodes coming out weekly.

The South Westerlies - 2020 - Date TBD

In this Irish six-part comedy-drama, Orla Brady (*Mistresses*) plays Kate, an environmental consultant for a Norwegian energy firm. She's asked to go undercover among Irish protestors and help eliminate their objections to a wind farm near their small coastal town. Her task's difficulty is compounded by the arrival of a surfer who bears a strong resemblance to her son.

The Sum of Us - 1994 - September 14

Russell Crowe stars in this touching comedy about a father and gay son who are complete opposites but get on very well.

Unfortunately, new relationships eventually put a strain on their bond.

Wisting - 2019 - September 7

This Norwegian drama follows homicide detective William Wisting as he investigates the possibility of an American serial killer living in Norway.

BritBox

The Bletchley Circle: San Francisco - 2020 - Date TBD

This spin-off to The Bletchley Circle was renewed for a second season in 2019, with filming in late 2019 and an expected air date of 2020. No firm date has been announced at time of print.

Don't Forget the Driver - 2019 - September 2020

Toby Jones (Detectorists) takes on another comedy role in this series about a depressed single dad who works as a coach driver. His mundane existence is shaken up when he takes a group across the English Channel and finds a migrant stowed away in his wheel arch. Jones co-wrote the series with playwright Tim Crouch.

Amazon's Prime Video

Truth Seekers - 2020 - Autumn 2020 premiere

This supernatural comedy series sees Nick Frost and Simon Pegg as ghost hunters who unintentionally uncover a conspiracy that could wipe out the human race.

Topic

Release - 2020 - September 3

Completed before the pandemic, this series sees a fictional virus changing the lives of a group of people.

Sundance Now

Des - Dates TBD

Based on the novel *Killing for Company* by Brian Masters, this series follows Scottish serial killer Dennis Nilsen. He was arrested in 1983 and ultimately convicted of six counts of murder (though he was likely guilty of more). David Tennant stars.

A Discovery of Witches, Series 2 - 2021 - Expected January, no firm date

The long-awaited second series of this show about a reluctant witch/historian is expected to hit Sundance Now in early 2021.

One Lane Bridge - 2020 - September 17

While working a murder investigation, a young Maori detective accidentally awakens a spiritual gift that may harm the case.

HBO

The Gilded Age - 2021 - Date TBD

Created by Downton Abbey writer Julian Fellowes, this period drama follows a wealthy American family during the boom years of the 1880s. Production was delayed by COVID-19, and it's believed filming will start in Autumn 2020.

The Third Day - 2020 - September 14

With three interconnected stories, this series follows the journeys of a man and woman who arrive on a strange island at different times. The series was filmed in the UK and includes Brits Jude Law, Paddy Considine,

and Emily Watson among the cast members. Though originally set to premiere in both the US and UK in May, post-production was slowed down due to the pandemic. It's said to be premiering on September 14th in the US.

The Undoing - 2020 - October 25

A successful New York therapist sees her life start falling apart when she publishes her first book. Though American, Hugh Grant is among the stars.

Netflix

Lucifer, Season 5: Part 1 - 2020 - August 21

Tom Ellis (*Miranda*) stars in this American series about what happens when the devil gets bored with Hell and decides to give LA a try. In this first half of the (expected) final series, they begin to wrap up the storyline between Lucifer and Chloe.

Rebecca - 2020 - October 21

Lily James and Keeley Hawes star in this adaptation of Daphne du Maurier's classic novel by the same name.

Young Wallander - 2020 - September 3

This *Wallander* prequel focuses on the experiences of Kurt Wallander as a recently graduated police officer in his 20s.

IMDb TV

Alex Rider - 2020 - November 13

Based on the *Alex Rider* novels by Anthony Horowitz (*Foyle's War*), this series follows a London teenager who's been recruited by the Department of Special Operations to

infiltrate an academy for the wayward children of the very rich.

PBS Masterpiece

All Creatures Great and Small - 2020 - Expected January 2021

This remake of the much-loved classic Yorkshire veterinary series is expected to hit screens in January 2021. It's based on the books by James Herriot.

Elizabeth is Missing - 2019 - Expected January 3/4

Glenda Jackson stars as a woman trying to solve two mysteries while suffering from dementia. Her only friend has gone missing, and she's not sure what information she can trust.

Flesh & Blood - 2020 - Expected October 4/5

When a widow finds unexpected romance with a retired surgeon, her family's reactions are mixed. A web of lies and secrets brings chaos and eventually, murder. This one's full of crazy relatives, dark secrets, and for good measure, a nosy neighbor played by Imelda Staunton.

Miss Scarlet and the Duke - 2020 - Autumn 2020

When Eliza Scarlet is left destitute after her father's death, she can either get married or take over his detective agency. Because she's living in the 1880s and it's deemed inappropriate for a woman to take part in the trade, she gets a partner - Scotland Yard's Detective Inspector William Wellington, "The Duke".

Roadkill - 2020 - Expected November 1/2

Hugh Laurie stars as a self-made, scheming politician with humble roots. He's ambitious and looking for more, but there are many who'd like to bring him down.

The Trouble with Maggie Cole - 2020 - Expected October 18/19

Dawn French brings us this new comedy-drama about the dangers of gossip. She plays Maggie Connors, a seaside village busybody who likes to ignore the saying that "those who live in glass houses shouldn't throw stones.

Van der Valk - 2020 - Expected September 13/14

This reboot of the 1970s series will see Marc Warren (Beecham House) as Commissaris Piet Van der Valk. Set in modern Amsterdam, it's a major departure from the original Nick Freeling novels.

INDEX

Hulu
Agatha Christie's Ordeal by Innocence - Prime Video
Agatha Raisin - Acorn TV
Age Before Beauty - BritBox
Ain't Misbehavin' - Acorn TV
Air Ambulance ER - IMDb TV, Tubi
Air Farce New Year's Eve Special - Best of British TV
Alan Davies: As Yet Untitled - BritBox
Alexandria: The Greatest City - Prime Video, Acorn TV
Alfred Hitchcock Presents - Peacock
Alfresco - BritBox
Alias Grace - Netflix
Alibi - Acorn TV
All Aboard! - BritBox
All Creatures Great & Stuffed - Best of British TV
All Creatures Great and Small - BritBox
All in Good Faith - Acorn TV
All's Well That Ends Well (1981) - BritBox
Allotment Wars - Best of British TV
Always Greener - Prime Video
Amazing Interiors - Netflix
Ambassadors - Pluto
Amber - Prime Video
Ambulance - Tubi
American Gods - Starz
Amnesia - Prime Video, Acorn TV
An Accidental Soldier - Acorn TV
An Adventure in Space & Time - BritBox
An Hour to Save Your Life - Tubi
An Inspector Calls - BritBox
Ancient Egypt - Life and Death in the Valley of the Kings - Prime Video, Pluto
Ancient Rome: The Rise and Fall of an Empire - BritBox
And Then There Were None - Acorn TV
Anglo-Saxon Attitudes -

Acorn TV
Angry Britain - Best of British TV
Animal 24/7 - Tubi
Animal A&E - Prime Video
Animal Madhouse - Tubi
Animal Park - IMDb TV
Animal Rescue School - Tubi
Animal Rescue Squad - Prime Video
Animal Squad - Prime Video
Anna Karenina (2000) - Acorn TV
Anna Karenina (1978) - Pluto
Anna's Wild Life - Prime Video
Anne of Green Gables: Fire and Dew - PBS Masterpiece
Anne With An "E" - Netflix
Anner House - Acorn TV
Anthem for Doomed Youth: The War Poets - BritBox
Antiques Roadshow - BritBox, Pluto
Antony and Cleopatra (1981) - BritBox
Anzac Girls - Acorn TV
Apple Tree Yard - PBS Masterpiece, Hulu
Appropriate Adult - Prime Video
Arabian Nights - Pluto
Archangel - Pluto
Archangel - IMDb TV
Are You Being Served? (1972) - BritBox
Are You Being Served? (2016) - BritBox
Are You Being Served? Again! - BritBox
Aristocrats - BritBox
Armadillo - BritBox
Around the World in 80 Faiths - BritBox
Art Deco Icons: Britain's Bling and Glamour - Prime Video, Tubi
Art of the Heist - Acorn TV
Arthur and George - PBS Masterpiece
As Time Goes By - BritBox
As You Like It (1978) - BritBox

Asylum - Prime Video
At Home With the Braithwaites - Prime Video, Tubi
At Home with the Georgians - Acorn TV
At Last the 1948 Show - BritBox, Tubi
At Your Service - Tubi
Atlantis - Hulu
Atlantis High - Prime Video
Auction - Tubi
Autumnwatch - BritBox
Avenue 5 - HBO Max, HBO
B.B. King: The Life of Riley - Topic
Babs - Topic
Baby Baby - Tubi
Baby Ballroom - Netflix
Baby Beauty Queens - Tubi
Baby Hospital - Tubi
Back Home - Acorn TV
Back to Life - Showtime
Bad Education - Netflix
The Ballroom Boys - Acorn TV
Ballykissangel - BritBox
The Ballymurphy Precedent - IMDb TV
Balthazar - Acorn TV
Banana - Prime Video
Bancroft - BritBox
Band of Gold - Prime Video
Bang - Acorn TV
Banged Up - IMDb TV
Banished - BritBox, Prime Video, Hulu
The Bank - Best of British TV
Baptiste - PBS Masterpiece
The Baron - BritBox
Baroque - Prime Video, Acorn Tv
Barristers - Acorn TV
Bath, England - Prime Video
Battle Castle - Prime Video
Battle of Kings: Bannockburn - IMDb TV
Battlefield Recovery - Netflix
The Bay - BritBox
The BBC at War - BritBox
BBC's Lost Sitcoms - BritBox
Beat My Build - Inside Outside
Beau Geste - Prime Video

Beaver Falls - Prime Video
Bed of Roses - Acorn TV, Prime Video
Bedlam - Prime Video, Hulu, Pluto
Beecham House - PBS Masterpiece
Behaving Badly - Acorn TV
Behind Enemy Lines - Netflix
Being Erica - Prime Video, Hulu
Being Human - Prime Video, Tubi, Pluto
Being Human (CAN) - Sundance Now
The Bench - Prime Video
Benidorm - BritBox
Best in Paradise - BritBox
Best Laid Plans - Tubi
The Best of Agatha Christie - Acorn TV
Best of British Heritage Railways - Prime Video
The Best of Men - PBS Masterpiece
The Betrayal - Best of British TV
Between - Netflix
Big Dreams Small Spaces - Inside Outside
The Big Family Cooking Showdown - Netflix
The Big Flower Fight - Netflix
The Big House Reborn - Acorn TV, Prime Video
Big School - Pluto
Big Sky - Prime Video
Big Star's Little Star - Best of British TV
Biggie & Tupac - Topic
Bill - BritBox
Billionaire Boy - BritBox
Birds of a Feather - Acorn TV
Black Books - Prime Video, Tubi, Hulu
Black Earth Rising - Netflix
Black Harbour - IMDb TV, Pluto
Black Mirror - Netflix
Black Mirror: Bandersnatch - Netflix
Black Widows - Acorn TV, Prime Video

Black Work - Sundance Now, Acorn TV
Blackadder - Prime Video, Hulu, BritBox
The Blake Mysteries: Ghost Stories - BritBox
Blandings - Prime Video, BritBox, Tubi
Bleak House (2005) - BritBox
Bleak House (1985) - Prime Video
Bleak House (2005) - Hulu
The Bleak Old Shop of Stuff - Prime Video
The Bletchley Circle - PBS Masterpiece
The Bletchley Circle: San Francisco - BritBox
Bliss - BritBox
Blood - Acorn TV
Blood Ties - Prime Video, Pluto
Blue Murder - IMDb TV, BritBox, Tubi
The Blue Rose - Prime Video, Acorn TV
Bluestone 42 - Pluto
Bodily Harm - Acorn TV
Body and Soul - Prime Video
Bodyguard - Netflix
Bollywood: The World's Biggest Film Industry - Acorn TV
Bomb Girls - Acorn TV, Pluto
Bomber Boys - Prime Video
Bonekickers - Prime Video
Boomers - Acorn TV
Boon - BritBox
Booze Britain - Tubi
Boozed Up Brits Abroad - Tubi
Borderline - Netflix
The Borgias - Netflix
Born to Kill - Sundance Now
Bottersnikes and Gumbles - Netflix
Bounty Hunters - Prime Video, Tubi
Boy Meets Girl (2009) - Prime Video, Tubi
Boy Meets Girl (2015) - BritBox
The Boy with the Topknot - Acorn TV

Bramwell - Prime Video, BritBox
Brand New House on a Budget - Tubi
Brassic - Hulu
Brave New World - Peacock
Breathless - PBS Masterpiece
Brexitcast - BritBox
Brick by Brick: Rebuilding Our Past - Tubi, Pluto
The Bridal Coach - Tubi
Brideshead Revisited - BritBox, Tubi
Bridges that Built London - Prime Video
Bridget & Eamon - Prime Video, Tubi
The Brief - Prime Video
Brief Encounters - Sundance Now, Acorn TV
The Brilliant Brontë Sisters - Acorn TV
Brilliant Gardens - Prime Video
Bringing Babs Home - Topic
Britain AD: King Arthur's Britain - Prime Video
Britain by Narrowboat - Prime Video
Britain on Call - Best of British TV
Britain's Best Bakery - IMDb TV, Pluto
Britain's Best Canals - Prime Video
Britain's Best Drives - Prime Video
Britain's Biggest Adventures with Bear Grylls - BritBox
Britain's Bloodiest Dynasty - Sundance Now, Acorn TV
Britain's Bloody Crown - Sundance Now, Acorn TV
Britain's Poshest Nannies - Best of British TV
Britain's Railways Then & Now: LNER - Prime Video
Britain's Railways: Then and Now - Prime Video
Britain's Real Monarch - Prime Video
Britain's Royal Weddings - BritBox

Britain's Secret Homes - Best of British TV

Britain's Secret Treasures - BritBox

Britain's Tudor Treasure - BritBox

Britain's Outlaws: Highwaymen, Pirates, and Rogues - Prime Video

Britannia - Prime Video

The Britannia Awards - BritBox

British Bouncers - Prime Video

British Inland Waterways - Prime Video

British Passions on Film - Prime Video

British Railway Journeys - Prime Video

British Railways - Prime Video

British Royal Heritage: The Royal Kingdom - Prime Video

Brits Behind Bars - Best of British TV

Broadchurch - Netflix

Broadmoor: A History of the Criminally Insane - Prime Video

Broken - BritBox

The Brokenwood Mysteries - Acorn TV

The Broker's Man - Prime Video, Acorn TV

Bromwell High - Pluto

Brontë Country: The Life and Times of Three Famous Sisters - Prime Video

The Brontë Sisters - Prime Video

Brotherhood - Showtime

Brushstrokes: Every Picture Tells a Story - Prime Video

The Buccaneers - Prime Video

Bucket - BritBox

Budgie - Tubi

Build a New Life in the Country - Tubi

Build a New Life in the Country Revisits - Tubi

Building Dream Homes - Prime Video

Building Ireland - Prime Video

Burnistoun - Netflix

Butterfly - Hulu

Byways of Steam: In Stephenson's Country - Prime Video

Byways of Steam: In the Valleys and the Mountains - Prime Video

C.B. Strike - Cinemax

Cabins in the Wild with Dick Strawbridge - Netflix

Cadfael - Prime Video, BritBox, Tubi

Caligula with Mary Beard - Acorn TV

Call Security - Best of British TV

Call the Midwife - Netflix

Camelot - Tubi

Cameraman to the Queen - BritBox

Camomile Lawn - Tubi, Acorn TV

Campion - BritBox

Can a Computer Write a Hit Musical - Acorn TV

Can't Cope, Won't Cope - Netflix

Capital - Acorn TV, Topic

Captain Scarlet & the Mysterons - Prime Video

The Capture - Peacock

Care - Acorn TV

Caroline Quentin's National Parks - BritBox

Cars, Cops, & Criminals - Tubi

The Cars That Made Britain Great - Pluto

Carters Get Rich - Tubi

The Case - Acorn TV, Pluto

Case Histories - IMDb TV, Tubi, Pluto

Castle Builders - Prime Video

Castles and Palaces of Europe - Prime Video

Casualty - BritBox

Casualty 1900s: London Hospital - BritBox

The Casual Vacancy - HBO Max, HBO

Catastophe - Prime Video

Catherine the Great - HBO Max, HBO

Catherine's Family Kitchen - Tubi

Caught on Camera - Netflix

Celebrity Restaurant in Our Living Room - Tubi

Celtic Britain - Prime Video, Pluto

The Celts - Prime Video

The Celts: Blood, Iron, and Sacrifice with Alice Roberts and Neil Oliver - Prime Video

The Champions - BritBox

Chancer - Prime Video

Charles & Diana: Wedding of the Century - BritBox

Charles Dickens: The Man That Asked for More - Prime Video

Charles Dickens' London Life - Prime Video

Charles I: Downfall of a King - Prime Video

Charles II: The Power and the Passion - BritBox

Charlie Jade - Prime Video

Chasing Shadows - Acorn TV

Chatsworth - Prime Video

Cheat - Sundance Now

Chef's Protégé - Tubi

Chernobyl - HBO Max, HBO

Chewin' the Fat - Netflix

The Child in Time - PBS Masterpiece

Children's Hospital - Tubi

Chiller - Prime Video, Tubi

Chimerica - Topic

Choccywoccydoodah - Tubi

Christopher and His Kind - BritBox

Churchill: Blood Sweat, & Oil Paint - Prime Video, Acorn TV

The Churchills - Acorn TV

Churchill's Secret Agents: The New Recruits - Netflix

Churchill: The Darkest Hour - BritBox

Cider with Rosie - Acorn TV

Cilla - Acorn TV

The City & the City - Prime Video, BritBox

City Homicide - IMDb TV, Hulu, Tubi

City of Vice - Prime Video

Civil War - Prime Video, Acorn TV

Civil War: The Untold Story - Acorn TV

Civilisation - BritBox

Cla'am - Topic

Clarissa & the King's Cookbook - Inside Outside

Clash of the Santas - BritBox

Classic British Steam Engines - Prime Video

Classic Doctor Who - BritBox

Classic Doctor Who Comic Con Panel - BritBox

Classic Mary Berry - IMDb TV

Clean Break - Acorn TV

Cleverman - Netflix

Click and Collect - BritBox

Click for Murder - Netflix

Clink - Prime Video

Clique - Hulu

Clone - Tubi

Close to the Enemy - Sundance Now, Acorn TV

Cloudstreet - Acorn TV

Coalition - BritBox

Coast - BritBox

Coastal Railways with Julie Walters - Acorn TV

Cocaine - Netflix

The Code (2014) - Netflix, Acorn TV

The Code (2011) - Netflix

Code 9 - Pluto

Code Blue: Murder - BritBox

Code of a Killer - Acorn TV

Codebreakers: The Secret Geniuses of World War II - BritBox

Cold Blood - BritBox

Cold Feet - Prime Video, BritBox

Cold Feet: The New Years - BritBox

Cold Squad - Prime Video

Collateral - Netflix

Collision - PBS Masterpiece

Colonel March of Scotland Yard - Prime Video

The Colour of Magic - IMDb TV

Come Dine With Me - Best of British TV

The Comedy of Errors (1983) - BritBox

Come Home - Topic

Comfort Eating - Prime Video, Tubi

The Commander - Acorn TV

Conspiracies - Netflix

Constable: A Country Rebel - Prime Video

Conviction: Murder at the Station - Pluto

Conviction: Murder in Suburbia - Pluto

Cook Yourself Thin UK - Tubi

Cop Car Workshop - Pluto

The Cops - Prime Video

Coronation Street - BritBox, Hulu

The Coronavirus Newscast - BritBox

The Coroner - BritBox

Corrie at Christmas - BritBox

Count Arthur Strong - Acorn TV, Tubi

Countryfile Autumn Diaries - BritBox

Countryfile Spring Diaries - BritBox

Coupling - Prime Video, Hulu

Crackanory - Prime Video

Cracker (UK) - BritBox

Cracker (US) - Tubi

Cracking the Shakespeare Code - Prime Video

Cradle to Grave - Acorn TV

Cranford - BritBox

Crashing - Netflix

Crazy Delicious - Netflix

Crazyhead - Netflix

Creeped Out - Netflix

The Crest - IMDb TV

Crime & Violence in England - Prime Video

Crime and Punishment - Prime Video

Crime Story - BritBox

Criminal Justice - Hulu

Criminal: United Kingdom - Netflix

Crims - Prime Video, Tubi

The Crimson Field - PBS Masterpiece

The Crimson Petal and the White - Sundance Now, Tubi

Critical - Pluto

The Crown - Netflix

Crown and Country - Prime Video

Crownies - Prime Video

Cruise of the Gods - BritBox

Cruising the Cut - Prime Video

The Cry - Sundance Now

Cuckoo - Netflix

Cuffs - Prime Video

Cut from a Different Cloth - Prime Video

Cymbeline (1982) - BritBox

Daleks' Invasion Earth 2150 A.D. - BritBox

Dalziel & Pascoe - BritBox

Damned - BritBox

Damned Designs: Don't Demolish My Home - Inside Outside

Dan Snow's Norman Walks - Prime Video

Dancing on the Edge - PBS Masterpiece, Starz

Danger Man, aka Secret Agent - Prime Video

Danger Mouse - Netflix

Danger Mouse: Classic Collection - Netflix

Daniel & Majella's B&B Road Trip - Prime Video

Daniel Deronda - Prime Video, Hulu

Dark Angel - Prime Video

Dark Heart - BritBox

Dark Matter - Netflix

The Darling Buds of May - Prime Video, BritBox, Tubi

David Copperfield (1999) - BritBox, Prime Video, Hulu

David Copperfield (1986) - Prime Video

David Jason's Secret Service - Prime Video, Acorn TV

David Suchet on the Orient

Express - BritBox

David Suchet's Being Poirot - Acorn TV

Da Vinci's Demons - Starz

Days of Majesty - BritBox

DCI Banks - Prime Video, Hulu

Dead Boss - Prime Video, Hulu

Dead Good Job - BritBox

Dead Lucky - Sundance Now, Acorn TV

Dead Man's Shoes - Pluto

Dead Set - Netflix

Deadwater Fell - Acorn TV

Deadwind - Netflix

Dear Murderer - Acorn TV

Death Comes to Pemberley - PBS Masterpiece

Death in Paradise - BritBox

Death Over Dinner - Topic

Decline and Fall - Acorn TV

Decoding the Future - BritBox

The Deep - Prime Video, Pluto

Deep Water - PBS Masterpiece, Acorn TV

Degrassi : Next Class - Netflix

Delicious - Acorn TV

The Delivery Man - Prime Video, Acorn TV

Dennis and Gnasher Unleashed - Netflix

Derek - Netflix

Derek Acorah's Ghost Towns - Prime Video

Dermot Bannon's Incredible Homes - Tubi

Derry Girls - Netflix

Desi Rascals - Prime Video

Design Doctors - Prime Video, Tubi

Designer Darlings - Tubi

Desperate Romantics - Prime Video, BritBox, Pluto

The Detectives - Prime Video, Acorn TV

Detectorists - Acorn TV, Prime Video

The Devil's Mistress - Tubi, Pluto, Prime Video

Diana: The New Evidence - IMDb TV

Diary of a Teenage Virgin - Best of British TV

Dickensian - Prime Video, BritBox

Digging for Britain - Acorn TV

Dinner Party Wars - Best of British TV

The Diplomat - Pluto

Dirk Gently (UK) - BritBox

Dirk Gently's Holistic Detective Agency (US) - Hulu

Discover England - Prime Video

Discover Ireland - Prime Video

Discover Scotland - Prime Video

Discovering Britain - Acorn TV

Discovering Korean Food with Gizzi Erskine - Inside Outside

Discovering the World - Tubi

Do or Die - Prime Video

Doc Martin - Acorn TV, Hulu, Tubi, Pluto

Doctor at Large - Tubi

The Doctor Blake Mysteries - BritBox

Doctor Finlay - Acorn TV

Doctor Foster - Netflix

Doctor Thorne - Prime Video

Doctor Who - HBO Max

Doctor Who Specials - BritBox

Doctor Who: Tales Lost in Time - Prime Video

Doctor Who: The Doctors Revisited - BritBox

Doctor Zhivago - BritBox

The Dog Rescuers - Pluto, Tubi

Dombey and Son (1983) - Prime Video

Dombey and Son (2015) - Prime Video

Dominion Creek - Acorn TV

Donal MacIntyre - Prime Video

Donovan - Prime Video

Double Your House for Half the Money - Prime Video, Tubi

Down from London - Topic

Downton Abbey - Prime Video, Peacock

Dr. Who and the Daleks - BritBox

Dream Corp LLC - Hulu

Drifters - Prime Video, Pluto

Drovers' Gold - Prime Video

Dublin Murders - Starz

Dunkirk - BritBox

Durham County - Prime Video

The Durrells in Corfu - Prime Video

East of Everything - Acorn TV

East West 101 - Acorn TV

EastEnders - BritBox

Edge of Heaven - BritBox

Edge of the Universe - Netflix

Edinburgh: More than Words - Prime Video

The Edinburgh Show - BritBox

Edward & Mary: The Unknown Tudors - Acorn TV, Prime Video

Edward and Mrs. Simpson - IMDb TV

Edwardian Farm - Tubi

Elizabeth I (2014) - Prime Video

Elizabeth I (2006) - HBO Max, HBO

Elizabeth I & Her Enemies - Acorn TV

Elizabeth I: Killer Queen - Prime Video

Elizabeth I: The Virgin Queen - PBS Masterpiece

Elizabeth I: War on Terror - Prime Video

Elizabeth R - BritBox

Elizabeth: Queen, Wife, Mother - Best of British TV

Emerald Falls - BritBox

Emergency Firefighters - Prime Video, Tubi

Emma - BritBox

Emmerdale - Prime Video, BritBox

Empire - Acorn TV

Empire: The Soul of Britannia - Prime Video

Endeavour - PBS Masterpiece, Prime Video

The End of the F***ing World - Netflix

Enemy at the Door - Prime Video

England's Forgotten Queen: The Life and Death of Lady Jane Grey - IMDb TV

The English Game - Netflix

The English Gentleman - Prime Video

English Gypsies - Prime Video

Enid Blyton Adventure Series - IMDb TV

Enid Blyton Secret Series - IMDb TV

Enterprice - Topic

Episodes - Showtime

The Escape Artist - PBS Masterpiece

Escape to the Chateau - Peacock

Escape to the Country - IMDb TV

Escorts - Best of British TV

Eternal Law - IMDb TV, Tubi, Pluto

Everyday Miracles - Netflix

Excalibur: Behind the Movie - PBS Masterpiece

Executive Stress - Acorn TV

Exhibition on Screen: History's Greatest Artists - Prime Video

Exile - PBS Masterpiece, Tubi, Topic

Extras - Netflix

Extreme A&E - Tubi

Extreme Ghost Stories - Pluto

Extremely Dangerous - BritBox

The Fades - Prime Video, Hulu, Pluto

The Fall - Sundance Now, Prime Video, BritBox, Tubi

Family Business - Acorn TV

The Family Farm - Acorn TV

Family Tree - Prime Video, HBO Max, HBO

Fanny by Gaslight - Prime Video

Fanny Hill - Acorn TV

Far From the Madding Crowd - PBS Masterpiece

Farewell Tina - Best of British TV

The Farm Fixer - Prime Video

The Farmer's Country Showdown - Tubi

Fat Men Can't Hunt - Tubi

Father and Son - BritBox

Father Brown (1974) - BritBox

Father Brown (2013) - BritBox

Father Ted - Prime Video, BritBox, Pluto

Fawlty Towers - BritBox

The Fenn Street Gang - IMDb TV

The Field of Blood - Prime Video, Acorn TV, Pluto

Fields of Gold - BritBox

Fifth Gear - Pluto

Fight Club: A History of Violence - Pluto

Finding Joy - Acorn TV

Fingersmith - Sundance Now

First Homes - Tubi

The First Silent Night - Prime Video

The Five - Netflix

Five by Five - BritBox

Five Days - HBO Max, HBO

Five Days: The Train - Acorn TV

Fix Her Up - Prime Video

Flack - Showtime

Fleabag - Prime Video

Flickers - Prime Video

Flood - Prime Video

Florence Nightingale - BritBox

Flowers - Netflix

The Flying Scotsman Steam Train Comes Home - Prime Video

The Flying Scotsman: A Rail

Romance - Prime Video

The Flying Scotsman: Running the Legend - Prime Video

Food Glorious Food - Inside Outside

Footloose in England: Along the Ridgeway - Prime Video

Footloose in Ireland - Prime Video

Footloose in London: All the Best Sights of our Capital - Prime Video

Footloose in London: Undiscovered and Unusual - Prime Video

Footloose in Scotland: The West Highland Way - Prime Video

Footloose in the Cotswolds, Part 1 - Prime Video

Footloose in the Cotswolds, Part 2 - Prime Video

The Force: Manchester - Prime Video

Foreign Exchange - Prime Video

Forensic Investigators - Pluto

The Forsyte Saga - PBS Masterpiece

Foyle's War - Acorn TV

The Fragile Heart - Acorn TV

The Frankenstein Chronicles - Netflix

Frankie - BritBox, Pluto

Frankie Drake Mysteries - PBS Masterpiece

Fred Dinenage Murder Casebook - Prime Video, Pluto

Free Rein - Netflix

The French Collection - Tubi

French Fields - Acorn TV

Fresh Fields - Acorn TV

Fresh Meat - Prime Video

Freud - Netflix

The Fried Chicken Shop: Life in a Day - Best of British TV

Friday Night Dinner - Prime Video

From Darkness - BritBox

From Father to Daughter - Acorn TV

From Russia With Cash - Best of British TV

From There to Here - Prime Video

Frontier - Netflix

Frontline Police - Best of British TV

Fun fact - BritBox

Funny is Funny: A Conversation with Normal Lear - BritBox

Gadget Man - Prime Video

Galway, Ireland: Busy Streets and Irish Music in the Pubs - Prime Video

Game of Thrones - HBO Max, HBO

Gameface - Hulu

Gangsters: Faces of the Underworld - Pluto

The Garden Pantry - Inside Outside

Garden Rescue - Inside Outside

Gardeners' World - Inside Outside, BritBox

Gardens of the National Trust - Prime Video

Gauguin: The Full Story - Prime Video

Gavin & Stacey - Prime Video, BritBox

The Genius of Roald Dahl - Acorn TV

Genius of the Ancient World - Acorn TV, Netflix

Genius of the Modern World - Netflix

Gentleman Jack - HBO Max, HBO

Gentlemen, The Queen - BritBox

The Gentle Touch - Prime Video

George III: The Genius of the Mad King - IMDb TV

Get a Life - Tubi

Get Even - Netflix

Get Growing - Inside Outside, Prime Video

Getting High for God? - Topic

Getting On - Prime Video, Hulu, Pluto

Getting the Builders In - Tubi

Ghost Chasers - Pluto

Ghosts - HBO Max

The Ghost Squad - Pluto

Gibraltar: Britain in the Sun - Best of British TV

Gideon's Daughter - BritBox

The Gil Mayo Mysteries (aka Mayo) - BritBox

Giri/Haji - Netflix

Girlfri3nds (2012) - Tubi

Girlfriends (2018) - Acorn TV

Girls to Men - Best of British TV

Girls with Autism - BritBox

Give a Pet a Home - Tubi

Glitch - Netflix

Glorious Gardens from Above - Prime Video

Glow Up - Netflix

Go Girls - Prime Video

God Save the Queen - Prime Video

Gold Digger - Acorn TV

Golden Years - Acorn TV

Good Cop - BritBox

The Good Karma Hospital - Acorn TV

Good Morning Britain - BritBox

Good Omens - Prime Video

Gordon Behind Bars, aka Ramsay Behind Bars - Pluto

Gordon Ramsay's The F Word - Hulu

Gordon Ramsey's 24 Hours to Hell & Back - Hulu

Gordon Ramsey's Ultimate Home Cooking - Hulu

Gracepoint - Prime Video, Tubi

Grafters - Prime Video, Tubi

The Grand - IMDb TV

Grand Designs - IMDb TV, Netflix, Tubi

The Grand Tour - Prime Video

Grand Tours of Scotland's Lochs - Prime Video

Grand Tours of the Scottish Islands - Prime Video

Grantchester - PBS Masterpiece, Prime Video

Great Artists with Tim Marlow - Prime Video

The Great British Baking Show - Netflix

The Great British Baking Show: The Beginnings - Netflix

The Great British Benefits Handout - Prime Video

The Great British Countryside - BritBox

Great Cars: British Elegance - Prime Video

The Great Chelsea Garden Challenge - BritBox

Great Escape: The Untold Story - BritBox

Great Estates of Scotland - Prime Video

Great Expectations (1999) - BritBox, Prime Video

Great Expectations (1981) - Prime Video

The Great Fire - PBS Masterpiece

The Great Gardens of England - Prime Video

The Great Hip Hop Hoax - IMDb TV

Great Houses with Julian Fellowes - PBS Masterpiece

Great Interior Design Challenge - Inside Outside, Pluto

Great Lighthouses of Ireland - Prime Video

Great Night Out - Best of British TV

Great Performances: Macbeth - PBS Masterpiece

The Great Train Robbery - Prime Video, Acorn TV

Greatest Events of WWII in Colour - Netflix

Greatest Gardens - Prime Video, Tubi

The Green Park - Prime Video

Green Wing - Prime Video, Tubi

Grime Fighters - Tubi
Ground Force - Prime Video
Ground Force Revisited - Prime Video
Guardians of the Night - Prime Video
Guerrilla - Showtime
The Guilty - Prime Video
Gunpowder - HBO Max, HBO
The Gypsy Matchmaker - Prime Video
H2O: Just Add Water - Netflix
Hadrian's Wall: Antonine Wall - Prime Video
The Hairy Biker's Christmas Party - BritBox
Hairy Bikers Everyday Gourmets - BritBox
Hairy Bikers: Pubs that Built Britain - Prime Video, Tubi
Hairy Bikers' Bakeation - BritBox
Half Moon Investigations - Prime Video
Half-Built House - Prime Video
Halloween: Feast of the Dying Sun - Prime Video
Hamish Macbeth - Prime Video, Acorn TV
Hamlet, Prince of Denmark (1980) - BritBox
Hammer House of Horror - Prime Video, Tubi
Hang-Ups - Hulu
Happyish - Showtime
The Harbour: Aberdeen - Prime Video
Harbour Lives - Best of British TV
Hard Sun - Hulu
Hard Times - Prime Video
Harlots - Hulu
Harrow - Hulu
Harrow: A Very British School - Prime Video
Harry - Acorn TV
Haven - Netflix
Heartbeat - BritBox, Tubi, IMDb TV
The Heart Guy - Acorn TV
Heartland - Netflix

Hearts & Bones - Prime Video, BritBox
Heat of the Sun - Prime Video
The Heist at Hatton Garden - BritBox
The Helen West Casebook - Acorn TV
Helicopter ER - Tubi
Helicopter Search & Rescue - Prime Video, Tubi
Hello Ladies - HBO Max, HBO
Hell's Kitchen - Peacock, Hulu, Tubi
Henry and Anne: The Lovers Who Changed History - PBS Masterpiece
Henry IV: Parts 1 and 2 (1979) - BritBox
Henry IX - Acorn TV
Henry IX: Lost King - PBS Masterpiece, Acorn TV
Henry V (1979) - BritBox
Henry VI: Parts 1-3 (1983) - BritBox
Henry VII: Winter King - Prime Video
Henry VIII (1979) - BritBox
Hetty Wainthropp Investigates - BritBox
Hidden (2011) - Acorn TV, Tubi
Hidden (2018) - Acorn TV
Hidden Britain by Drone - Acorn TV
Hidden Europe - Tubi
Hidden: World's Best Monster Mystery - Loch Ness - BritBox
Highlands and Islands: Where Scotland's Heart Beats Loudest - Prime Video
Him - BritBox
Him & Her - Pluto
Hinterland - Netflix
His Dark Materials - HBO Max, HBO
History 101 - Netflix
The Hitchhiker's Guide to the Galaxy - Prime Video, BritBox, Hulu
Hitler's Circle of Evil - Netflix

Hitmen - Peacock
Hoarder SOS - Inside Outside
Hoarders, Get Your House in Order - Inside Outside
Hoff the Record - Netflix
Holbein: Eye of the Tudors - Prime Video
Holby City - BritBox
Hold the Sunset - BritBox
Hollyoaks - Hulu
Home & Away - Prime Video
Home Away from Home - BritBox
Home Fires - Prime Video
Home of Fabulous Cakes - IMDb TV, Tubi
Home of the Year: Ireland - Prime Video, Tubi
Homefront - BritBox
Homes By Design - Tubi
The Home Show - Prime Video
Homes Under the Hammer - Inside Outside
Honey, I Bought the House - Tubi
Horrible Histories - Prime Video, Hulu
Horrible Histories: Formidable Florence Nightingale - BritBox
The Hotel - Tubi
The Hotel Fixers - Prime Video
Hot Tub Britain - Best of British TV
Hotel of Mum and Dad - Best of British TV
Hound of the Baskervilles - BritBox
The Hour - Acorn TV
House Swap - Inside Outside
The House that 100k (GBP) Built - Prime Video, Tubi
The House that 100k Built: Tricks of the Trade - Prime Video, Tubi
The House that Dripped Blood - Tubi
How Gay is Pakistan? - Topic
How to Cook Well With Rory

O'Connell - Tubi

How to Get Ahead - Prime Video

How to Haggle for a House - Inside Outside

How to Live Mortgage Free with Sarah Beeny - Netflix

Howards End - Prime Video, Starz

Hugh the Hunter - Topic

Humans - Prime Video

Hunderby - Hulu

Hunted - Cinemax

Husbands from Hell - Tubi

Hustle - Prime Video, Tubi

Hyperdrive - Pluto

I Am a Killer - Netflix

I May Destroy You - HBO Max, HBO

The Ice House - BritBox

I, Claudius - Acorn TV

Idris Elba: King of Speed - IMDb TV

Imagine a School: Summerhill - IMDb TV

The Impressionists - Prime Video

The Inbetweeners - Netflix, Tubi

The Inbetweeners Movie - Tubi

The Incredible Journey of Mary Bryant - IMDb TV, Pluto

The Indian Detective - Netflix

The Indian Doctor - Prime Video, Acorn TV

The Innocents - Netflix

In Plain Sight - BritBox

In the Dark - BritBox

In the Flesh - Prime Video, Hulu

Injustice - Acorn TV

In-Law Wedding Wars - Best of British TV

Innocent - Sundance Now

Insert Name Here - BritBox

Inside Claridges - Best of British TV, BritBox

Inside Men - Pluto

Inside No. 9 - BritBox, Hulu

Inside the Ambulance - Prime Video, Tubi

Inside the Court of Henry VIII - PBS Masterpiece

Inside the Crown: Secrets of the Royals - IMDb TV

Inside the Freemasons - Netflix

Inside the Merchant - Prime Video

Inside the Real Narcos - Netflix

Inside the Tower of London: Crimes, Conspiracies, Confessions - Prime Video

Inside the World's Toughest Prisons - Netflix

Inspector Lewis - PBS Masterpiece

The Inspector Lynley Mysteries - BritBox

Inspector Morse - BritBox

The Instant Gardener - BritBox

Intelligence (2005) - Netflix

Intelligence (2020) - Peacock

Interior Design Masters - Netflix

Intruders - Prime Video, Hulu, Topic

The Investigator: A British Crime Story - Netflix

The Invisibles - Acorn TV

Ireland with Ardal O'Hanlon - Prime Video

Ireland's Wild River - Prime Video

The Irish Mob - Netflix, Pluto

The Irish Pub - Prime Video, Tubi

The Irish R.M. - Acorn TV

Iron Men - Prime Video

Island at War - Prime Video

Isle of Man: From the Air - Prime Video

Isolation Stories - BritBox

It Came From Connemara - IMDb TV

The IT Crowd - Netflix

Ivanhoe - Prime Video

Jack Irish - Acorn TV

Jack Taylor - Acorn TV

Jack the Ripper - Prime Video

Jack the Ripper Revealed - Prime Video

Jack the Ripper: Conspiracies - Prime Video

Jack the Ripper: The Definitive Story - Prime Video

Jack Whitehall at Large - Netflix

Jack Whitehall: Christmas With My Father - Netflix

Jack Whitehall: I'm Only Joking - Netflix

Jack Whitehall: Travels with My Father - Netflix

Jackson's Wharf - Prime Video

James & Thom's Pizza Pilgrimage - Tubi

James Acaster: Repertoire - Netflix

James Martin Home Comforts - Tubi

James Martin's Mediterranean - Tubi

James Martin's United Cakes of America - Tubi

James May's Man Lab - Prime Video

James May's Toy Stories - Prime Video

Jamestown - PBS Masterpiece

Jamie and Jimmy's Food Fight Club - Pluto

Jamie: Keep Cooking and Carry On - Hulu

Jamie's Quick and Easy Food - Hulu

Jamie's American Road Trip - Topic

Jamie's Food Escapes - Topic

Jamie's Super Food - Topic

Jane Austen Country: The Life and Times of Jane Austen - Prime Video

Jane Austen: Life - Prime Video

Jane Eyre (1983) - Prime Video

Jane Eyre (2006) - Prime Video, Hulu, BritBox

Janet King - Acorn TV

Jason and the Argonauts - Tubi

Jekyll & Hyde - BritBox

Jennie: Lady Randolph Churchill - Acorn TV

Jericho - Acorn TV

Jericho of Scotland Yard - Acorn TV

Jessica - Prime Video

The Jewel in the Crown - PBS Masterpiece

Jimmy Doherty's Escape to the Wild - Inside Outside

The Job Lot - BritBox

Joe 90 - Prime Video

Jonathan Creek - BritBox, Pluto

The Jonathan Ross Show - Best of British TV

Joseph Campbell: Mythos 1 - Acorn TV

The Joy of Techs - IMDb TV

Julia Bradbury's Coast and Country Walks - Acorn TV

Julius Caesar (1979) - BritBox

Julius Caesar with Mary Beard - Prime Video

The Jury - Prime Video, BritBox

Just Another Immigrant - Showtime

Justice - BritBox

K-9 - Pluto

K9 & Company: A Girl's Best Friend - BritBox

The Kangaroo Gang - Tubi

Kat & Alfie: Redwater - BritBox

Kath & Kim - Netflix

Kavanagh QC - Prime Video, BritBox, Tubi

Keeping Faith - Acorn TV

Keeping the Castle - Acorn TV

Keeping Up Appearances - BritBox

The Kennedys - Prime Video, Hulu

The Kettering Incident - Prime Video

Kevin McCloud's Escape to the Wild - Inside Outside

Keys to the Castle - Prime Video

Kids on the Edge - Tubi

Killed By My Debt - BritBox

Killer Net - Acorn TV

Killer Roads - Tubi

Killer Women with Piers Morgan - Netflix

Killing Eve - Hulu

Kim's Convenience - Netflix

King Arthur's Britain - Acorn TV

King Arthur's Lost Kingdom - Prime Video

King Gary - Prime Video

King Lear (2018) - Prime Video

King Lear (1982) - BritBox

King of Scots - Prime Video

Kingdom - Acorn TV, Hulu

Kirstie's Vintage Home - BritBox

Kiss Me First - Netflix

Kitchen Criminals - Inside Outside

Kitchen Nightmares - IMDb TV, Hulu, Tubi

Know the British - Prime Video

The Kumars - Best of British TV

L'Accident - Acorn TV

Ladette to Lady - Tubi

Ladhood - Hulu

Ladies of Letters - Acorn TV

Lady Chatterley - Acorn TV

Laid - Prime Video

Land Girls - Acorn TV, Netflix

Lanester - Prime Video

Lark Rise to Candleford - BritBox, Hulu

Last Contact - Prime Video

The Last Days of Anne Boleyn - Prime Video

The Last Detective - BritBox

The Last Kingdom - Netflix

Last of the Summer Wine - BritBox

The Last Post - Prime Video

Last Tango in Halifax - Netflix

Laura McKenzie's Traveler - Tubi

Law & Order: UK - Sundance Now

The League of Gentlemen - BritBox

Legends - Hulu, IMDb TV

Legends of King Arthur - Prime Video

Legends of Power with Tony Robinson - Prime Video

Len and Ainsley's Big Food Adventure - Prime Video

Les Misérables - PBS Masterpiece

Les Petits Meurtres D'Agatha Christie - Acorn TV

The Letdown - Netflix

The Letter for the King - Netflix

The Level - Acorn TV

Leverage - Sundance Now. Tubi

Lewis (Pilot) - BritBox

Liam Dale's Ghostly Trails: Haunted Great Britain - Prime Video

Liar - Sundance Now

Licence to Thrill: Paul Hollywood Meets Aston Martin - BritBox

The Life and Crimes of William Palmer - Prime Video

The Life and Death of King John (1984) - BritBox

Life in Squares - Prime Video

Life of Crime - BritBox

The Life of Verdi - Acorn TV

Life on Mars - BritBox

Life's Too Short - HBO Max, HBO

The Lights Before Christmas - BritBox

The Lights Before Christmas: Luminous London - BritBox

Like Father Like Son - Acorn TV

The Lilac Bus - Acorn TV

Lillie - Prime Video

Lily Allen: From Riches to Rags - IMDb TV, Tubi

Limmy's Show - Netflix

Line of Duty - Acorn TV, BritBox, Prime Video, Hulu

Lip Service - Hulu, Tubi, Pluto

Little Boy Blue - BritBox

Little Britain USA - HBO Max, HBO
Little Devil - Prime Video
Little Dorrit (2008) - Prime Video, Pluto
Little Dorrit (1987) - Starz
The Little Drummer Girl - Sundance Now
Liverpool 1 - Prime Video, Acorn TV
The Living & the Dead - Prime Video
Living in the Shadow of World War II - Prime Video, Acorn TV
Living the Dream - BritBox
Living the Tradition: An Enchanting Journey into Old Irish Airs - IMDb TV
Loaded - Netflix
Location, Location, Location - Tubi
Loch Ness - Sundance Now, Acorn TV
London Irish - Prime Video, Tubi
London Kills - Acorn TV
London Road - BritBox
London Spy - Netflix
London: A City in Time - Prime Video
London: A Tale of Two Cities - Prime Video
London's Burning - IMDb TV
Looking for Victoria - BritBox
Lord Montague - Prime Video
Lords and Ladles - Acorn TV
Lorna Doone (1976) - Acorn TV
Lorna Doone (2000) - Prime Video
Lost in Austen - BritBox, Tubi
Lost Kingdoms of Africa - Acorn TV
Louis Theroux - BritBox
Louis Theroux's Altered States: Choosing Death - Topic
Louis Theroux's Altered States: Take My Baby - Topic

Love Hurts - Acorn TV
Love in a Cold Climate - Prime Video
Love Island - Hulu
Love Lies Bleeding - Prime Video
Love London - Prime Video, Pluto
Love Your Garden - Inside Outside
Love, Lies, & Records - Acorn TV
Love/Hate - Prime Video
Love's Labour's Lost - BritBox
Lovejoy - PBS Masterpiece, Acorn TV
Lucifer - Netflix
Lucy Worsley's 12 Days of Tudor Christmas - PBS Masterpiece
Lucy Worsley's Royal Myths and Secrets - PBS Masterpiece
Lunch Monkeys - Prime Video, Tubi
Luther - Prime Video, Starz
Macbeth (1983) - BritBox
Madame Bovary - Prime Video
Made Over By - Tubi
Maeve Binchy Echoes - Acorn TV
The Magical World of Trains - Prime Video
Magic Numbers: Hannah Fry's Mysterious World of Maths - Prime Video, Acorn TV
Maigret (1992) - BritBox
Maigret (2016) - BritBox
Make Me Perfect - Tubi
Make My Home Bigger - Prime Video, Tubi
The Making of a Lady - PBS Masterpiece
The Mallorca Files - BritBox
Man & Beast with Martin Clunes - Prime Video
Man Down - Netflix
Man in an Orange Shirt - PBS Masterpiece
Man Like Mobeen - Netflix
Man Stroke Woman - Tubi,

Pluto
Manhunt - Acorn TV
Mansfield Park (2007) - PBS Masterpiece
Mansfield Park (1983) - Prime Video
The Man Who Cracked the Nazi Code - IMDb TV
The Man Who Killed Richard III - IMDb TV
The Man Who Lost His Head - Acorn TV
Mapp and Lucia (1985) - BritBox
Mapp and Lucia (2014) - BritBox
Marcella - Netflix
Marco's Great British Feast - BritBox
Margaret - BritBox
Margaret: The Rebel Princess - PBS Masterpiece
Market Forces - Prime Video
Market Kitchen - Inside Outside
Marley's Ghosts - BritBox
Married to a Celebrity - Tubi
Martin Chuzzlewit - Prime Video
Martin Clunes & a Lion Called Mugie - Prime Video
Martin Clunes: A Man and His Dogs - IMDb TV
Martin Clunes: Heavy Horsepower - Prime Video
Martin Clunes: Islands of America - Acorn TV
Martin Clunes: Islands of Australia - Acorn TV
Martin Clunes: Last Lemur Standing - Prime Video
Marvellous - Acorn TV
Mary Berry's Absolute Favourites - BritBox, Tubi
Mary Berry's Country House Secrets - BritBox
Mary Berry's Foolproof Cooking - Tubi
Masterpiece - Tubi
Masterpiece: Indian Summers - Prime Video
Masterpiece: The

Chaperone - PBS Masterpiece
Masterpiece: Wind in the Willows - PBS Masterpiece
Maxxx - Hulu
Mayday - Acorn TV
The Mayor of Casterbridge - Acorn TV
McCallum - Acorn TV
McLeod's Daughters - IMDb TV, Acorn TV, Tubi, Pluto
McMafia - Sundance Now
Measure for Measure (1979) - BritBox
Medieval Lives - Acorn TV
Meet the Adebanjos - Netflix
Meet the Romans - Prime Video, Pluto
Meghan & Harry: A Revolutionary Romance - BritBox
Memories of Scotland - Prime Video
Men Behaving Badly - IMDb TV, Tubi
The Merchant of Venice (1980) - BritBox
Merlin - Netflix, Tubi, Pluto, Prime Video
Merlin's Apprentice - Tubi
The Merry Wives of Windsor (1982) - BritBox
MI-5 - BritBox
Middlemarch - Prime Video
Midsomer Murders - Acorn TV, BritBox, Tubi, Pluto, IMDb TV
Midsomer Murders Favourites - BritBox
Midsomer Murders: 20th Anniversary Documentary - BritBox, Acorn TV
Midsomer Murders: Neil Dudgeon's Top 10 - Acorn TV
Midwinter of the Spirit - Sundance Now, Acorn TV
The Mighty Boosh - Hulu
The Mill - Prime Video, Tubi
Million Pound Menu - Netflix
Million Pound Properties - Prime Video, Tubi
Millionaire Basement Wars - Tubi
Mind Games - Acorn TV
Mind Your Language - Prime Video
The Miniaturist - PBS Masterpiece
Miranda - IMDb TV, Hulu
Miriam's Big American Adventure - Topic
Misfits - Hulu
Miss Austen Regrets - Prime Video, BritBox
Miss Fisher & The Crypt of Tears - Acorn TV
Miss Fisher's Murder Mysteries - Acorn TV
Miss Marple - BritBox
Miss Sherlock - HBO Max, HBO
Missing - Acorn TV
The Missing - Prime Video, Starz
Missing Persons Unit - IMDb TV, Prime Video
The Mixer - Prime Video
Mo - BritBox
Mobile - Prime Video
Moby Dick (1998) - Prime Video, Pluto
Moby Dick (2011) - Prime Video
Mock the Week - BritBox
Modern Irish Food - Tubi
Moll Flanders - Tubi
Mom P.I. - Prime Video
The Monarchy - BritBox
Monarchy with David Starkey - Acorn TV
Monday Monday - Tubi
Monkman & Seagull's Genius Guide to Britain - Topic
Monroe - IMDb TV
Monty Don's Paradise Gardens - Acorn TV
Monty Python and the Holy Grail - Netflix
Monty Python Before the Flying Circus - Netflix
Monty Python Best Bits - Netflix
Monty Python Conquers America - Netflix
Monty Python Live (Mostly):
One Down, Five to Go - Netflix
Monty Python Live at Aspen - Netflix
Monty Python Live at the Hollywood Bowl - Netflix
Monty Python: The Meaning of Live - Netflix
Monty Python's Almost the Truth - Netflix
Monty Python's Fliegender Zircus - Netflix
Monty Python's Flying Circus - Netflix
Monty Python's Life of Brian - Netflix
Monty Python's Personal Best - Netflix
Monumental Challenge - BritBox
The Moodys - Acorn TV
Moone Boy - Hulu
The Moonstone (1972) - BritBox
The Moonstone (2016) - BritBox, Prime Video
The Moors Murders - Prime Video
The Moorside - BritBox
Moses Jones - Topic
Most Haunted - Prime Video, Pluto
Mother's Day - BritBox
MotherFatherSon - Starz
Motherland - Sundance Now
Mount Pleasant - Acorn TV
Mount Royal - Prime Video
Moving On - Prime Video, BritBox
Mr. and Mrs. Murder - Acorn TV
Mr. Bean - Prime Video, BritBox, Pluto, Hulu
Mr. Palfrey of Westminster - Acorn TV
Mr. Selfridge - PBS Masterpiece
Mr. Stink - BritBox
Mr. Young - Netflix
Mrs. Biggs - Acorn TV
The Mrs. Bradley Mysteries - BritBox
Mrs. Brown - BritBox

Mrs. Brown's Boys - BritBox

Mrs. Wilson - PBS Masterpiece

Ms. Fisher's Modern Murder Mysteries - Acorn TV

Much Ado About Nothing (1984) - BritBox

Mum - BritBox

MumDem - Prime Video

Mummy's Little Murderer - IMDb TV

Murder Call - Prime Video

Murder City - Prime Video

Murder Investigation Team - Acorn TV

Murder Maps - Netflix

Murder on the Homefront - PBS Masterpiece

Murder Rooms: Mysteries of the Real Sherlock Holmes - Prime Video

Murder Trial: The Disappearance of Margaret Fleming - Sundance Now

Murder, Mystery, and My Family - BritBox

Murder, She Wrote - Peacock, IMDb TV

Murdered by My Boyfriend - BritBox

Murdered by My Father - BritBox

Murdered for Being Different - BritBox

Murderland - Acorn TV

Murdertown - Prime Video

Murdoch Mysteries - Acorn TV, Hulu

Murdoch Mysteries: The Movies - Acorn TV

Murphy's Law - Prime Video, Acorn TV

The Musketeers - Hulu

My Boy Jack - BritBox

My Dream Derelict Home - Prime Video

My Dream Farm - Prime Video

My Flat Pack Home - Tubi

My Hotter Half - Netflix

My Kitchen Rules, aka MKR + UK - Pluto

My Life is Murder - Acorn TV

My Life on a Plate - Tubi

My Mad Fat Diary - Hulu

My Mother & Other Strangers - Prime Video

My Pet Shame - Tubi

My Transgender Kid - Best of British TV

My Uncle Silas - Prime Video

My Welsh Sheepdog - Prime Video, Acorn TV

Mysteries of Stonehenge - Prime Video

Mysterious Places of Scotland and Ireland: Swans of Loch Lomond - Prime Video

The Mystery of Agatha Christie with David Suchet - Prime Video

The Mystery of Mary Magdalene - BritBox

Mystery Road - Acorn TV

Nadiya's Time to Eat - Netflix

The Name of the Rose - Sundance Now

Narnia's Lost Poet: The Secret Lives and Loves of C.S. Lewis - Prime Video, Acorn TV

Narrowboat Houseboating Through the English Countryside - Prime Video

The Nativity - Prime Video

Nature: What Plants Talk About - Prime Video

Neighbourhood Blues - Prime Video

Nero: The Obscure Face of Power - Tubi

The Nest - Acorn TV

Neverland - Prime Video

New Blood - BritBox

The New Tomorrow - IMDb TV, Pluto

Newton's Law - Acorn TV

New Tricks - Prime Video, Hulu

New Worlds - Acorn TV

Newzoids - BritBox

Next of Kin - Sundance Now

Nicholas and Alexandra: The Letters - PBS Masterpiece

Nick Knowles: Original

Home Restoration - Tubi

Nigel Slater Eating Together - Tubi

Nigellissima - BritBox

The Night Manager - Prime Video

The Nightmare World of HG Wells - Prime Video

The Nile: 5000 Years of History - Prime Video, Acorn TV

The No. 1 Ladies' Detective Agency - HBO Max, HBO

No Offence - Acorn TV

No Ordinary Party - Tubi

No Tears - Acorn TV

Normal People - Hulu

Northanger Abbey - PBS Masterpiece

Northern Lights - BritBox

Not Safe for Work - BritBox, Topic

Not the Nine O'Clock News - BritBox

Nothing Trivial - IMDb TV

The Nurse - Prime Video

Nurses Who Kill - Netflix

Nursing the Nation - Tubi

NW - BritBox

The Office - BritBox, Hulu, Topic

Off the Beaten Track - Acorn TV

The Oldenheim 12 - Acorn TV

Older Than Ireland - IMDb TV, Tubi

Oliver Twist (2007) - BritBox, Prime Video, Hulu

Oliver Twist (1985) - Prime Video

The Only Way is Essex - Prime Video, Hulu, Tubi, Pluto

On the Ballykissangel Trail - Prime Video

On the Whisky Trail: The History of Scotland's Famous Drink - Prime Video

On the Yorkshire Buses - IMDb TV

One Born Every Minute - Prime Video, Tubi, Pluto

One Born Every Minute UK: What Happened Next? - Tubi

One Foot in the Grave - BritBox

One Night - BritBox

One Night Stand with Anne Sibonney - IMDb TV

Only Fools and Horses - BritBox

Only When I Laugh - Prime Video

Operation Homefront - Inside Outside

Operation Ouch - Netflix

Ordinary Lies - BritBox

Othello (1981) - BritBox

The Other One - Acorn TV

The Other Wife - Tubi

Our Cops in the North - BritBox

Our Friends in the North - BritBox

Our Girl - BritBox, Prime Video, Tubi

Our Lives: I'm a Teenage Grandmother - Best of British TV

Our Lives: The Men With Many Wives - Best of British TV

Our Mutual Friend - Prime Video

Outlander - Starz

Outnumbered - Hulu, Prime Video, Best of British TV, Tubi

Outrageous Fortune - IMDb TV

Over Ireland - Prime Video

Over the Rainbow - Acorn TV

Oxford Street - Prime Video, Tubi

Pacific Heat - Netflix

The Palace - Prime Video, Pluto

The Pale Horse - Prime Video

Panorama: Fighting Coronavirus - The Scientific Battle - BritBox

Parade's End - HBO Max, HBO

The Paradise - Prime Video

Paradox - Prime Video, Hulu, Pluto

Paranoid - Netflix

Parents - Prime Video, Acorn TV, Tubi

Park Life: London - Tubi

Party Tricks - Prime Video, Acorn TV

The Passing Bells - Prime Video, BritBox

Patrick Melrose - Showtime

Paul Hollywood Pies & Puds - Inside Outside

Paul O'Grady: For the Love of Dogs - BritBox

Pawnbrokers - Prime Video

Peak Practice - Prime Video, Tubi, Pluto

Peaky Blinders - Netflix

Peep Show - Prime Video, Hulu, Tubi

Penance - Sundance Now

Penelope Keith's Hidden Coastal Villages - Acorn TV

Penelope Keith's Hidden Villages - Acorn TV

Penelope Keith's Village of the Year - Acorn TV

Penny Dreadful - Showtime

People Just Do Nothing - Netflix

Pericles, Prince of Tyre (1984) - BritBox

Perry Mason - HBO Max, HBO

Personal Services Required - Tubi

Pet School - Prime Video

Pete vs. Life - Prime Video, Pluto

Picnic at Hanging Rock - Prime Video

The Pickwick Papers - Prime Video

Pie in the Sky - PBS Masterpiece, Acorn TV

The Pillars of the Earth - Starz

Pine Gap - Netflix

Pinocchio - Prime Video

Pitching In - Acorn TV

Place of Execution - Acorn TV

Plus One - Prime Video, Tubi, Pluto

The Poirot Collection - Acorn TV

Poirot: Super Sleuths - Acorn TV

The Poison Tree - Acorn TV

Poldark (1975) - Acorn TV

Poldark (1996) - BritBox, Prime Video

Poldark (2015) - Prime Video

Poldark Revealed - PBS Masterpiece

Pollyanna - PBS Masterpiece

Pompeii: The Last Day - BritBox

Pompidou - Prime Video

Porridge (1974) - BritBox

Porridge (2016) - BritBox

Posh Neighbours at War - Prime Video

Pramface - Prime Video

Preserved Lines - Prime Video

Press - PBS Masterpiece

Prey - Prime Video, Hulu

Pride & Prejudice (1995) - BritBox, Hulu

Pride and Prejudice (1980) - Prime Video

Prime Minister's Questions - BritBox

Prime Suspect - BritBox, Hulu

Prime Suspect: Tennison - Prime Video

Primeval - Hulu, Pluto

Prince Charles at 70 - PBS Masterpiece

Prince Charles: The Royal Restoration - Prime Video

Princess Elizabeth: The Early Years with Jane Dismore - Prime Video

Prison: First and Last 24 Hours - Pluto

The Prisoner - Tubi, Pluto, Prime Video

The Prisoner of Zenda - Prime Video

Prisoners' Wives - Tubi, Prime Video, Acorn TV

The Private Lives of the Tudors - Prime Video

Project Restoration - Prime Video, Tubi
The Promised Life - Acorn TV
Proof - Prime Video
The Protectors - Prime Video
Psychoville - BritBox
Public Enemies - Prime Video
Pulp: A Film About Life, Death and Supermarkets - Topic
Puppy Love - BritBox
QI - BritBox
The Quatermass Experiment - BritBox
Queen and Country - PBS Masterpiece
The Queen at 90 - IMDb TV
The Queen at War - PBS Masterpiece
Queen Elizabeth's Battle for Church Music - Acorn TV
Queen Elizabeth's Secret Agents - PBS Masterpiece
Queen Victoria's Letters: A Monarch Unveiled - Prime Video
Queens of Mystery - Acorn TV
Question Time - BritBox
Quirke - BritBox
Quizeum - Tubi
Rachel Allen Home Cooking - Tubi
Rachel Allen: Easy Meals - Pluto
Rachel Allen's Cake Diaries - Prime Video, Pluto
Rachel Allen's Dinner Parties - Tubi
Rachel Khoo's Kitchen Notebook: London - BritBox
Rachels' Coastal Cooking - BritBox
The Rain - Netflix
The Rainbow - Prime Video
Railway Round-Up - Prime Video
Raised by Wolves - Sundance Now, Acorn TV
Rake - Prime Video, Acorn

TV, Netflix
Ramsay's Best Restaurant - Pluto
The Real Dr. Zhivago - Acorn TV
The Real Middle Earth - IMDb TV
Rebecca - PBS Masterpiece
Rebecka Martinsson - Acorn TV
The Rebel - Acorn TV
Rebellion - Netflix
Rebus - Acorn TV, BritBox
The Rector's Wife - Acorn TV
Red Dwarf - BritBox
Red Rock - Prime Video
The Red Shadows - Sundance Now
Reg - BritBox
Reggie Perrin - Acorn TV
Reilly, Ace of Spies - PBS Masterpiece, Acorn TV
Relative Strangers - Acorn TV
Rellik - Cinemax
Remarkable Places to Eat - Tubi
Remember Me - PBS Masterpiece
Renaissance Unchained - Prime Video
The Repair Shop - Netflix
Republic of Doyle - Prime Video, Netflix
Requiem - Netflix
The Restaurant - Sundance Now
Restaurant in Our Living Room - Tubi
Restless - Sundance Now, Acorn TV
Restoration Home - Prime Video, Tubi, Pluto, IMDb TV
Restoration Man - Tubi
Restoration Man Best Builds - Tubi
Retail Therapy - Tubi
Retribution - Netflix
The Return - Acorn TV
Return of the Black Death - Prime Video
Rev. - BritBox
Revenge Porn - Best of British TV

Richard Hammond's Engineering Connections - IMDb TV, Pluto
Richard Wilson On the Road - Prime Video, Pluto
Rick Steves's Europe - Prime Video
Rillington Place - Sundance Now
Ripper Street - Netflix
Ripping Yarns - BritBox
The Rise of the Nazi Party - Acorn TV
Rita - Netflix
Rita & Me - Best of British TV
The Rivals of Sherlock Holmes - Acorn TV
River - Prime Video, BritBox
Riviera - Sundance Now
Robin Hood - Prime Video, Pluto
Rocket's Island - Prime Video
Rococo Before Bedtime - Prime Video, Acorn TV
Roman Britain: From the Air - Prime Video
Roman Mysteries - Prime Video
Rome: Empire Without Limit - Prime Video, Acorn TV, Pluto
Romeo and Juliet (1978) - BritBox
The Rook - Starz
Room to Improve - Prime Video, Tubi
Rosehaven - Sundance Now
Rosemary & Thyme - BritBox
Ross Kemp: Back on the Frontline - IMDb TV
Ross Kemp: Return to Afghanistan - IMDb TV
Rovers - Prime Video, Pluto
Rowan Atkinson Presents: Canned Laughter - BritBox
The Royal - BritBox, Tubi, IMDb TV
Royal Babies - BritBox
The Royal Bodyguard - Best of British TV
Royal Britain: An Aerial History of the Monarchy -

Prime Video
Royal Celebration - BritBox
The Royal Edinburgh
    Military Tattoo - BritBox
The Royal House of Windsor
    - Netflix
Royal Paintbox - PBS
    Masterpiece
The Royals - Prime Video
The Royal Today - BritBox
Royal Upstairs Downstairs -
    Inside Outside
Royal Variety Performance -
    Best of British TV, BritBox
Royal Wives at War - PBS
    Masterpiece
Royals & Animals: 'Til Death
    Do Us Part - Prime Video
The Royle Family - Prime
    Video
Rubens: An Extra Large
    Story - Prime Video
Rumpole of the Bailey - PBS
    Masterpiece, Acorn TV
Run (2013) - Prime Video,
    Acorn TV, Hulu, Topic
Run (2020) - HBO Max, HBO
Rural Britain: A Novel
    Approach - Prime Video
The Ruth Rendell Mysteries -
    Prime Video
The Ruth Rendell Mysteries:
    Next Chapters - BritBox
Safe - Netflix
Safe House - Sundance Now
The Saint - Prime Video,
    Acorn TV, Tubi
Sally4Ever - HBO Max, HBO
Salt Beef and Rye - Prime
    Video, Tubi
Sam's Game - Prime Video,
    Tubi
The Sandbaggers - BritBox
Sanditon - PBS Masterpiece
Sando - Acorn TV
Sapphire and Steel - Prime
    Video
Sara Dane - IMDb TV
Sarah Jane Adventures -
    HBO Max
Save Me - Starz
Savile Row - Acorn TV
Scapegoat - Prime Video
The Scapegoat - Acorn TV

Scarborough - BritBox
The Scarlet Pimpernel -
    Acorn TV
Scarlet Woman: The True
    Story of Mary Magdalene -
    Prime Video
Schitt's Creek - Netflix
The Schouwendam 12 -
    Acorn TV
Scotch! The Story of Whisky
    - Prime Video, Acorn TV,
    Tubi
Scott & Bailey - Prime Video,
    BritBox, Hulu
The Scottish Covenanters -
    Prime Video
Scottish Myths and Legends
    - Prime Video
Scrotal Recall (aka Lovesick)
    - Netflix
Seachange - Acorn TV
Seachange: Paradise
    Reclaimed - Acorn TV
Second Sight - Prime Video
Secret Agent - Acorn TV,
    Tubi
Secret City - Netflix
Secret Daughter - Acorn TV
Secret Diary of a Call Girl -
    Showtime
Secret Eaters - Tubi
Secret Gardens of England -
    Prime Video
Secret Life of the Human
    Pups - Best of British TV
Secret Nature - IMDb TV
Secret Removers - Inside
    Outside
Secret Smile - Prime Video
Secret State - Sundance
    Now
Secrets and Lies - Prime
    Video
Secrets from the Sky -
    BritBox
The Secret History of the
    British Garden - Inside
    Outside
The Secret Identity of Jack
    the Ripper - Prime Video
The Secret Life of Us - Prime
    Video
The Secret of Crickley Hall -
    Prime Video, Hulu

Secrets of Britain - PBS
    Masterpiece
Secrets of Britain's Great
    Cathedrals - PBS
    Masterpiece
Secrets of Great British
    Castles - Netflix
Secrets of Highclere Castle -
    PBS Masterpiece
Secrets of Iconic British
    Estates - PBS Masterpiece
Secrets of the Gay Sauna -
    Best of British TV
Secrets of the Irish
    Landscape - Prime Video
Secrets of the Magna Carta -
    Prime Video
Secrets of the Manor House
    - PBS Masterpiece
Secrets of the Six Wives -
    PBS Masterpiece
Secrets of the Stones -
    Prime Video, Tubi
Seesaw - Acorn TV
Sense and Sensibility (2008)
    - Hulu, Prime Video
Sensitive Skin - Acorn TV
Serial Killer with Piers
    Morgan - Netflix
Serving the Royals: Inside
    the Firm - Prime Video
Seven Dwarves: The
    Wedding - Best of British
    TV
Seven Wonders of the
    Commonwealth - BritBox
Seventy With a Six-Pack -
    Best of British TV
Sex Education - Netflix
The Shadow Line - Pluto
Shakespeare & Hathaway -
    BritBox
Shakespeare in Italy -
    BritBox
Shakespeare's Stratford -
    Prime Video
Shameless - Hulu, Tubi,
    Pluto
Shameless (US) - Showtime
The Shard: Hotel in the
    Clouds - Best of British TV,
    BritBox
Sharon Horgan's Women -
    Prime Video

Sharpe - BritBox
Shaun the Sheep: Adventures from Mossy Bottom - Netflix
The Shelbourne Hotel - Prime Video, Tubi
Sherlock - Netflix
Sherlock Holmes - BritBox
Sherlock Holmes & the Case of the Silk Stocking - BritBox
Sherlock Holmes Against Conan Doyle - Prime Video
Sherlock Holmes and the Leading Lady - Prime Video
Sherlock Holmes: Incident at Victoria Falls - Prime Video
Sherlock Holmes: The Classic Collection - Tubi
Shetland - BritBox
She-Wolves: England's Early Queens - Acorn TV
Shoreline Detectives - Prime Video, Acorn TV
Shut Up & Play the Hits - Topic
Sick Note - Netflix
The Silence - Prime Video, Acorn TV, Pluto
Silent Witness - Prime Video, BritBox
Silk - Prime Video, Hulu
Simon Amstell: Set Free - Netflix
The Simple Heist - Acorn TV
Simply Nigella - Pluto
Sinbad - Prime Video
Single Father - BritBox
Single-Handed - Acorn TV, IMDb TV
Sisters (IT) - Acorn TV
Sisters (AU) - Netflix
Sisters of War - Acorn TV
The Six Wives of Henry VIII - BritBox
Skins - Netflix
Skye's the Limit - Prime Video
The Slap - Acorn TV
Slings & Arrows - Acorn TV
Smack the Pony - Tubi
Small Animal Hospital -

Prime Video, Tubi
Small Island - BritBox
Smart Travels with Rudy Maxa - Prime Video
The Smoke - Prime Video
Smoke and Steam - Prime Video
Snowdonia 1890 - Prime Video, Tubi
Soldier Soldier - Prime Video
Some Assembly Required - Netflix
Some Girls - Prime Video
The Sommerdahl Murders - Acorn TV
Song of Granite - Topic
Soundbreaking: Stories from the Cutting Edge of Recorded Music - Acorn TV
Space: 1999 - Tubi
Spaced - IMDb TV, Hulu, Tubi
The Spanish Princess - Starz
The Special Needs Hotel - Prime Video
Speed with Guy Martin - Pluto
Spendaholics - Tubi
Spies of Warsaw - Prime Video
Spirit Breaker - Prime Video
The Spirit of England: Part 1 - Prime Video
The Spirit of England: Part 2 - Prime Video
Spitting Image - BritBox
The Split - Sundance Now, Hulu
Springwatch - BritBox
Spy - Hulu, Tubi
Spying on the Royals - PBS Masterpiece
The Spy Who Went Into the Cold - Prime Video, Acorn TV
State of Mind - Prime Video
State of the Union - Sundance Now
Stella Blomkvist - Sundance Now
Step Dave - IMDb TV
Stephen Tompkinson's Australian Balloon Adventure - Prime Video

Sticks and Stones - BritBox
Still Game - Netflix
Still Life: A Three Pines Mystery - Acorn TV
Still Standing - Prime Video
Stingray - Prime Video
Stonemouth - BritBox
The Story of Europe - Prime Video
The Story of London - Prime Video
The Story of Luxury - BritBox
The Story of Math - Acorn TV
The Story of Tea: The History of Tea & How to Make the Perfect Cup - Tubi
The Story of the Mini - Prime Video
The Story of Women and Power - Prime Video, Acorn TV
Straight Forward - Sundance Now, Acorn TV
Stranded - Prime Video
The Stranger - Netflix
The Street - Prime Video, BritBox
Street Hospital - Tubi
Strike Back - Cinemax
Striking Out - Sundance Now, Acorn TV
Strippers - Best of British TV
Stunt Science - Netflix
Suffragettes - BritBox
Sunday Night at the Palladium - Best of British TV
Sunderland 'Til I Die - Netflix
Sunny Bunnies - Netflix
The Sunshine Makers - Topic
Supermarket Secrets - BritBox
Supersized Hospitals - Tubi
Supply and Demand - Acorn TV
Surgery School - IMDb TV
Susan Calman's Fringe Benefits - BritBox
Suspects - Acorn TV
The Suspicions of Mr. Whicher: Beyond the Pale -

BritBox, Pluto

The Suspicions of Mr. Whicher: The Murder at Road Hill House - BritBox, Pluto

The Suspicions of Mr. Whicher: The Murder in Angel Lane - BritBox, Pluto

The Suspicions of Mr. Whicher: The Ties That Bind - BritBox, Pluto

The Sweeney - BritBox

Swingin' Christmas - BritBox

Switch - Prime Video

Sword of Honour - Acorn TV

The Syndicate - Prime Video

The Syndicate: Playing for Keeps - Acorn TV

Taggart - BritBox

The Take - IMDb TV

Taken Down - Acorn TV

Tales from Northumberland with Robson Green - BritBox

Tales from the Coast with Robson Green - BritBox

Tales from the Royal Wardrobe - PBS Masterpiece

Tales of the City - Acorn TV

Tales of the Unexpected - Prime Video, Tubi

The Talisman - Prime Video

The Taming of the Shrew (1980) - BritBox

Tea with the Dames - Hulu

Teachers - Tubi

The Tempest (1980) - BritBox

The Tenant of Wildfell Hall - Prime Video

Terrahawks - Pluto

Terry Jones' Great Map Mystery - Prime Video, Pluto

Terry Pratchett's Going Postal - Prime Video, Acorn TV

Terry Pratchett's Hogfather - Prime Video, Pluto

Tess of the D'Urbervilles - Prime Video

Testament - Acorn TV

That Day We Sang - BritBox

That's My Boy - Prime Video

Theatreland - Acorn TV

Thelma's Big Irish Communions - Tubi

Then There Were Giants - IMDb TV

There She Goes - BritBox

Therese Raquin - Acorn TV

They've Gotta Have Us - Netflix

The Thick of It - Prime Video, BritBox, Hulu

The Thin Blue Line - BritBox

Thirteen - Prime Video

This Farming Life - BritBox

This is Personal: The Hunt for the Yorkshire Ripper - Prime Video

This Way Up - Hulu

Thomas & Sarah - Prime Video

Thorne: Scaredy Cat - BritBox, Acorn TV

Thorne: Sleepyhead - BritBox, Acorn TV

Three Girls - BritBox

Three Sovereigns for Sarah - PBS Masterpiece

Thriller - Prime Video, Tubi

Through the Garden Gate: A Diary of the English Countryside - Prime Video

Thunderbirds - Prime Video

Tidelands - Netflix

The Time of Our Lives - Prime Video, Acorn TV

Time Team - Prime Video, Acorn TV, Tubi

Timon of Athens (1981) - BritBox

Tin Star - Prime Video

Tina & Bobby - BritBox

Tiny Plastic Men - Prime Video

Tipping the Velvet - BritBox

Titus Andronicus (1985) - BritBox

To Build or Not to Build - Tubi

The Toilet: An Unspoken History - IMDb TV

To the Ends of the Earth - Prime Video, Pluto

To Walk Invisible: The

Brontë Sisters - Prime Video

Toast of London - Netflix

Together - Acorn TV

Tom Jones - Prime Video

Tony Robinson's Gods and Monsters - Prime Video

Tony Robinsons's Crime and Punishment - Prime Video

Top Boy - Netflix

Torchwood - HBO Max

Touching Evil - Prime Video

The Tower - Prime Video

Tower Block Kids - Tubi

Traffik - Acorn TV

The Tragedy of Coriolanus (1984) - BritBox

The Tragedy of Richard III (1983) - BritBox

Trailer Park Boys - Netflix

Train 48 - Prime Video

Traitors - Netflix

Transsiberian - Topic

Trauma - BritBox

Trauma Rescue Squad - Tubi

Travel Man - Hulu, Pluto

Travel Scotland with James McCreadie - Prime Video

Travelers - Netflix

Travels by Narrowboat - Prime Video

Treasure Gardens of England - Prime Video

Treasure Houses of Britain - Prime Video, Acorn TV

Treasure Island - Pluto

The Trench - Acorn TV

Treyvaud Travels - Prime Video

Trial & Retribution - Acorn TV

The Tribe - IMDb TV

Trinity - Tubi

Trivia - Prime Video, Acorn TV

Troilus and Cressida (1981) - BritBox

Trolley Dollies - Prime Video

Trouble in Poundland - Tubi

Troy: Fall of a City - Netflix

Truckers - Pluto, Tubi, Prime Video

Trust - Prime Video, Acorn TV

The Truth Will Out - Acorn TV

The Tube: Going Underground - Prime Video

Tudor Monastery Farm at Christmas - PBS Masterpiece, Prime Video, Tubi

The Tudors - Showtime, Netflix

The Tunnel - Prime Video

Turn Up Charlie - Netflix

Turning Green - Acorn TV

Tutankhamun - BritBox

Twelfth Night (1980) - BritBox

The Two Gentlemen of Verona (1983) - BritBox

Two's Company - Prime Video

Ultimate Force - Pluto, Tubi

Uncle - Prime Video, Hulu

Under Capricorn - Acorn TV

Underbelly - Prime Video

Undercover - Prime Video

Unfinished Portrait: The Life of Agatha Christie - BritBox

Unforgotten - PBS Masterpiece, Prime Video

United - Prime Video, Acorn TV

Unreal Estate - Tubi

Up All Night: The Minicab Office - Best of British TV

The Up Series - BritBox

Up the Women - BritBox

Upright - Sundance Now

Upstairs Downstairs (1971) - BritBox

Upstairs Downstairs (2010) - BritBox, Hulu

Upstart Crow - BritBox

Van Helsing - Netflix

Vanity Fair (1987) - Prime Video

Vanity Fair (1998) - Prime Video

Vanity Fair (2018) - Prime Video

Vera - BritBox, Acorn TV

Vera Postmortem - BritBox

Very British Problems - Prime Video, Tubi

Vexed - Prime Video, Acorn TV, Netflix

The Vicar of Dibley - BritBox

The Vice - Prime Video

The Viceroys - Acorn TV

Vicious - PBS Masterpiece, Tubi

The Victim - BritBox

Victoria - PBS Masterpiece, Prime Video

Victoria and Albert: The Wedding - PBS Masterpiece

Victoria Wood's A Nice Cup of Tea - Acorn TV

Victorian Farm - Tubi

Victorian Farm: Christmas Special - Tubi

Victorian House of Arts and Crafts - Acorn TV

Vidago Palace - Acorn TV

Vienna Blood - PBS Masterpiece

The Village - BritBox

Vincent - IMDb TV, Tubi

Vincent Van Gogh: Painted with Words - BritBox

Vintage Roads: Great and Small - Acorn TV

Vintage Steam Trains: Great British Steam - Prime Video

Virgin Atlantic: Up in the Air - BritBox

The Virtues - Topic

Visit Wales with Rachel Hicks - Prime Video

W1A - Netflix

Wainwright Walks - Acorn TV

Waiting for God - BritBox

Waking the Dead - BritBox

Walking Through History With Tony Robinson - Prime Video

Walks Around Britain - Prime Video

Walks Around Britain: The Great Glen Way - Prime Video

Walks With My Dog - Prime Video, Acorn TV, Tubi

Wallander - BritBox

Wallis Simpson: The Secret Letters - Prime Video

Wanderlust - Netflix

Wanted - Netflix

War & Peace - Acorn TV

Warren - Prime Video

Wasted - Hulu

Watership Down - Netflix

The Way Back - Acorn TV

The Way We Live Now - Prime Video

We Hunt Together - Showtime

Weapons of Mass Production - Topic

WED Talks - BritBox

Wedding SOS - Tubi

Wedding Town - Best of British TV

The Week the Women Came - Best of British TV

We'll Meet Again - Prime Video

Wentworth - Netflix

Westminster: Behind the Closed Doors - Prime Video

Westside - Prime Video

What Remains - BritBox

What the Durrells Did Next - PBS Masterpiece

What the Neighbours Did - Tubi

What to Do When Someone Dies - Acorn TV

Where the Heart Is - Prime Video

Whisky: The Islay Edition - IMDb TV

Whistlestop Edinburgh: Scotland's Beautiful Capital - Prime Video

White Dragon - Prime Video

White Gold - Netflix

White Heat - BritBox

The White Princess - Starz

The White Queen - Starz

White Teeth - Acorn TV

White Van Man - Best of British TV, Prime Video, Tubi

Whitechapel - Prime Video, Hulu

Whites - Prime Video, Acorn TV

Whose Line is it Anyway: Australia - Best of British TV

Whose Line Is It Anyway? - Hulu

Wide Sargasso Sea - Acorn TV

The Widow - Prime Video

The Widower - PBS Masterpiece

Wild Animal Rescue - Tubi

Wild at Heart - Acorn TV, Tubi, Pluto, IMDb TV

Wild Bill - BritBox

Wild Decembers - Acorn TV

The Wild Roses - Prime Video

William and Mary - Prime Video

The Windermere Children - PBS Masterpiece

The Windermere Children: In Their Own Words - PBS Masterpiece

Windsor Castle: After the Fire - Prime Video

The Windsors - Netflix

The Windsors: A Royal Family - PBS Masterpiece

The Wine Show - Hulu

Winter - Acorn TV

Winterwatch - BritBox

Win the Wilderness - Netflix

Wire in the Blood - Acorn TV

Wired - Prime Video, Pluto

Wish Me Luck - Prime Video

Wisting - Sundance Now

The Witcher - Netflix

Witches: A Century of Murder - Netflix

Without Motive - BritBox

The Witness - IMDb TV, Topic

Wolcott - Prime Video

Wolf Hall - PBS Masterpiece

Wolfblood - Tubi, Pluto, Prime Video

The Woman in White - PBS Masterpiece

The Woman Who Ate Her House - Best of British TV

Women in Love - Prime Video

The Women of World War

One - BritBox

Wonderland - Prime Video

Workin' Moms - Netflix

World on Fire - PBS Masterpiece

The World's Most Extraordinary Homes - Netflix

World War II in Colour - Netflix

World Without End - Starz

The Worricker Trilogy - PBS Masterpiece, Prime Video

The Worst Week of My Life - Best of British TV, Acorn TV

The Worst Witch - Netflix

Would I Lie to You? - BritBox

WPC 56 - Prime Video, BritBox

Wreckers - Acorn TV

The Wrong Mans - Hulu

Wuthering Heights (2012) - Topic

Wuthering Heights (2009) - PBS Masterpiece

Wycliffe - Prime Video, BritBox, IMDb TV

Wyonna Earp - Netflix

Year of the Rabbit - Topic

Years and Years - HBO Max, HBO

Yes, Minister - BritBox

Yes, Prime Minister - BritBox

The Yorkshire Vet - Acorn TV, Tubi

York, UK - Prime Video

You Deserve This House - Inside Outside

You, Me, & Them - Best of British TV, Acorn TV, Prime Video

Young Dracula - Prime Video, Pluto

Young Hyacinth - BritBox

Young Lions - Prime Video

Young Wallander - Netflix

Young, Gifted, and Classical: The Making of a Maestro - Acorn TV

The Young Person's Guide to Becoming a Rock Star - Tubi

Young, Rich, and

Househunting - Tubi

Zen - BritBox

159

COMMON QUESTIONS

Why am I seeing ads on Amazon?

There are two reasons you may see ads on Amazon:

- You're watching a "free with Prime Video" show. If a show has the "Prime" banner that tells you it's free with membership, it will frequently show ads for other Amazon shows.
- You're watching a show on IMDb TV. It's a free-with-ads service that integrates with Amazon (since Amazon owns IMDb), and it plays all sorts of different ads (not just Amazon show ads).

Sometimes, a show may be on both IMDb TV *and* a subscription service you use. For example, McLeod's Daughters is on both Acorn TV and IMDb TV. It's very easy to accidentally watch the IMDb TV version and get loads of ads.

Though it varies by device, you can usually fix this by going to your computer, visiting Amazon, and adding the show to your watchlist - making sure you're on the page that mentions your subscription.

If you're on a Roku or similar device, you'll often see two options for viewing, and you can select the subscription rather than IMDb TV.

The Amazon system is a bit wild, so in some cases there's an entirely separate show page for the IMDb TV version and the subscription version - and not in others. If you continue to have trouble with it, contact Amazon's support for help.

In some cases, you may find it beneficial to take your subscription direct to the company in question - but of course, some people find that shows stream more smoothly through Amazon, and others just like having all the billing in one central location.

How do I watch these channels on my TV? I don't have a smart TV and I don't want to watch on my laptop or tablet.

There are a lot of different ways you can do this, but we'll focus on the simplest. For around $30 (base model), you can buy a device called a Roku. They sell them at Walmart, Target, Best Buy, Amazon, and even some pharmacies and convenience stores. It's our top recommendation because they're easy to use and the remote control has big print and few buttons.

A Roku plugs into your television and you can connect it to your internet wirelessly. Then, you can add channels like Acorn TV, BritBox, or Tubi. Some are free (like Tubi), while others require you to set up a monthly subscription with the company in question (like Acorn or BritBox).

You also have the option of subscribing to Amazon's Prime Video service - and then subscribing to your other channels through the Amazon app so all the billing goes through one place.

You only pay for the Roku device one time. There's no monthly cost associated with having a Roku, and if you were so inclined, you could buy one and only use the free channels.

Nearly all channels offer free trials (usually either 7 or 30 days), and the vast majority allow you to log in online and cancel your account without calling anyone on the phone and waiting on hold.

Some cable companies do offer Acorn TV or BritBox, but we generally don't recommend it if you're able to subscribe another way. We see a lot of reader complaints about poor service or inability to cancel without lengthy phone calls to customer service.

Why is Amazon charging me for — show?

This is another area that causes a lot of misunderstanding and frustration. Amazon offers a giant video marketplace, and there are different types of access within the system.

- **IMDb TV Shows** - Shows in this "section" are free to all with ads.
- **Prime Video** - If you're an Amazon Prime member (or purely a Prime Video member), you get access to a larger set of programmes which are included in the price of membership. Sometimes, only the older seasons of a show are included in this membership.
- **Channel Subscriptions** - Dozens of channels make their programming available through Amazon's platform. That includes Acorn TV, BritBox, Sundance Now, and many of the others in this guide. You pay for these channels on top of the basic Amazon Prime or Prime Video fee. An Acorn TV or BritBox subscription won't give you access to all British TV shows on Amazon - only those offered by Acorn TV or BritBox.
- **Rentals & Purchases** - Some shows are not included in any of the plans above (or you may choose to buy/rent them instead of subscribing to a channel). It's a bit like when we all went to the local video store for things not offered on our cable packages. If you really wanted to see it, you could pay a bit extra to get it right away…or wait and hope it showed up on one of your channels eventually.

Made in the USA
Monee, IL
24 October 2020